CITIZEN JOURNALISM

Simon Cottle
General Editor

Vol. 1

PETER LANG
New York • Washington, D.C./Baltimore • Bern
Frankfurt am Main • Berlin • Brussels • Vienna • Oxford

CITIZEN JOURNALISM

Global Perspectives

EDITED BY
Stuart Allan and Einar Thorsen

PETER LANG
New York • Washington, D.C./Baltimore • Bern
Frankfurt am Main • Berlin • Brussels • Vienna • Oxford

Library of Congress Cataloging-in-Publication Data

Citizen journalism: global perspectives / edited by Stuart Allan, Einar Thorsen.
p. cm. — (Global crises and the media; vol. 1)
Includes bibliographical references and index.
1. Citizen journalism. 2. Online journalism. I. Title.
PN4784.C615 C58   070.4'3—dc22   2009012804
ISBN 978-1-4331-0296-7 (hardcover)
ISBN 978-1-4331-0295-0 (paperback)
ISSN 1947-2587

Bibliographic information published by **Die Deutsche Bibliothek**.
Die Deutsche Bibliothek lists this publication in the "Deutsche
Nationalbibliografie"; detailed bibliographic data is available
on the Internet at http://dnb.ddb.de/.

Cover design by Clear Point Designs

The paper in this book meets the guidelines for permanence and durability
of the Committee on Production Guidelines for Book Longevity
of the Council of Library Resources.

Table OF Contents

Series Editor's Preface

We live in a global age. We inhabit a world that has become radically interconnected, interdependent, and communicated in the formations and flows of the media. This same world also spawns proliferating, often interpenetrating, "global crises".

From climate change to the war on terror, financial meltdowns to forced migrations, pandemics to world poverty and humanitarian disasters to the denial of human rights, these and other crises represent the dark side of our globalized planet. Their origins and outcomes are not confined behind national borders and they are not best conceived through national prisms of understanding. The impacts of global crises register across 'sovereign' national territories, surrounding regions and beyond and they can also become subject to systems of governance and forms of civil society response that are no less encompassing or transnational in scope. In today's interdependent world, global crises cannot be regarded as exceptional or aberrant events only, erupting without rhyme or reason or dislocated from the contemporary world (dis)order. They are endemic to the contemporary global world, deeply enmeshed within it. And so too are they highly dependent on the world's media.

How global crises become signaled and defined, staged and elaborated in the world's media proves critical to wider processes of recognition and response, and can enter into their future course and conduct. In exercising their symbolic and communicative power the world's media variously inform processes of public understanding, but so too can they dissimulate the nature of the threats that confront us and marginalize those voices that seek to mobilize forces for change. The scale of death and destruction involved in different global crises or the potentially catastrophic nature of different global threats are no guarantee that they will register prominently, if at all, in the world's media, much less that they will be defined therein as "global crises." So-called "hidden wars" and "forgotten disasters" still abound in the world today and because of their media invisibility can go unnoticed, commanding neither recognition nor wider response.

The series *Global Crises and the Media* sets out, therefore, to examine not only the media's role in the *communication* of global threats and crises but also how the media today complexly enter into their very *constitution*, enacting them on the public stage and shaping their course around the world. More specifically, the volumes in this series seek to: 1) contextualize the study of global crisis reporting in relation to wider debates about the changing flows and formations of world media communication; 2) address how global crises become variously communicated and contested in the media around the world; 3) consider the possible impacts of media global crisis reporting on public awareness, political action and policy responses; 4) showcase the very latest research findings and discussion from leading authorities in their respective fields of inquiry; and 5) contribute to the development of positions of theory and debate that deliberately move beyond national parochialisms and/or geographically disaggregated research agendas. In these ways the specially commissioned books in the *Global Crises and the Media* series aim to provide a sophisticated and empirically engaged understanding of the media's role in global crises and thereby contribute to academic and public debate about some of the most significant global threats, conflicts and contentions in the world today.

Citizen Journalism: Global Perspectives, edited by Stuart Allan and Einar Thorsen, chimes well with these stated aims. Their collection of chapters written by academics working in this field contributes new global perspectives on the rise of citizen journalism around the world, exploring its diverse expressions and emphasizing its close affinity with crises, catastrophes, and contemporary struggles for justice. As the editors observe at the outset, there has long been a close association between citizen journalism and the reporting of crises for it is in situations of crises, they suggest, that ordinary people are often "compelled to adopt the role of a reporter" and "bear witness to crisis events unfolding around them." This collection builds on these claims—empirically, conceptually and theoretically—when examining diverse situations of crisis. Whether, for example, eyewitness accounts and the critical responses of ordinary people to Hurricane Katrina in the US and the Wenchuan earthquake in China; the use of warblogs and the hybrid links between civil society and news social movements in protests against the political, legal, and humanitarian crisis of the Iraq war; the role of citizen journalism in the fight for human rights, democracy and dignity across regions and inside different countries, including Brazil, India, Iran, Palestine, China, and Vietnam; the online promotion of awareness and action in Antarctica about climate change; or the part played by citizen media in recent political crises and contests including violent elections in Kenya, the amplification of contentious campaign remarks in Barack Obama's US electoral campaign, and the role of social networking and citizen-sourced content in Australia's federal elections.

Citizen journalism though certainly not without historical precedents, has evolved rapidly across recent years and is expressive of the surrounding culture, organizational structures, and politics of civil societies. Much hangs, clearly, on what exactly is meant by "citizenship" and also "journalism" and the plural meanings and projects now pursued in respect of both. More generally, citizen journalism has proved to be creatively adept at putting to work the now constantly updating and superseding communication technologies that have become widely available. These highly portable, low-cost, discreet, digitized communication technologies that are easily plugged into and uploaded to the world wide web have become for many an integral part of everyday life and medium for the conduct of social relations. Animated by differing conceptions of both "citizenship" and "journalism," and practiced under very different political regimes around the world, "citizen journalism(s)" now assert their presence *outside, through,* and *within* today's mainstream news media.

Citizen journalism variously enters into and informs today's world news ecology with its overlapping formations and flows of news, mainstream and alternative news media, and new interactive technologies of news dissemination and user-generated content. Though still in large part structured in dominance by Western news corporations and news flows from the "West to the rest," today's world news ecology also incorporates established and emergent non-Western news formations and a plethora of alternative news forms and outlets generating news contra-flows and/or circulating oppositional views and voices—from the "rest to the West", the local to the global. Mainstream newspapers and broadcasting news services have become surrounded by and wired into the world wide web, where most also seek a virtual news presence of their own and negotiate as they do so the internet's enhanced connectivity, interactivity, and cacophony of voices that now emanate from the exponentially expanding blogosphere(s).

Mainstream news organizations for the most part, however, decline to surrender their traditional editorial control, agenda-setting functions or gatekeeper authority when deciding who is permitted to enter "their" news domain, under what conditions, when and how. But all are nonetheless cognizant of the added value that forms of citizen journalism can now bring when packaged inside their own news presentations—especially when reporting crises and catastrophes. Here first-hand testimonies, visceral accounts, and graphic images help to dramatize and humanize stories, injecting emotion, and urgency into the stories of people's plight and pain. And, possibly, such raw images and graphic accounts can also sometimes help to undergird a mediated ethics of care or even the necessary politics of what should be done.

While corporate news organizations seek to expand market share and colonize communications space *around* the globe, citizen journalism it seems has managed to insinuate itself *inside* corporate news packages while simultaneously *staking out* independent platforms of news delivery and world-wide dissemination. As citizen journalism progressively ingratiates itself into today's differentiated news ecology so inevitably it unsettles, reconfigures, or simply bypasses traditional hierarchies and relations of communicative power. At least that's the democratic promise and often heard claim of citizen journalism. But how accurate are these claims when approached in global context?

Citizen Journalism: Global Perspectives digs expertly beneath the rhetorical veneer of citizen journalism whether glossed in celebratory or cynical terms and does so in twenty-one focused and tightly argued chapters. Together these help to document, analyze, conceptualize, and theorize the richly differentiated forms and expressions of citizen journalism in the world today—and the part they perform within diverse crisis situations. The collection examines the fast-developing rise of citizen journalism in diverse countries and political contexts around the world but the "global" is more than the aggregation of different countries and national perspectives of course, and here the collection also includes discussion and analysis of how citizen journalism originated *in* particular national contexts, crises, and contests intervenes *across* countries and continents and secures a transnational or even global presence within the "global news arena."

In these and other ways, the chapters in this book help to illustrate the increasingly complex flows and formations of today's world news ecology and how citizen journalism enters within them to communicate and condition the course of different crises and political contests around the globe. Stuart Allan and Einar Thorsen's *Citizen Journalism: Global Perspectives,* then, offers a timely, authoritative and cutting-edge collection that should be of interest to all those interested in looking behind the inflated claims and undue cynicism that too often surround the rise of citizen journalism in the world today. The authors in this volume offer by far a more grounded, more measured, and more nuanced appreciation of citizen journalism, its diverse forms and political expressions and contribution to shifting relations of communicative power—especially in situations of crisis.

Simon Cottle,
Series Editor

Introduction

STUART ALLAN AND EINAR THORSEN

When "citizen journalism" makes the headlines it is often for the wrong reasons. A case in point occurred in October 2008 with respect to iReport.com, a news website operated by CNN, the cable news network. It relies entirely upon news stories submitted by ordinary members of the public. While its tagline "Unedited. Unfiltered. News" highlights its approach, iReport describes its own agenda this way:

> Lots of people argue about what constitutes news. But, really, it's just something that happens someplace to someone. Whether that something is newsworthy mostly depends on who it affects—and who's making the decision. On iReport.com, that is you! So we've built this site and equipped it with some nifty tools for posting, discovering and talking about what you think makes the cut.

It continues:

> Use the tools you find here to share and talk about the news of your world, whether that's video and photos of the events of your life, or your own take on what's making international headlines. Or, even better, a little bit of both.

Although iReport is owned and operated by CNN (controlled, in turn, by Time Warner, Inc.), a statement from the network on the website affirms that "it makes no guarantees about the content or the coverage" to be found there. News items submitted by users "are not edited, fact-checked or screened before they post," with only those bearing the mark "On CNN" having been properly vetted by the network for use in its own news reports. Responsibility for the quality of the reporting, it follows, rests not with CNN but rather with "you, the iReport.com community."

The website has enjoyed a good reputation since its launch in the summer of 2006. It has proven to be a remarkably popular source of alternative news and is widely credited for having made important contributions to the reporting of breaking stories—including the use of a student's cell-phone video footage during the April 2007 shootings at Virginia Tech University (the sound of gunfire from inside an adjacent building being captured). iReporter items covering California wildfires, as well as Midwest floods, similarly helped to bring the website to prominence. User statistics suggest that as many as 20,000 items can be posted per month. However, on the morning of October 3, 2008, a posting by one iReporter would spark an extraordinary controversy that would ensure this experiment in citizen journalism would be subjected to intense scrutiny from across the mediascape.

During early trading on Wall Street, an anonymous individual—identified only as "Johntw"—posted this apparent "news" item:

> Steve Jobs [CEO of Apple, Inc.] was rushed to the ER [Emergency Room] just a few hours ago after suffering a major heart attack. I have an insider who tells me that paramedics were called after Steve claimed to be suffering from severe chest pains and shortness of breath. My source has opted to remain anonymous, but he is quite reliable. I haven't seen anything about this anywhere else yet, and as of right now, I have no further information, so I thought this would be a good place to start. If anyone else has more information, please share it.

The impact of the report, which appeared to resonate with recent concerns about the state of Jobs's health, was as sudden as it was severe. Within minutes, Apple's stock price spiraled to a 17-month low (a plunge worth almost $5 billion of market value) as the rumor gained momentum across the internet. Seeking to verify the story, Silicon Alley Insider (a business blog) managed to reach an Apple spokesperson on the telephone; she promptly denied it, which brought the story to a grinding halt in less than an hour after it began. As the day wore on, the company's stock price managed to recover much of its lost ground, but in the opinion of some commentators the damage to the credibility of CNN—and its decision to "tap into the citizen journalism craze" (Sandoval, 2008)—was all but irreversible.

All too aware of the pointed questions being posed about the principles underpinning its public news initiative, CNN moved swiftly to respond. A statement was quickly released to journalists clarifying its position:

> iReport.com is an entirely user-generated site where the content is determined by the community. Content that does not comply with Community Guidelines will be

removed. After the content in question was uploaded to iReport.com, the community brought it to our attention. Based on our Terms of Use that govern user behavior on iReport.com, the fraudulent content was removed from the site and the user's account was disabled.

Despite CNN's resolve to reaffirm the gate-keeping role attributed to the site's community of users, criticism from rival news organizations—and from across the blogosphere—was fierce. The network's "brand," in the eyes of some, was badly tarnished by this "imbroglio," with some critics expressing their astonishment that it could be so naïve as to trust the site's users to safeguard its reputation for quality reporting.

Henry Blodget (2008), blogging at Silicon Alley Insider, was among the first to weigh in, declaring that citizen journalism "apparently just failed its first significant test." Others insisted that the problem revolved around the absence of agreement over acceptable editorial standards, including those determining who can be a CNN iReporter (technically anyone, given that all that is required to register is the completion of an online form, and an email address). Still others maintained that the real issue was the inadequacy of "health warnings" on the site, that is, the necessity of adding "unverified" to "unedited" and "unfiltered." In sharp contrast, for those defending the site, blame deserved to be placed elsewhere. "The (iReport) story's been picked up by numerous sites as a failure of citizen journalism," Arnold Kim (2008) of MacRumors.com observed. "It's nothing of the sort.... The real reason it gained traction is the reporting of it on mainstream blog sites." It was the latter sites, such as Silicon Alley Insider, that in his view gave the false report sufficient credibility to frighten market traders. Meanwhile Adam Ostrow (2008), a blogger at Mashable, pointed out that internet rumors impacting the stock market was a longstanding problem, suggesting that this "blunder" was hardly "the beginning of the end for citizen journalism." Blogger Jeff Jarvis (2008) at BuzzMachine concurred. In contending that the web had proven to be "almost as fast at spreading truth [i.e., Apple's statement about Jobs's health] as it is at spreading rumors," he asked: "Is this a story of citizen journalism and its failings or of professional journalism and its jealousies?"

Not surprisingly, given the bold—even, at times, apocalyptic—pronouncements being made regarding the very future of journalism in this regard, there is little sign that differences in fervently held opinions will be resolved any time soon. Even where there is a shared sense that major news organizations—struggling to cope with slashed budgets in recessionary times—will be increasingly relying upon the appropriation of first-person news reporting, views differ markedly over who should be held responsible for any lapses in quality. While some believe that the occasional mishap should not be allowed to undermine a news organization's commitment to empowering citizens to be reporters, a praiseworthy form of democratization in their eyes, others discern in such incidents a portent of crisis that threatens to unravel the very integrity of the journalistic craft itself.

Against this backdrop, it is worth observing how these tensions reverberate in various national contexts around the globe. A comparative perspective, we believe, is invaluable for securing fresh insights into the factors shaping the emergence and evolution of citizen journalism as a phenomenon in its own right. In Britain, for example, debates over whether important distinctions between "professional" and "amateur" reporting are becoming dangerously blurred are often framed in terms of public service. In the case of the BBC, the role of user-generated content (UGC—its preferred term for citizen journalism) has gradually become a key feature of its newsgathering process, even though reservations remain. Speaking at an e-Democracy conference on November 11, 2008, the BBC's director of news Helen Boaden (2008) outlined what she perceived to be the main challenges at stake for its online provision. "Our journalism is now fully embracing the experiences of our audiences, sharing their stories, using their knowledge and hosting their opinions," she declared; "we're acting as a conduit between different parts of our audience; and we're being more open and transparent than we have ever been." The "accidental journalism" performed by ordinary citizens during the London bombing attacks in July 2005 was a watershed, in her view, "the point at which the BBC knew that newsgathering had changed forever" (see also in this volume Allan, Chapter 1, and Liu et al., Chapter 3). Members of the public contributed an extraordinary array of reports via emails, texts, digital photographs, and videos to help document what was happening that day.

Since then, the BBC has become much more proactive in soliciting this type of content from its audiences. In Boaden's words:

> It's not just a "nice to have"—it can really enrich our journalism and provide our audiences with a wider diversity of voices than we could otherwise deliver. As well as voices we might not otherwise hear from, there are stories about which we would never have known.... For many of our audiences, this has opened their eyes to something very simple: that their lives can be newsworthy—that news organisations don't have a monopoly on what stories are covered. Indeed, that news organisations have an appetite for stories they simply couldn't get to themselves and they value information and eye witness accounts from the public—as they always have done. (Boaden, 2008)

In learning to accept the tenet that "someone out there will always know more about a story than we do," the BBC has embraced citizen newsgathering as a vital resource. At the heart of its news provision is a recently established "UGC Hub"—a 24/7 operation—staffed by 23 people to handle what on an average day typically amounts to 12,000 emails and about 200 photographs and videos. This newly forged relationship, Boaden is convinced, represents a positive opportunity for journalism to improve in a way that reinforces informed citizenship. "Smart news organisations are engaging audiences and opening themselves up to the conversation our audiences clearly want," she contends. In addition to helping to preserve the BBC's core journalistic values of accuracy, fairness, and diversity of opinion, she adds, this type of interactivity reaffirms a commitment to reporting in the public interest. "In order to survive," Boaden concludes, "journalism must be trusted."

This normative alignment of citizen journalism with the public interest can be thrown into even sharper relief in countries where the basic principles of press freedom cannot be taken for granted. In seeking to make their claim for such principles, bloggers have often paid a very high personal price for challenging the interests of the powerful and the privileged with alternative forms of news reporting. Repressive governments around the world have sought to place strict limits on the blogosphere, refusing to recognize the right of the citizen—let alone the citizen journalist—to express himself or herself freely, without prior restraint or censorship.

In Malaysia, around the time of the CNN iReport incident discussed above, Raja Petra Kamaruddin, responsible for the country's best-known political blog, *Malaysia Today*, was imprisoned based on allegations of "spreading confusion" and "insulting the purity of Islam." Having been arrested on September 12, 2008, under the Internal Security Act, invoked during a government clampdown on opposition voices, he was being detained without trial. Long considered a "thorn in the side" of the Malaysian government because of criticisms conveyed on his blog, Raja Petra was one of three critics being held for two years—a sentence renewable indefinitely—under the act (the other two being another blogger, Syed Azidi Syed Aziz, and Chinese-language journalist Tan Hoon Cheng). *Malaysia Today* continued to publish, thanks to the efforts of Marina Lee Abdullah, wife of Raja Petra, and colleagues using a variety of strategies to elude official attempts to block the website. (Strategies included publishing the blog on a mirror site, as well as using new web addresses in foreign countries.) Suddenly, on November 7, 2008, the charges against Raja Petra were dropped, due largely to pressure brought to bear by Reporters Without Borders. The 58-year-old blogger, according to the campaigning organization, was "constantly harassed" while he was being held in a Kuala Lumpur police station. "He was put in a cell with no window and with just a plank of wood for a bed, and was subjected to lengthy interrogation sessions designed to demonstrate that he was a bad Muslim. The police also deprived him of sleep" (RWB, 2008). Evidently the release had been ordered by a court ruling based on the view that the government had overstepped its authority in arresting him for comments on his blog where no immediate threat to national security was apparent. While a previous charge of sedition was still pending against him at the time of his release, Raja Petra vowed to be back online within 24 hours. "I already have two articles that I wrote in prison," he stated, "and I'm waiting to post them" (cited in Fuller, 2008; see also CPJ, 2008).

In those countries where the state equates dissent with criminality, the indefatigable determination of ordinary citizens to speak truth to power is remarkable. The rise of the network society, to use Manuel Castells's (2000) term, is rewiring the planet in ways that have profound implications for the geo-politics of informational power and control. And yet there is little doubt that familiar—that is to say, Western—conceptions of what counts as citizen journalism risk appearing to be merely academic, in the worst sense of the word, in countries where ordinary people lack basic access to electricity. In civil-war-torn Liberia, for example, Alfred Sirleaf's efforts to perform a role akin to the citizen journalist are a case in point. As the managing editor of The Daily Talk, he writes up news and editorials on a chalkboard positioned on the street outside his "newsroom" hut every day, thereby providing passersby with important insights into what is happening in Monrovia. Equipped with his "nose for a good scoop," this "self-taught newshound" scours newspapers—and calls on an informal network of friends acting as correspondents—for the information necessary to keep everyone "in the know."

News stories—three or four of which are displayed each morning—are concisely written, relying on street words that people actually use themselves (thus "big stealing" rather than "embezzlement," for example). "I like to write the way people talk so they can understand it well," he told The New York Times. "You got to reach the common [person]" (cited in Polgreen, 2006). Crucially, Pru Clarke (2008) points out, Sirleaf has recognized two significant points:

> First, that the war continued because the young soldiers and their supporters didn't have access to any information. [Warlord Charles Taylor] brainwashed them into believing that fighting for him would bring them riches and power. They believed Taylor's fraudulent claims to be the rightful leader, and that Taylor's enemies would subjugate them if they won. They needed to hear the truth if they were to see Taylor for what he was, and to stop fighting.
>
> Sirleaf also realized that after a decade of war more than half the Liberian people were illiterate. Those who could read couldn't understand the flowery, overblown prose of the government-sanctioned newspapers. (I still struggle to understand them!) Neither could they afford to pay for them. (Clarke, 2008)

For those unable to read words on a chalkboard, there are symbols: a blue helmet hanging beside the board means that the story involves the United Nations peacekeeping force, while a chrome hubcap represents the president (the "iron lady" of Liberian politics). In previous years Sirleaf's dedication to citizen reporting has met resistance from those in power during the Taylor regime; he was arrested and spent a brief spell in prison, then went into exile while his newsstand was torn down. Today, with his plywood hut rebuilt, he remains steadfast in his belief that what he is doing matters for the country's emergent democracy. "Daily Talk's objective is that everybody should absorb the news," he maintains. "Because when a few people out there make decisions on behalf of the masses that do not go down with them, we are all going to be victims" (cited in Polgreen, 2006).

The brief examples of citizen journalism touched upon above—from the US, Britain, Malaysia, and Liberia—usefully highlight a number of the pressing issues to be examined in the course of this book's discussion. Taken together, they are indicative of a communication continuum that stretches from global news organizations, such as CNN and the BBC, to the lone voices of individuals struggling to be heard against dauntingly formidable odds. Celebratory proclamations about the "global village" engendered by Web 2.0 ring hollow when we are reminded, in turn, that the majority of the world's population has never made a telephone call, let alone logged on to a computer.

Accordingly, *Citizen Journalism: Global Perspectives* will endeavor to delve beneath the rhetoric of globalization in seeking to examine the spontaneous actions of ordinary people—more often than not in the wrong place at the wrong time—compelled to adopt the role of reporter. Time and again, their motivation is to bear witness to crisis events unfolding around them. This collection, in taking this crisis dimension as its point of departure, draws together 21 original, thought-provoking chapters. It investigates the emergent ecology of citizen journalism in the West, including the United States, United Kingdom, Europe, and Australia, in conjunction with its inflection in a variety of other nations around the globe, including Brazil, China, India, Iran, Iraq, Kenya, Palestine, South Korea, Vietnam, and even Antarctica. In so doing, it strives to engage with several of the most significant topics for this important area of inquiry from fresh, challenging perspectives. Its aim is not to set down the terms of debate, but rather to encourage new forms of dialogue.

OVERVIEW OF *CITIZEN JOURNALISM: GLOBAL PERSPECTIVES*

Section One: Eyewitness Crisis Reporting

In Chapter 1, Allan sets the scene for the book's discussion by exploring what counts as "citizen journalism" from varied historical perspectives. Beginning with a brief overview of the emergence of the internet as a "new news medium," he proceeds to examine several crises where the reporting of ordinary citizens made a vitally important contribution. Examples include natural disasters (such as earthquakes and hurricanes), political scandal, and the tragedies of terrorism, conflict, and war, among others. Allan's aim is to discern the emergent ecology of citizen journalism as it has been negotiated through the exigencies of crisis reporting.

The Iraq war provides the backdrop for Wall's (Chapter 2) analysis of the recent wave of warblogs—"a feisty new genre of blog that focused specifically on the terrorism wars"—written by Iraqis from within the war zone, and milblogs, written by current or former soldiers. Of particular interest is the way in which institutional forces have sought to censor and intimidate bloggers and even to use their "grassroots authenticity as a cover for sophisticated war information operations." Despite this, she argues, citizen journalism is poised to have a central position in the future "as amateurs play an even larger role in providing audiences with first-hand information about the world."

Citizens' eyewitness photography—especially where the use of a cell or mobile telephone equipped with a camera is concerned—is increasingly playing a significant role in crisis reporting. In Chapter 3, Liu, Palen, Sutton, Hughes, and Vieweg explore the genre of photo-blogging in relation to six distinct crises, several of which were of global significance. They single out for special attention the evolving role of Flickr, the prominent photo-sharing website, to show how it serves as a community forum for crisis-related photojournalism. Of particular interest, they point out, are efforts underway to develop a set of normative criteria to guide the nature of social practice around photographic content during emergency response and recovery efforts.

The idea that citizen journalism can help victims of crisis is also the focus of Vis's (Chapter 4) assessment of the performance of Wikinews in the aftermath of Hurricane Katrina, which struck the US coast in 2005. She illustrates how collaborative citizen journalism acted as a clearinghouse for disaster relief information, including messages from individuals willing to help the homeless. Moreover, Vis demonstrates how the Wikinews community, in striving to report on the crisis and its aftermath, dealt with issues such as the perceived "bias" of certain eyewitness reports submitted by ordinary citizens. The site's Neutral Point of View policy, she argues, was sorely tested, especially in relation to the first-person reporting of lawlessness during the relief effort.

Empowerment is a crucial tenet of citizen journalism in India, a democracy with over one billion people. Sonwalkar (Chapter 5) argues that this new form of reporting is having an influential political function in highlighting social problems, such as the impact of severe poverty on those at the margins of public life. In a society where women, for example, "are seen as inferior and, in many cases, subjected to domestic violence," blogging has enabled pressure groups to spark public discussion and debate "in a way that the mainstream news media have never done." Citizen journalism, Sonwalkar points out, is being increasingly recognized as a powerful force in this regard.

Citizen journalism from within a conflict zone is the focus of Zayyan and Carter's (Chapter 6) discussion, which explores how bloggers in the Occupied Palestinian Territories "have helped to tell a truth different from the one frequently related in the mainstream media in many countries." Many of these citizen journalists choose to write in English instead of Arabic so as to reach a global audience with their message and to plea for basic human rights. Zayyan and Carter argue that in so doing, "Palestinian citizen journalism is shifting the terms of debate on the conflict in the Middle-East." This reporting embodies a "simple hope," namely that by raising awareness of their suffering, "pressure will be brought to bear on politicians around the world to help end it."

In Chapter 7, Nip assesses citizen journalism's response to the Wenchuan earthquake in southwestern China in May 2008. She reveals how citizen journalists were the first to report the earthquake both to a Chinese and international audience, providing eyewitness reports and expressions of personal emotion—grief, anger, and sympathy. Moreover, in a rare moment of openness under the Communist government, citizen journalists were also able to investigate and critique officials' handling of the disaster. Such reporting did not completely evade state censorship, however, and Nip further discusses new government tactics such as infiltration of citizen-generated content—that is, paying for people to post content supporting the government as a strategy to subvert opposition and manage this new form of public discourse.

Rounding out this section, Thorsen (Chapter 8) explores how scientists researching the climate-change crisis in Antarctica are using blogging as a means to communicate directly with the public. He argues that citizen journalism can function as a form of educational outreach, giving us seemingly unmediated access to scientists who are recording the effects of climate change first-hand. This emergent form of science reporting is shown to provide an important contrast to traditional forms of journalism, where the process of climate change is a difficult fit for conventional, event-led news agendas.

Section Two: Citizen Journalism and Democratic Cultures

Khiabany and Sreberny (Chapter 9) address questions of citizenship and journalistic professionalism in an authoritarian regime by exploring the re-inflection of a more Western conceptualization of citizen journalism in relation to Iran's radically different political setting. The Persian blogosphere, they demonstrate, provides a space for trade unions, radical student groups, and women's movements to voice their plight, which is otherwise ignored by the traditional, state-controlled mass media. They show how citizenship and journalism are both experiencing a revival through innovative and alternative forms of expression in response to the political context.

Children and young adults are often sidelined in debates surrounding citizenship and journalism. In thinking of children as citizens "in the making," Guedes Bailey (Chapter 10) explores the importance of "Newspaper Clubs" in Brazil, a project conceived and implemented by the Brazilian NGO "Communication and Culture" in partnership with public schools (local and state government). Since 1995, newspaper clubs have empowered children by giving them a voice as reporters of community affairs, thereby socializing them as informed and active citizens. Guedes Bailey's chapter also highlights the continued significance of print-based publications in the developing world, where many people—in particular children and young adults—have "no access to computers and have little or no information about, or practice with, communications technologies skills."

One of the most frequently cited examples of citizen journalism is the role of OhmyNews during the 2002 South Korean presidential election, a time when democracy itself was perceived to be in a crisis of legitimacy. Woo Young (Chapter 11) illustrates how the website functions as a counterbalance to the otherwise conservative media, maintaining that citizen journalism is integral to improving the country's democratic system as it ensures that the diversity of South Korea's public opinion is recognized. Indeed, the popularity of the citizen reporting at the heart of OhmyNews has made it the largest, most influential online newspaper in the country.

Despite Vietnam being listed as one of the 13 "enemies of the internet" in 2006 by Reporters Without Borders, Nguyen (Chapter 12) argues that citizen journalism has "developed quite vigorously" there. Indeed, he illustrates how it has seen a spectacular rise in recent years, establishing a reputation for breaking news—often reporting events that would have been ignored by mainstream media as too controversial. In this way, citizen journalists are helping to create a realm of debate where the authority of the state can be called into question. The blogosphere has prospered, in Nguyen's view, not simply because of technological advances, but also because of the governing regime's "confident tolerance" in allowing such activities to take place.

While such tolerance is more often associated with Western democracies, Carpentier, De Brabander, and Cammaerts (Chapter 13) demonstrate in their analysis of the Belgian peace movement that citizen journalism is a vital means to enable alternative or activist voices to be heard. They argue that the "active presence of the Indymedia.be (volunteer) staff members" at peace marches and associated events "highlights the interweaving of citizen journalism and peace activism."

That is, activists both report and actively support the objectives of such activities. They suggest that citizen journalism needs "to be seen as an inseparable part of civil society," since this form of participatory media enables citizens to "be active in one of many (micro-)spheres relevant to daily life, organize different forms of deliberation, and exert their rights to communicate."

Citizen journalism is frequently associated with political activists seeking to challenge society's established institutions and power relations. In Chapter 14, Salter explores the position of Indymedia's citizen journalists in relation to libel, security laws, and incitement, drawing on recent examples where both private and state actors have attempted to shut its operations down. Salter argues that citizen journalists cannot simply "claim the rights afforded to journalists," since the "privilege is dependent upon adherence to the rules" of law. Such activist citizen journalism, it follows, "will always be at a disadvantage compared to mainstream journalism—politically, economically, culturally and legally," which has important implications for democratic dissent.

Peaceful protests are in stark contrast to some of the practices uncovered during the 2007 Kenyan presidential election crisis by Zuckerman (Chapter 15). He reveals how bloggers took on the role of reporters in documenting the election process and mapping the violence that ensued following the disputed result, providing a crucial source of information following the government's ban on live media. However, citizen media and text messaging were also used in a more sinister way to mobilize different ethnic groups against each other. Attempts at moderating such hateful content led Kenya's leading bulletin board site to shut down, while the government decided to block bulk text messages. Technologies "useful for reporting and peacemaking," Zuckerman warns, "are also useful for rumor mongering and incitement to violence."

The 2007 Australian federal election, in contrast, will be remembered for more peaceful reasons, most notably the incumbent prime minister losing his seat and the increasingly significant role of citizen media during the campaign. In Chapter 16, Bruns, Wilson, and Saunders explore the tension that developed between bloggers and mainstream media such as *The Australian*, with the latter attacking citizen journalists for having the audacity to criticize its election analysts. Experiences from the authors' involvement in the hyperlocal citizen journalism project, Youdecide2007, are also shared. Based on this experiment, the chapter concludes with a proposal to "transcend the stale 'professional-amateur' dichotomy" by putting forth a concept of "journalism as social networking." The authors here highlight four dimensions in which they argue "professional practice is changing to accommodate citizen-generated content."

The 2008 US presidential election marked a historic shift in American politics through the election of Barack Obama. One of the key characteristics of this campaign was the influence of the internet, which is explored by Fiedler in Chapter 17. His discussion begins with the occasion on which Obama encountered Mayhill Fowler, a citizen journalist, at a campaign fundraising event that was off-limits to the mainstream press. Obama's off-the-cuff remarks about the reasons why some working-class voters might feel embittered about politics, dutifully relayed by Fowler in a blog, sparked news headlines around the world. This was a crisis of an unusual sort for the Obama campaign to address, one that helped to reveal the changing nature of election campaigns in the age of the internet.

Section Three: Future Challenges

Reese and Dai, in Chapter 18, explore the role of citizen journalists acting as media critics, arguing that the Chinese blogosphere is increasingly featuring posts and comments that represent a new form of public deliberation. Nationalism, they argue, suits the interests of the Chinese government, which has given citizens free range in criticizing the Western media—attacking CNN for discrepancies in its coverage of the Tibet riots and negative framing of the Olympic Torch relay, for instance. Moreover, they demonstrate how citizen reporters also critique domestic professional journalistic principles, forcing action on issues that would otherwise have been ignored. In the context of globalization, they contend, these developments point to new ways of understanding social change.

Mainstream media are increasingly appropriating citizen journalism content—broadly encapsulated under the umbrella of "user-generated content" (UGC)—in part to avoid perceptually undermining traditional journalism's occupational values. Singer and Ashman (Chapter 19) pick up on this tension from the perspective of "journalists at Britain's *Guardian* newspaper and its internationally popular website," exploring how journalism practice is changing as it is forced to accommodate content from—and interaction with—its audience. Journalists' responses are positioned in relation to traditional occupational values of authenticity, autonomy, and accountability. While "user-generated content" and audience interaction are cautiously embraced, journalists remain wary of the challenges inherent in negotiating new relationships with citizen contributors.

Few technological innovations invite forms of use as distinct from traditional journalistic practice as wikis. Bradshaw examines the emergence of wiki-based citizen journalism in Chapter 20, evaluates its strengths and weaknesses, and proposes a taxonomy of its different forms. Wikis are "blogs 2.0," he argues, since their technology forces a collaborative practice that transcends the linear communications flow of blogs and discussion forums. Wikis offer a single place for the distributed discussion of blogs to take place, where the community deliberates to reach (ongoing) consensus by making changes to the original text.

The book draws to a close with Deuze's (Chapter 21) assessment of the future of citizen journalism from three different perspectives: industry, audience, and convergence culture. The future of citizen journalism, he argues, "is about creating brand communities around the news"—often where communities of interest already exist, which explains the success of "hyperlocal" initiatives. Deuze calls into question the promise and practice of online audience interaction, suggesting that "none of these forms of distributed conversation have real, permanent, or stable political power." Beyond these critical perspectives, he settles on a more positive note by exploring how convergence culture may enable "a future citizen journalism where professional reporters and engaged citizens indeed co-create a public sphere within their communities of reference."

These brief chapter overviews begin to make apparent several pressing reasons why the contributors to *Citizen Journalism: Global Perspectives* have sought to participate in the debates traversing these pages. It is hoped that the respective chapters, individually and collectively, will help to provide the basis for new dialogues to emerge regarding citizen journalism today, as well as about where it may be heading tomorrow. In drawing attention to how crisis events in particular throw into sharp relief the imperatives underpinning this evolution, the importance of this dialogue becomes all the more apparent. At stake is nothing less than the future of journalism itself. "We used to call mainstream journalism the 'first draft of history,'" Dan Gillmor (2005) has observed. "Now, I'd argue, much of that first draft is being written by citizen journalists. And what they're telling us is powerful indeed." In agreeing with this view, we would add that it signals a further challenge, namely for all of us to discover new ways to recast the rigid, zero-sum dichotomies of the "professional versus amateur" debate. This will necessarily entail thinking anew about the social responsibilities of the citizen as journalist while, at the same time, reconsidering those of the journalist as citizen.

REFERENCES

Blodget, H. (2008) "Apple denies Steve Jobs heart attack report." Silicon Alley Insider, 3 October.

Boaden, H. (2008) "The role of citizen journalism in modern democracy." Keynote speech at the e-Democracy conference, RIBA, London, 13 November.

Castells, M. (2000) *The rise of the network society* (2nd ed.). Oxford: Blackwell.

Clarke, P. (2008) "The Daily News: Liberia." *World Vision Report*, 28 September.

CPJ (2008) "Blogger held on sedition charges." *Committee to Protect Journalists*, 7 May.

Polgreen, L. (2006) "All the news that fits: Liberia's blackboard headlines." *The New York Times*, 4 August.

Fuller, T. (2008) "Malaysian court frees jailed blogger." *International Herald Tribune*, 7 November.

Gillmor, D. (2005) "Tsunami and citizen journalism's first draft." *Dan Gillmor on Grassroots Journalism, Etc.*, 6 January.

Jarvis, J. (2008) "Citizen journalism ruins the world (again)." BuzzMachine, 6 October.

Kim, A. (2008) "Citizen journalism not a failure, blogs a failure?" MacRumors.com, 3 October.

Ostrow, A. (2008) "Steve Jobs health scare: citizen journalist costs Apple shareholders billions." Mashable, 3 October.

RWB (2008) "Interior minister orders blogger held for two years under draconian security law." Reporters Without Borders, 23 September.

Sandoval, G. (2008) "Who's to blame for spreading phony Jobs story?" *DigitalMedia*, 4 October.

SECTION ONE: EYEWITNESS CRISIS REPORTING

CHAPTER ONE

Histories OF Citizen Journalism

STUART ALLAN

At a time when current debates over what should count as "citizen journalism" are being hotly contested, it is not surprising that disagreements about its origins tend to be similarly charged. Any one "history of citizen journalism" subjected to close scrutiny is bound to reveal an array of competing, even contradictory, histories. Much will depend on the preferred definition of "citizen journalism" being employed—or even of "history," for that matter—let alone the perspective, interests, and motivation of the person marshalling selected facts into a compelling narrative. No such history will be entirely innocent of politics, no matter how self-reflexive the history writer may be about her or his personal views or predispositions.

In light of these challenges, it may be tempting to begin a critical history by adopting an etymological approach. Is it possible to determine when the phrase "citizen journalism" initially emerged in public discourse? Similarly, we might ask, at what point did it cross the threshold and enter into the journalistic lexicon? Bearing in mind the obvious—namely that there is no singular, essential definition awaiting discovery—such efforts might usefully seek to trace those occasions when the term figures in deliberations over the status of the "amateur" in relation to that of the "professional," some of which, of course, go back to the earliest days of something recognizable as "journalism" in the first place. From the vantage point of today, these disputes over the meaning of terms are revealing, with bold proclamations shaped as much by their silences as by their assertions.

While there is little danger that consensus is about to emerge any time soon, it is nonetheless important to recognize the extent to which competing conceptions of citizen journalism revolve around crisis reporting. More often than not, commentators will point to the gradual unfolding of an over-arching narrative that began to consolidate in the immediate aftermath of the South Asian tsunami of December 2004. This was the decisive moment, they contend, when citizen journalism became a prominent feature on the journalistic landscape. The remarkable range of first-person accounts, camcorder video footage, mobile and digital camera snapshots—many of which were posted online through blogs and personal webpages—being generated by ordinary citizens on the scene (holiday-makers, in many instances) was widely heralded for making a unique contribution to mainstream journalism's coverage. One newspaper headline after the next declared citizen journalism to be yet another startling upheaval, if not outright revolution, being ushered in by internet technology. News organizations, it was readily conceded, were in the awkward position of being dependent on this "amateur" material in order to tell the story of what was transpiring on the ground. "Never before has there been a major international story where television news crews have been so emphatically trounced in their coverage by amateurs wielding their own cameras," observed one British newspaper. "Producers and professional news cameramen often found themselves being sent not to the scenes of disaster to capture footage of its aftermath, but to the airports where holiday-makers were returning home with footage of the catastrophe as it happened" (*The Independent*, January 3, 2005).

Despite its ambiguities, the term "citizen journalism" appeared to capture something of the countervailing ethos of the ordinary person's capacity to bear witness, thereby providing commentators with a useful label to characterize an ostensibly new genre of reporting. In the years since the tsunami, it has secured its place in journalism's vocabulary (for better or otherwise in the view of many news organizations), more often than not associated with a particular crisis event. It is described variously as "grassroots journalism," "open source journalism," "participatory journalism," "hyperlocal journalism," "distributed journalism," or "networked journalism" (as well as "user-generated content"), among other terms, but there is little doubt that it is recasting crisis reporting's priorities and protocols in profound ways.

This chapter, in privileging for consideration a number of these crisis events, shall draw particular attention to how citizen journalism is transforming what was once considered to be the exclusive domain of the professional. In acknowledging the formative significance of those occasions in which ordinary people found themselves caught up in events that compelled them to temporarily adopt the role of a journalist in relaying what was happening around them, however, it is important not to overstate their impact as sudden, prodigious departures from previous convention. That is to say, we need to avoid reaffirming the implicit premise that this is a history punctuated by technology-driven revolutions in reportorial form, practice, or epistemology. The appeal of this illusion of linearity, where one dramatic breakthrough follows another in a logical, rational sequence unfolding under the rippling banner of progress, is difficult to resist. But resist it we must. The identification of technical innovations is crucial, yet equally noteworthy are the uneven ways in which these innovations are taken up, modified, and recrafted to render them fit for purpose. Such a focus on the situated materiality of technology pinpoints the ways in which the citizen journalist's commitment to bear witness is shaped by the lived negotiation of its affordances and possibilities, as well as by its pressures and constraints. This chapter's discussion thus aims to complicate some of the more technology-determined accounts of citizen journalism's emergence. In so doing, I shall argue that a more nuanced treatment will help to secure fresh insights into the nature of what it is to be a journalist, and also why it matters for the reporting of crises today.

"A NEW NEWS MEDIUM"

Journalists, when interviewed about their personal recollections about the arrival of the internet in the newsroom, often use phrases such as "Back in the old days…" when referring to events that took place a mere decade or so ago. The researcher, when sifting through transcripts of the interview material afterward, may be forgiven for feeling like an archaeologist of sorts, someone gently removing sand from chiselled hieroglyphics in order to unravel the enigmas of classical antiquity.

Journalist and academic John Naughton (1999) has vivid memories of this time in a British context. "For decades," he writes, "the Net was below the radar of mainstream journalism—its practitioners didn't even know of its existence. When I used to tell newspaper colleagues that I'd been using email from home since 1975, they would make placatory noises and check the route to the nearest exit" (p. 30). It was around 1995, he recalls, that the situation began to change, when "the conventional media realised something was up." Precisely what was up, of course, was anything but clear. He observes:

> At first the Net was treated as a kind of low-status weirdo craze, akin perhaps to CB radio and the use of metal-detectors. Then it became the agent of Satan, a conduit for pornography, political extremism and subversion. Next it was the Great White Hope of Western capitalism, a magical combination of shopping mall and superhighway which would enable us to make purchases without leaving our recliners. Then

it was the cosmic failure because it turned out that Internet commerce was—shock! horror!—*insecure*. And so it went, and goes, on, an endless recycling of myths from newspaper clippings, ignorance, prejudice, fear, intellectual sloth and plain, ornery malice. (p. 30)

Naughton proceeds to note the irony that the hostility some print journalists have directed toward the internet is very similar to that which their 1950s counterparts aimed at early television newscasts. "Then, as now, the first instinct was to rubbish and undermine the intruder," he comments. "Television news, said the newspapers, would be vulgar and sensational. There would be fewer words in an entire thirty-minute news bulletin than in half a page of *The Times*. And so on" (p. 31). A further line of attack was to challenge the credibility of the internet as a news provider, typically by characterizing online sites as being inherently untrustworthy—and lacking in the objectivity, professionalism, and independence members of the public expected. It was only when it became apparent that people were turning to the internet for their "hot" or "breaking" news, despite such dire warnings, that newspapers began, ever so reluctantly, to rethink their relationship to their internet rivals.

Given the significance of breaking news in this regard, it is not surprising that so many of the early indications of citizen journalism's potential—long before the term itself was employed—emerged during crisis events. News flashes about earthquakes in California, home of the fledgling software industry, were a case in point. First in 1989 in San Francisco, but more substantively in Northridge (20 miles west-northwest of Los Angeles) on January 17, 1994, "the global computer network buzzed into action," to quote from an Associated Press wire service report (AP, January 18, 1994). One early user, evidently a Prodigy subscriber with a wireless modem, alerted the world about the predawn earthquake before mainstream media broke the news. Within 20 minutes of the incident, users began offering first-hand accounts of their experiences, including descriptions of the destruction they had personally witnessed. Others relayed information updates gleaned from the television and radio news coverage to hastily configured newsgroups. While distant users sent emails inquiring about the well-being of relatives, local people with long-distance telephone connections offered to make calls on behalf of those temporarily denied the service in the quake area. Some even offered to help organize rescue operations. For journalist Jon Katz (1994), this electronic response suggested that "a new news medium" had been born. "No information structure has ever been able to do anything remotely like it," he argued, seeing in this activity a basis to project an optimistic appraisal of what he termed "the new information culture."

Other commentators, as one would expect, were less convinced by this "network of computer networks" increasingly being called "the internet" in news reports. Paul Andrews, writing in the *Seattle Times*, argued that when "the traditional information infrastructure is disrupted—jammed phone lines, power outages, wrecked highways in the case of the quakes and government censorship in the [then-Soviet Union] coup—the Internet shines." On such occasions, when the internet is "the only game in town," it acquires "far more legitimacy, substance and credibility" than would be the case otherwise. Indeed, in Andrews's view, when the internet competes with other media, it is promptly revealed to be "a noisy and cumbersome sideshow," effectively little more than "the haunt of amateurs, poseurs and incompetents" (*The Seattle Times*, April 30, 1995). For those sharing this line of argument, real journalism did not take place on the internet.

And yet, as Naughton observed above, it was in 1995 that the situation began to change. Indeed, historical accounts often state that this was the year when users in the West "fell in love" with the internet. If the web was in effect three years old by then, its presence was slowly becoming a reality for increasing numbers of people due to the popular take-up of online services using Netscape's refashioned browser software. (In the United States, for example, the Microsoft Network, or MSN, was launched in July and had acquired over 500,000 subscribers by the end of the year.) Now it was possible to click a mouse to access information on a computer database directly on the web, as opposed to typing addresses such as "Telnet 192.101.82.300" to retrieve it. The release of Microsoft's Windows 95 operating system in August was front-page news around the world, a clear sign that personal computing was becoming increasingly mainstream. It would be some time, however, before the internet would be widely regarded as a news source in its own right, a transformation brought about in large part by its capacity for crisis reporting.

CRISIS REPORTING

Historical assessments of online news in its infancy often underscore the significance of crisis events in the latter half of the 1990s—precedents of form and practice, including the reporting of the Oklahoma City bombing, the crash of TWA flight 800, the Heaven's Gate mass suicide, and the death of Princess Diana—with respect to their contribution to the growing status of the internet as a news source. Each of these and related instances help to pinpoint the emergent ecology of online news, that is, the ways in which its rudimentary reportorial conventions were undergoing a socially contingent process of appropriation, consolidation, and reinflection (see also Allan, 2006).

It is against this backdrop of shifting priorities between "old" and "new" media that the crisis sparked by a "renegade cyber-journalist," Matt Drudge, needs to be situated. On January 17, 1998, Drudge posted a "world exclusive" on his fledgling website, the Drudge Report, alleging that President Bill Clinton had conducted a sexual affair with White House intern Monica Lewinsky. The ensuing scandal engulfed the Clinton Administration while, at the same time, making Drudge a household name. His website had been set up years earlier, when he worked in the gift shop at CBS television, to share "little morsels of studio rumors" (his words) that he happened to overhear from time to time. Working from his apartment in Los Angeles, he rapidly established an online following for his postings, despite making no pretense of being a journalist. Described in a newspaper profile as a "cheerful 29-year-old, looking out of place on the Boulevard of Broken Dreams," he explained how the site operated. "I use a beat-up Packard Bell 486 desktop running Windows 3.1, with a 28.8 modem. And Netscape Navigator 1.1. I keep going back to earlier versions because they're easier to use." In the same interview, he expressed his surprise about the growing interest in his site generated by the mainstream media. "Here I am, I write this thing out in my boxer shorts with my cat, as if I'm passing notes in high school," he stated. Then, suddenly, "I'm getting mentioned on Rush Limbaugh's radio show—that's 20 million listeners—and the *New York Times* are giving out my address too" (cited in *The Independent*, July 29, 1996).

In the immediate aftermath of the Lewinsky revelations, Drudge's personal philosophy—"anyone can report anything"—was subjected to intense scrutiny in the press, with much of the commentary scathing in its critique. Drudge himself was well aware that his relaxed attitude to fact-checking invited scorn, but he saw much of the criticism as being elitist in nature, steadfastly refusing to take the blame for an erosion of journalism's standards. "I'm a citizen first and a reporter second," he insisted. "The people have a right to know, not the editors who think they know better. You should let people know as much as you know when you know" (cited in AP, February 1, 1998).

This familiar argument, well rehearsed over the course of journalism's history, was suddenly striking a different chord—in the view of some, a deeply disturbing one—in the era of "instant news" on the internet. The following year, a crisis of an entirely different order would throw into sharp relief the contours of a related set of imperatives shaping the emergence of what would be called "citizen journalism" in the years to follow.

"The first internet war," as it was widely dubbed by journalists and press commentators, was being waged over the reporting of Kosovo in 1999. "The battle for hearts and minds is being fought on the net," declared newspaper reporter Simon Rogers, an observation that underscored the rapidly growing significance of web-based journalism (*The Guardian*, March 26, 1999). Deserving of particular attention, other observers agreed, was the way these new forms of reporting afforded members of the public in distant places an unprecedented degree of access and immediacy to breaking news in the war zone. This emergent genre of digital war coverage was attracting attention in its own right, including the extent to which it invited a self-reflexive critique among journalists about the relative challenges these technologies posed for the integrity of reportorial practice.

Those welcoming the arrival of digital technologies—the internet, but also satellite dishes, laptops, cell or mobile telephones, audio and video recorders, and the like—encountered the reservations of critics, many of whom were skeptical about the relative advantages to be gained by "cyber-journalism" where improving war reporting was concerned. In retracing the contours of this debate today, it is remarkable to observe how novel the idea that the internet could be used as an alternative platform for the eyewitness accounts of ordinary citizens seemed to be. Time and again, press reports acknowledged how the inclusion of first-person accounts of those caught up in the conflict—including those of a "cyber-monk" offering eyewitness reports from a 12th-century monastery, a young Albanian teenager's emails describing daily life sent to her "electronic pen pal" in the United States (who shared them with news organizations), as well as bulletin-board postings relaying, in horrific detail, what NATO's definition of "collateral damage" following a bombing raid looked like up close—shaped public perceptions of what was actually happening on the ground (see also Matheson & Allan, 2009). In so doing, this "underground," "populist," or "amateur" journalism (as it was variously labelled in the press), performed by ordinary citizens using the web, fostered a heightened sense of personal engagement for "us" with the distant suffering of "them."

This sense of connection afforded by citizen reporting during a crisis proved to be one of the few bright spots on September 11, 2001. Less than 10 minutes after the first passenger jet struck the World Trade Center, eyewitness accounts began to appear on the web. People were desperate to put into words what they had seen, to share their experiences, even when they defied comprehension. "This unfathomable tragedy," online writer Rogers Cadenhead observed, "reminds me of the original reason the internet was invented in 1969—to serve as a decentralized network that couldn't be brought down by a military attack." Cadenhead's comment was made to newspaper reporter Amy Harmon, who interviewed him on September 11 about the way his WTC attack email discussion list was circulating news about what was happening. "Amateur news reporters on weblogs are functioning as their own decentralized media today," Cadenhead pointed out, "and it's one of the only heartening things about this stomach-turning day" (cited in *The New York Times*, September 12, 2001). The major news sites, typically associated with broadcasters and newspapers, were so overwhelmed by user demand that they could be reached only sporadically as efforts mounted to ward off the danger of complete "congestion collapse." The homepage of the popular Google.com search engine posted an advisory message that made the point bluntly:

> If you are looking for news, you will find the most current information on TV or radio. Many online news services are not available, because of extremely high demand. Below are links to news sites, including cached copies as they appeared earlier today. (Google.com, September 11, 2001)

Elsewhere on the web, however, hundreds of refashioned personal websites began to appear over the course of the day, making available eyewitness accounts, personal photographs, and, in some cases, video footage of the unfolding crisis.

Taken together, these websites resembled something of a first-person news network, a collective form of collaborative news-gathering. Ordinary people were transforming into "amateur newsies," to use a term frequently heard at the time, or instant reporters, photojournalists, and opinion columnists. Many of them were hardly amateurs in the strict sense of the word, however, as they were otherwise employed as professional writers, photographers, or designers. "Anyone who had access to a digital camera and a web site suddenly was a guerrilla journalist posting these things," said one graphic-designer-turned-photojournalist. "When you're viewing an experience through a viewfinder, you become bolder" (cited in CNET News, October 12, 2001). The contributions to so-called "personal journalism," or what some described as "DIY [Do-It-Yourself] reporting" or "citizen-produced coverage," appeared from diverse locations, so diverse as to make judgments about their relative accuracy difficult, if not impossible. This type of first-person news item was typically being forwarded via email many times over, almost always by people who did not actually know the original writer or photographer. Presumably for those "personal journalists" giving sincere, unapologetically subjective expression to their experiences, though, the sending of such messages had something of a cathartic effect. In any case, the contrast with mainstream reporting was stark. These first-hand accounts and survivor stories, in the words of reporter Pamela LiCalzi O'Connell, were "social history in its rawest, tear-stained form" (*The New York Times*, September 20, 2001).

EYEWITNESSES TO WAR

The vital contribution made by citizen photographers to enhance "our camera-mediated knowledge of war," to use Susan Sontag's (2003) evocative phrase, is being increasingly recognized. One especially noteworthy instance, which helped to crystallize both public and journalistic concerns about the imagery of the Iraq war, occurred in April 2004. The *Seattle Times* was able to print a photograph of military coffins being transported back from Iraq—the type of image the Pentagon had banned from media publication, ostensibly out of respect for the privacy of dead soldiers' families—because a civilian working in Kuwait International Airport, Tami Silicio, had emailed a shot taken on her digital Nikon Coolpix (3.2 megapixel) camera to a friend back in the United States. The shot in question showed rows of flag-draped coffins being secured into place on an Air Force cargo plane. Her friend, Amy Katz, forwarded it to Barry Fitzsimmons, photo editor at the *Seattle Times* (Silicio's hometown newspaper).

When the photograph arrived, "I just said wow," Fitzsimmons recalled. "The picture was something we don't have access to as the media" (cited in *Seattle Times*, April 18, 2004). In recognizing its extraordinary news value, he also knew that it was "too powerful an image just to drop into the newspaper" without first establishing the story behind it. Following several emails and telephone calls between Silicio and Fitzsimmons (and, later, staff reporter Hal Bernton), the decision was made to publish one of the images on the front page of the Sunday edition under the headline: "The somber task of honoring the fallen." In electing to run the photograph, news editors at the *Seattle Times* were aware that they would be contravening a policy adopted by the Pentagon in 1991, during the first Gulf War, to prohibit news organizations from photographing coffins at military bases. They similarly knew that the photograph was likely to spark strong reactions from readers, not all of whom would agree with the newspaper's position. "We're not making a statement about the course of the war," Fitzsimmons stated at the time. "Readers will make their own sense of the picture, their own judgment" (cited in *Seattle Times*, April 18, 2004).

The magnitude of the ensuing controversy caught everyone by surprise, it seemed, with the image promptly reproduced across the mediascape, including on the front pages of several other newspapers around the country. Matters intensified even further when Silicio was abruptly fired from her job in the cargo terminal two days later. Press accounts pointed to "avalanching public opinion" when describing the "onslaught of media requests for the photo" and the "blizzard of media inquiries" into what had happened. (*Seattle Times* editors found themselves being interviewed extensively, from *Good Morning America* to *NBC Nightly News*, over several days.) Maytag Aircraft Corporation, Silicio's and her husband's employer, claimed that her action was in breach of both company and base disclosure rules. (Its president was widely quoted as stating that the military had identified "very specific concerns.") The *Seattle Times* expressed its regret about her dismissal. "I'm happy the picture is out," Fitzsimmons stated, "but it broke my heart when I found out she lost her job" (cited in *Editor & Publisher*, April 22, 2004). The paper had alerted Silicio about possible risks when obtaining her permission to use the image, having rightly anticipated that there might be repercussions, but remained steadfast in the face of criticism. Managing editor David Boardman insisted that his paper's motives—like those of Silicio herself—were honorable, and there was no anti-war agenda at work. "[We] weren't attempting to convey any sort of political message," he explained, before expressing his disagreement with the military ban. "The Administration cannot tell us what we can and cannot publish" (cited in *Sydney Morning Herald*, April 23, 2004). Jim Vesely, the paper's editorial page director, described how "dumbfounded" staffers were by the public response from around the world— "at one point the emails were coming at one per second"—and how much they appreciated what were "overwhelmingly positive" reactions on the whole (cited in *Seattle Times*, May 2, 2004).

Although photographs of war and its aftermath have been taken by amateurs since the earliest days of the medium, suddenly it seemed that digitally generated imagery was being heralded—as well as criticized—for its transformative potential. "In an era when pictures and video can be captured and distributed across the world with a few clicks," Amy Harmon observed, "the traditional establishment—the military, the government, the mainstream media—appears to be losing control of the images of war." Digital technology, she pointed out, "is forcing a major shift in the expectation of what can be kept private, and it may ultimately hold everyone more accountable for their actions" (*The New York Times*, May 14, 2004). In addition to the Silicio case, the examples she cites include a website, TheMemoryHole.org, that posted further images of military coffins being shipped from Iraq (obtained through a Freedom of Information request), the grisly video of Nicholas Berg being decapitated by extremists, and various social networking sites where war images circulate. Most important in this regard, however, were the photographs of Iraqi prisoners being tortured by their American captors in the notorious Abu Ghraib prison 20 miles outside Baghdad. Despite the concerted efforts of human rights groups to draw news media attention to the disturbing allegations being made regarding the US military's mistreatment of Iraqi prisoners, their information was all but ignored by journalists for several months. The story finally broke when digital images casually snapped by soldiers inside Abu Ghraib, effectively documenting the maltreatment on an unimagined scale, found their way into the hands of the mainstream media. The ensuing scandal, according to the official line, revolved around the actions of some "bad apples" and was not indicative of systemic policies and procedures. Evidence to the contrary was readily available elsewhere on the internet.

Indeed, the disjuncture between official assertions about what was transpiring on the ground in Iraq and what was really happening there was a matter of intense dispute at a number of levels. In the months leading up to the US-led invasion, however, it was apparent that some of the best eyewitness reporting being conducted was that attributed to the warblog of one "Salam Pax" (a playful pseudonym derived from the Arabic and Latin words for peace), a 29-year-old architect living in middle-class, suburban Baghdad. His site, Where Is Raed, initially set up so that he could keep in touch with his friend Raed living in Jordan, was soon recast as a source of citizen reporting. Enraged by both Saddam Hussein's Baathist dictatorship and George W. Bush's motivations for the invasion, Salam documented life on the ground in Baghdad before and after the bombs began to drop. This was "embedded" reporting of a very different order, effectively demonstrating the potential of blogging as an alternative means of war reporting. Salam's posts offered readers a stronger sense of immediacy, an emotional feel for life on the ground, than more traditional news sites. As he himself would later reflect, "I was telling everybody who was reading the web log where the bombs fell, what happened...what the streets looked like." While acknowledging that the risks involved meant that he considered his actions to be somewhat "foolish" in retrospect, he nevertheless added: "It felt for me important. It is just somebody should be telling this because journalists weren't" (cited in transcript, CNN International, October 3, 2003).

Since the invasion, the number of warblogs appearing in occupied Iraq has multiplied at a remarkable rate. Such blogs provide web users from around the globe with viewpoints about what life is like for ordinary Iraqis, viewpoints otherwise likely to be routinely ignored or trivialized in their country's mainstream news media (see also Wall, Chapter 2 in this volume). The blog "Baghdadee" has as its tagline "An opportunity to hear from witnesses inside Iraq." "A Family in Baghdad" posts the online "diaries" of mother Faiza and sons Raed, Khaled, and Majid. This excerpt, written by Faiza, is indicative of its content:

> Wednesday, 21st, May 2003
> Electricity is on at the hours : 6–8 p.m., 2–4 a.m., the Americans are spreading news about achievements they have accomplished...but on actual grounds we see nothing... we don't know whether they are truthful or not.... The schools are open, they are teaching whatever, the importance being for the children to finish their school year. Some schools were destroyed during the war, so, they merged the students with others from another school, and made the school day in two shifts, morning and afternoon.... (afamilyinbaghdad.blogspot.com/)

"Baghdad Burning," posted under the name "Riverbend" (a "Girl Blog from Iraq"), posted this entry on August 7, 2004:

> 300+ dead in a matter of days in Najaf and Al Sadir City. Of course, they are all being called "insurgents." The woman on tv wrapped in the abaya, lying sprawled in the middle of the street must have been one of them too. Several explosions

rocked Baghdad today—some government employees were told not to go to work tomorrow.

So is this a part of the reconstruction effort promised to the Shi'a in the south of the country? Najaf is considered the holiest city in Iraq. It is visited by Shi'a from all over the world, and yet, during the last two days, it has seen a rain of bombs and shells from none other than the "saviors" of the oppressed Shi'a—the Americans. So is this the "Sunni Triangle" too? It's déjà vu—corpses in the streets, people mourning their dead and dying and buildings up in flames. The images flash by on the television screen and it's Falluja all over again. Twenty years from now who will be blamed for the mass graves being dug today? (riverbendblog.blogspot.com/)

Words from blogs such as these speak for themselves, their importance all too apparent for users looking beyond the narrow ideological parameters of much Western news coverage.

CONSOLIDATING CONVENTIONS

Histories of citizen journalism, we noted above, recurrently begin in the aftermath of the South Asian tsunami, when the term itself was appropriated into the journalistic lexicon. In the course of examining what I have characterized as the emergent ecology of citizen journalism, I have sought to open up for analysis the ways in which diverse modes of reportorial form, practice, and epistemology—typically defined too narrowly, in my view, around "revolutions" in technology—have been crafted through the exigencies of crisis reporting.

In bringing this discussion to where it can usefully serve as a starting point of sorts for the chapters to follow, it is necessary to briefly trace several further contours of these evolving dynamics. With the benefit of hindsight, the significance of the tsunami reporting for what was being increasingly described as a "citizen journalism movement" in the press became more apparent throughout 2005. The summer of that year, in particular, saw two crises unfold that appeared to consolidate its imperatives, effectively dispensing with claims that it was a passing "fad" or "gimmick" for all but its fiercest critics. The bombs that exploded in London on July 7, like the devastation wreaked by Hurricane Katrina the following month, necessarily figure in any evaluative assessment of how citizen journalism has re-written certain longstanding reportorial principles.

Particularly vexing for any journalist during a crisis is the need to secure access to the scene. On July 7, it was impossible to gain entry to London Underground stations because of tight security, which meant that the aftermath of the explosions was beyond reach and out of sight. On the other side of the emergency services' cordons, however, were ordinary Londoners, some of whom were in possession of mobile telephones equipped with digital cameras. These tiny lenses captured the scene of fellow commuters trapped underground, with many of the resultant images resonating with what some aptly described as an eerie, even claustrophobic quality. Video clips taken with cameras were judged to be all the more compelling because they were dim, grainy, and shaky, and—even more important—because they were documenting an angle to an event as it was actually happening. "Those pictures captured the horror of what it was like to be trapped underground," Sky News executive editor John Ryley suggested (cited in *Press Gazette*, July 14, 2005). "We very quickly received a video shot by a viewer on a train near King's Cross through a mobile," he further recalled. "And we had some heart-rending, grim stories sent by mobile. It's a real example of how news has changed as technology has changed" (cited in *Independent on Sunday*, July 10, 2005).

Many of these photographs, some breathtaking in their poignancy, were viewed thousands of times within hours of their posting on sites such as Flickr. com or Moblog.co.uk. It was precisely this quality that journalists and editors at major news sites were looking for when quickly sifting through the vast array of images emailed to them. "Within minutes of the first blast," Helen Boaden, BBC director of news, affirmed, "we had received images from the public and we had 50 images within an hour" (cited in *The Guardian*, July 8, 2005). "This is the first time mobile phone images have been used in such large numbers to cover an event like this," *Evening Standard* production editor Richard Oliver declared. It shows "how this technology can transform the newsgathering process. It provides access to eyewitness images at the touch of a button, speeding up our reaction time to major breaking stories." Local news organizations, in his view, were "bound to tap into this resource more and more in future" (cited in *National Geographic News*, July 11, 2005).

Later the same summer, as Hurricane Katrina caused severe destruction along the Gulf Coast in the United States, citizen journalism was once again at the fore. Voices from within major organizations were quick to concede that it was augmenting their news coverage in important ways. "I think Katrina was the highest profile story in which news sites were able to fill in the gaps where government wasn't able to provide information, where people were unable to communicate with each other," observed Manuel Perez, supervising producer of CNN.com. "A lot of the most compelling info we got was from citizen journalism" (cited in Online News Association, October 28, 2005). Lewis D'Vorkin, editor in chief of AOL News, in reflecting on the ways in which source material was generated by ordinary people, described the site as "the people's platform." The interactive nature of the online news experience, he believed, meant that it could offer "real-time dialogue" between users joining in to shape the news. In D'Vorkin's words:

> While citizen journalism has existed in forms through letters to the editor, "man on the street" interviews and call-in radio or television shows, the widespread penetration of the Web has promoted the citizen journalist to a new stature. With new technology tools in hand, individuals are blogging, sharing photos, uploading videos and podcasting to tell their firsthand accounts of breaking news so that others can better understand. What we did is the future of news, except it's happening now. (cited in WebProNews, September 6, 2005)

The significance of participatory journalism, where "everyday people" are able to "take charge of their stories," has taken this long to be properly acknowledged, in his view. "Can't do it in TV, can't do it in newspapers. That personal involvement is what the whole online news space is all about" (cited in *Los Angeles Times*, September 10, 2005). Michael Tippett, founder of NowPublic.com, concurred. In underscoring the extent to which journalism is being effectively democratized, he contended that perceptions of the journalist as an impersonal, detached observer were being swept away. "This is the real reality news," Tippett insisted. "People are uploading videos and publishing blog entries, saying, 'Let me tell you about my husband who just died.' It's a very powerful thing to have that emotional depth and first-hand experience, rather than the formulaic, distancing approach of the mainstream media" (cited in Lasica, 2005).

In the years since, there has been no shortage of crisis events that have similarly figured in appraisals of the changing nature of the relationship between "professional" journalism and its "amateur" alternatives. Examples are numerous, but any attempt to list them would likely include the citizen reporting of the Buncefield oil depot explosion in the United Kingdom, the Mumbai train bombings, the protesting monks of Myanmar, the execution of Saddam Hussein, or the Wenchuan earthquake, in addition to those already cited in this book's Introduction (not least the student's cell-phone reports during the shootings at Virginia Tech University). At the time of writing, the hostage crisis in Mumbai is coming to an end, with the role played by citizen journalists using the microblogging service Twitter feeds to relay vital insights warranting much comment in press accounts. Time and again, Twitter was singled out for praise as the best source for real-time citizen news. "Last night," Claudine Beaumont of the *Daily Telegraph* pointed out, "the social web came of age" (*The Daily Telegraph*, November 27, 2008). Stephanie Busari (2008) of CNN agreed: "It was the day social media appeared to come of age and signaled itself as a news-gathering force to be reckoned with." Still, if Twitter deserved praise as "a useful tool for mobilizing efforts and gaining eyewitness accounts during a disaster," she cautioned, doubts remained about its status as a trustworthy news source in its own right.

To close, it is readily apparent that what counts as journalism in the "network society" (Castells, 2000) is in a state of flux, with familiar reportorial principles being recast anew by competing imperatives of convergence in the mainstream media—and by those of divergence being played out in the margins by "the people formerly known as the audience," to use blogger Jay Rosen's (2006) apt turn of phrase. It follows, some might say, that it is too early to be even attempting a history of citizen journalism. Others disagree, pointing out that the ephemerality of the web dictates that now is the time to be documenting these consolidating, if still remarkably inchoate, processes. In aligning this chapter with the latter position, I hope its focus on crisis events will serve as a useful contribution to the emerging dialogue and debate about what such a history might entail.

REFERENCES

Allan, S. (2006) *Online news: journalism and the internet*. Maidenhead and New York: Open University Press.

Busari, S. (2008) "Tweeting the terror: how social media reacted to Mumbai." CNN, 27 November.

Castells, M. (2000) *The rise of the network society* (2nd ed.). Oxford: Blackwell.

Katz, J. (1994) "Online or not, newspapers suck." *Wired, 2.09*, September.

Lasica, J.D. (2005) "Citizens media gets richer." *Online Journalism Review*, 7 September.

Matheson, D., & Allan, S. (2009) *Digital war reporting*. Cambridge: Polity Press.

Naughton, J. (1999) *A brief history of the future: the origins of the internet*. London: Phoenix.

Rosen, J. (2006) "The people formerly known as the audience." *Pressthink*, 27 June.

Sontag, S. (2003) *Regarding the pain of others*. New York: Farrar, Straus and Giroux.

CHAPTER TWO

The Taming OF THE Warblogs: Citizen Journalism AND THE War IN Iraq

MELISSA WALL

In the spring of 2003, with the US-led invasion of Iraq underway, mainstream news media took note of the rising popularity of the warblog, a feisty new genre of blog that focused specifically on the terrorism wars. Like many other citizen journalism projects, the original warblogs were often independent sites created by their authors, yet dependent on a network of relationships with audiences, other bloggers, and the mainstream news media to sustain them.

Certain characteristics of warblogs, however, made them different. Warblogs did not focus on hyper-local news, instead concerning themselves, sometimes audaciously so, with international news and politics. While some, especially locally oriented, citizen journalism projects seek to bridge community divides, these frequently partisan, internationally focused warblogs tended to highlight differences of opinion and further increase political divisions. Another notable difference is that warbloggers eventually made themselves heard on their own terms by the mainstream media, which had initially scorned them. This acknowledgment has eluded many other independently operated citizen news projects. All of these characteristics made warblogs lively alternatives to the stolid, predictable reporting coming from mainstream corporate-owned media. Thus, warblogs have proven to be one of the most disruptive forms of citizen journalism and one of its greatest threats to traditional war reporting.

This chapter considers the rise and evolution of warblogs, focusing particularly on the more recent iterations of the warblog genre—Iraqi-penned blogs from the war zone, and milblogs, written by current or previous soldiers or other related supporters of Western military operations. Of particular interest here are the ways in which institutional forces have sought directly and indirectly to tame these successors to the original warblogs and what this tells us about the development of citizen journalism and war reporting.

CHANGING VOICES

As the "Global War on Terror" and specifically the war in Iraq have continued, blogs focusing on the conflicts have undergone an evolution in terms of whose voices are more likely to be heard. While many of the original warblogs were written by Western armchair pundits, one of the more striking changes in warblogging is that many are now written by Iraqis. Their growing numbers seem to reflect a pattern in citizen reporting about crises and sudden disasters in which those with the greatest resources may dominate the initial response, which is then followed by a broader spectrum of voices. While the groundwork for warblogging was laid primarily by Westerners inside and outside of Iraq and a much smaller number of local Iraqi blog pioneers, so many Iraqi-written blogs now exist that they are indexed by the aggregator Iraq Blog Count. Included blogs range from Baghdad Dentist, written by a 24-year-old dentist who likes Celine Dion music, to Atheeriraqi, a blog devoted to the promotion of atheism, to LGBTQ Iraq, which describes itself as a blog for the country's lesbian, gay, bisexual, and transgender community. Such blogs provide points of view that challenge the narrow representations of Iraq usually produced by traditional media and thus embody a fundamental characteristic of citizen journalism—that of expanding the ideological spectrum for news audiences.

However, a breakdown of these Iraqi blogs in terms of language in the spring of 2008 found that 77% were written in English, 13% in Arabic, and the rest a mix of both languages. This indicates that being heard on the global stage as a citizen journalist is easier if one writes in English. Coupled with the estimated number of Iraqis using the internet (0.1% of the population), it can be argued that these bloggers in fact represent only a small slice of Iraq (Junnarkar, 2007; OpenNet Initiative, 2007). Obviously, not all citizens are privileged enough to become citizen journalists, particularly in non-Western parts of the world.

The other prominent type of warblog has been the milblog, written mainly by military or related personnel. Some are similar to the original pundit-style warblogs; others simply provide a slice of soldier's life or that of family or other related groups, and a small number are critical of the wars or at least certain aspects of them. Examples of milblogs include Afghanistan Without a Clue, penned by a US Air Force captain and "dedicated to all those who sacrifice to rebuild Afghanistan be they American, Afghan or NATO" and Some Soldier's Mom, written by the mother of several military members including one discharged with severe post-traumatic stress, and which is emblematic of the military family blog. In terms of internet access, soldiers in Iraq or Afghanistan have unprecedented satellite internet connections, although on-the-ground access can vary from location to location. The rise of milbloggers writing from within the war zone itself suggests that in terms of international news reported from outside the West, citizen journalism—just like mainstream news reporting—is likely to be more easily done by Westerners. Citizen reporting may thus be still an elite activity in the global context.

AMPLIFYING WARBLOGS

By rapidly gaining public notice, warblogs became the focus of various efforts by larger enterprises to amplify—and oftentimes in the process benefit from—warbloggers' voices. This amplification ranges from seemingly benign activities such as republishing blog posts as books to using blog content to enhance another entity's money-making efforts. While enlarging audiences and providing broader circulation for bloggers have the potential to enhance a blogger's social (and economic) capital, at the same time amplification may also domesticate bloggers, ultimately affecting how and even whether they continue to blog. In this, warbloggers should serve as a warning for other citizen journalists.

This process of amplification has drawn several well-known bloggers into the Western commercial cultural stream. While mainstream journalists have traditionally arrived home from covering wars to pen their personal tomes, the appearance of bloggers among their ranks is new. Iraqi blogger Salam Pax of Where Is Raed? had his posts published as a book, Salam Pax: The Baghdad Blogger, by the Guardian Press, which also has had him blogging occasionally as well. His video blogging for the BBC has also been turned into a documentary that appeared on the alternative film festival circuit in the United States. Riverbend, the young Iraqi blogger of Baghdad Burning, has had two volumes of her posts published in the West and a stage play based on the books produced in New York and dramatized on BBC radio. A number of US soldier blogs were collected on a website at Slate magazine (associated with Doonesbury cartoonist Gary Trudeau) and re-packaged into a volume called The Sandbox. Military blogger and soldier Colby Buzzell parlayed his blog, CBFTW (Colby Buzzell Fuck The World), which was critical of the war effort and the Bush administration, into writing gigs with *Esquire* magazine and a book, *My War: Killing Time in Iraq*. Yet, publishing blog posts changes the very nature of blogging, an essentially ephemeral form whose very essence is based on immediacy. In addition, citizen media have been valued for providing ordinary people's perspectives on events: their non-professional qualities are part of what gives them value. Repackaging citizen reporting as a more traditional professional media product seems to inherently domesticate the sometimes-untamed voices and practices found on the blogs. Taken out of their original context, which allowed for interactivity and a sense of author accessibility, blogs as books do not seem quite so personal, so unauthorized.

Another process of amplification has been the recruitment of bloggers by Western professional and grassroots media groups to produce content. For example, the McClatchy newspapers' blog, Inside Iraq, has Iraqis write about their country. Milblogs have also been incorporated into mainstream coverage. British soldier Lachlan MacNeil blogged at Six Months in Afghanistan for *The Guardian*. Other, non-mainstream initiatives such as Alive in Baghdad have recruited and trained Iraqis to produce content for their vlog (video blog). Although self-identifying as alternative media, Alive in Baghdad still emphasizes "journalistic balance"— socializing Iraqis to follow professional Western journalism norms to make them palatable for redistribution to Western news outlets (Junnarkar, 2007).

Of course, it is no surprise that mainstream media are seeking warblogs out; clearly, they see the potential for free (or practically free) content from citizen reporters, not to mention potentially new audiences, and perhaps more credibility with new niches of readers. However, each initiative that seeks to incorporate Iraqi voices may ironically re-shape those voices, raising the question of whether a blog remains independent if incorporated into corporate projects. The rawness of their unpolished reports—perhaps marked by typos or offensive remarks—has provided citizen journalism forms such as blogging part of their credibility (Allan, 2006). Their very distance from professional values has been testament to the idea that they have not been influenced by larger forces in society. Socializing warbloggers into professional routines may smother their true voices and perspectives.

Other initiatives appear to be creating structures to monetize warblogs within non-traditional media enterprises. Milblogs are aggregated at Milblogging.com, a site created by J.P. Borda, who began blogging as a US National Guardsman from Afghanistan. (Borda also led the blogswarm against CNN news executive Eason Jordan, who had implied at a Davos forum that the US military targeted journalists in Iraq. Bloggers are credited with forcing Jordan's resignation.) Milblogging.com grew into the home of what it said was 1,100 military blogs in 23 countries. Most of the blogs support the war and tout the success of the invasion and occupation. Milblogging.com has hosted its own conference and bestows awards called the Milbloggies. Milblogging.com began having its content redistributed in 2006 by a much larger entity, Military.com, a portal for a private organization, Military Advantage, aimed at military personnel and related stakeholders that claims a membership of 30 million. Military Advantage was partly funded by The Mayfield Fund, U.S. Venture Partners, Primedia Ventures, and A&E Television Network until 2004, when it was purchased by Monster Worldwide for almost $40 million (Business Wire, 2004). Unlike the non-commercial grassroots aggregator, Iraq Blog Count, the Milblogging. com content on *Military.com* appears next to ads from major corporations such as General Motors and AT&T. Ironically, such connections raise the same sort of concerns the original warbloggers voiced about the lack of independence of mainstream news media from corporate control. They also reveal the lucrative potential for enterprises able to aggregate and repackage certain niches of citizen journalism content.

CULTIVATING BLOGS

The warblogosphere has also been targeted by governmental entities, particularly the US Department of Defense (DoD). This manipulation is exactly what critics of citizen news have long warned about: the lack of professional routines among bloggers and other citizens trying to collect information could make them more likely to commit ethical gaffes and more likely to be preyed upon by sophisticated entities seeking to take advantage of their lack of savvy or simply their lack of resources. Independently operated citizen media make easily identifiable targets for such manipulations. In some cases, all it takes to get content posted or altered is to convince a single person—the site's author—to buy into the idea or information being promoted. Indeed, a whole host of US government activities work to facilitate spreading various messages across blogs.

The DoD's head of new media operations has barnstormed across the United States, attending major blogging and technology conferences such as the Las Vegas BlogWorld Expo, where he sits on panels, shakes hands, and promotes the integration of bloggers within the Pentagon's own information apparatus. Meanwhile, at the US Central Command at MacDill Air Force Base in Florida, the Electronic Media Engagement Team (EMET) closely follows the milblogosphere, providing bloggers with press releases and other media materials, while facilitating interviews with military personnel. CENTCOM claims that the bloggers they supply material to "will pretty much post anything" that they are given with few questions asked (Sherman, 2006, p. 11). The main DoD website section for bloggers includes

Vclips from the Pentagon [television] Channel set up to facilitate embedding pre-packaged video onto a blog.

Another facet of this information strategy is embedding bloggers with the troops. Well-known conservative bloggers have traveled to Iraq to record the US military's success in an effort that they say counters the poor and misleading reporting done by mainstream media reporters. Many of these embedded pro-warbloggers such as Jeff Emanuel (a former director of a leading conservative blog, RedState.com and a self-described rescuer of US Private Jessica Lynch in his previous career in special operations) have a military background (Emanuel, 2006). Such credentials could both enhance their understanding of what they see as well as orient their interpretations toward a pro-military perspective.

The Pentagon has also implemented *DOD Live*, home of the Blogger Roundtables, conference calls on which select groups of bloggers are invited to ask questions of military personnel. These sessions often begin with a lengthy statement by a military officer or public affairs official that seems to set the parameters. Afterward, a transcript and audio file of the calls are posted on the DoD website, encouraging other bloggers to distribute the information. Typical headlines summarizing the calls are: "Brigade leaves Iraq region secure, revitalized," or "Colonel describes progress with Afghan army, police." The tone of the interactions is reflected in this question:

> Adm. Fox this is Mark Finkelstein from *Newsbusters* [a conservative blog] and I want to join with my blogging colleague in thanking you for your service. I know that, among other things, you scored the first kill of a Navy Mig during Desert Storm and that you've also been honored with the silver star. So it's a pleasure to speak with you. (DoD, 2007, p. 18)

Critics suggest that these bloggers are part of the Pentagon's use of surrogates to spread its point of view, which the admiral being questioned above seems to confirm when he thanks the bloggers for allowing the military to "get our message through the media filter directly to the American people" (DoD, 2007, p. 10; Silverstein, 2008).

By providing access and a steady source of information, the military can offer a seemingly attractive resource to usually cash-strapped citizen media, some of which are likely to see the military's efforts as something worthy of promoting and of great interest to their audiences. The military and its supporters might argue that there is little difference between a blogger remixing information culled from the Associated Press or information supplied by the Pentagon. Indeed, many conservative bloggers and their audiences might consider the latter a more believable source (Johnson & Kaye, 2006). Of course, the Associated Press, like other corporate news media, is generally not overtly attempting to change opinions and generate support for policies. Also, in some views, these sorts of programs being carried out by the military are unethical and potentially illegal in the United States because they constitute disseminating official domestic propaganda.

INTIMIDATING AND CENSORING BLOGS

Other means of co-opting or subduing blogs includes monitoring, intimidation, and censorship. And in this, the government reveals a different face, one that fears the power of citizen media, suggesting that it is not quite as in control as its other efforts indicate it wants to be. The US State Department has a team of personnel tracking blogs written in Arabic and other Middle Eastern languages such as Farsi and Urdu. The Digital Outreach Team posts comments on blogs representing a pro-US point of view and also works to challenge blog posts and comments that criticize the United States (Pincus, 2007). State Department officials bragged at a US Senate hearing that theirs was the only government it knows of openly engaging in this sort of heavy-handed practice (Federal News Service, 2008). The US director of National Intelligence Offices is also said to be tracking foreign blogs in hopes of co-opting them as "sources of intelligence," and a research paper, *Blogs and Military Information Strategy*, published by the Joint Special Operations University, recommended that the military pay bloggers to disseminate US government messages (Kinniburgh & Denning, 2006, p. 24; Shachtman, 2008c). Whether this has actually happened is not known. US-based civilian warblogs are also monitored by the US Central Command's Electronic Media Engagement Team, which contacts US bloggers writing about Iraq or Afghanistan when they perceive what is posted to be inaccurate or incomplete. As part of their contact, they request the blogger link to the command's own website. Obviously, such requests could serve as a form of intimidation. Indeed, without the backing of a powerful corporate sponsor or professional organization, citizen journalists seem quite vulnerable in such a conflict with powerful entities.

When the Anglo-American forces first invaded Iraq, soldier and other military personnel bloggers did not appear to be a consideration; since then, however, US military personnel writing blogs have been subject to monitoring by the Army Web Risk Assessment Cell, a 10-member team that tracks communication related to any aspect of the DoD (Jardin, 2006). In addition, the American, British, and Australian militaries have tried to limit or outright prevent soldiers from blogging. In the US military, Armed Forces Radio and Television public service announcements, screen savers, and fliers warn soldiers that "blogging is a major security risk" (Shachtman, 2008b, p. 4). Between 2006 and 2008

- The Australian Defence Force ordered soldier blogs be deleted and that no new ones be created.
- The Pentagon directed soldiers starting a blog to notify their superior officer and provide their unit, location, and even the contact information for their webmaster.
- The UK Ministry of Defense banned soldiers from blogging without prior authorization.
- The US Air Force was reported to be blocking access to websites that contained the word "blog" in their internet address. (Carne, 2006; Jones, 2007; Shachtman, 2008b)

Some freedom-of-expression advocates believe that such policies intimidate soldiers so much that they will no longer blog at all. Ironically, a US Electronic Frontier Foundation lawsuit resulted in data being released that showed soldiers' blogs rarely compromised security and at much lower rates than the Pentagon's own official sites (Shachtman, 2007).

Contrary to these often ham-handed attempts at control, some military researchers hold the opposite point of view, seeing blogs as information operations assets or, echoing Wilbur Schramm, "a combat multiplier in the information domain" (Robbins, 2007, p. 118), leading one general to argue that soldiers be allowed to blog so they could do some of the military's propaganda work in their off hours (Shachtman, 2008a). While bloggers appear to be a special target for military information operations, it is likely that other citizen media are included in this strategy. After all, the military has already established YouTube channels and pages on Flickr, MySpace, and Twitter. Clearly their visible engagements with citizen media are only just beginning.

CONCLUSION

While warblogs have become part of the fabric of today's war coverage, which includes citizen-produced content, many of the newest blogs—increasingly written directly from the conflict by Iraqi citizens, Western soldiers, and other amateurs—have become the focus not just of audiences but of the very commercial and ideological apparatuses their forerunners once mocked. The incorporation of the current warblogs into traditional news media reportage as well as into the communication products of other entities, including the Pentagon, has greatly expanded the types of voices producing war journalism. Yet these attentions seem to be a threat to warblogging's key characteristic: its independence. Critics' concerns about citizen journalists' gullibility or malleability may prove true as citizen media provide a potent means of propaganda for groups such as the US military, which in this case can use bloggers' grassroots authenticity as a cover for sophisticated war information operations.

Co-opting warblogs and other forms of citizen journalism may also homogenize their diverse voices, socializing amateurs to imitate professional production practices, thus resulting simply in a reproduction of existing forms of reporting, or at least narrow interpretations of them. Independent citizen media may have trouble generating content or attention if other citizens are being recruited to contribute to large-scale media organizations or other entities, as mainstream media simply "normalize" warblogging and other citizen media into another facet of their news products (Lowrey, 2006; Singer, 2005). When corporate media or other entities offer to host, aggregate, or collect citizen content, they further take away the incentive for citizens to independently post their content online within a context of their own creation or at least outside traditional media's control. Indeed, because one of the strengths of the blogosphere is said to lie in the "aggregate" of its multitude of voices (Reese et al., 2007, p. 259), when traditional media manufacture spaces for interested citizens, organic communities of original voices may increasingly fail to form online, possibly stifling the potential citizen media hold for innovation and creativity.

Yet, as corporate media's international news coverage shrinks, the market for citizen journalism from around the world will likely increase in the future as amateurs play an even larger role in providing audiences with first-hand information about the world. But just as with reality television shows, this citizen content may lead audiences to believe they are viewing something more authentic and unfiltered than they are likely to be actually seeing. These citizen contributors may also reflect global inequities, privileging elite voices. In the end, domesticating citizen journalism of all types—warblogs included—into corporate sites and providing watered-down versions of their former incarnations would appear to take away the potency of their original threat to traditional journalism and their promise of a new kind of war reporting.

REFERENCES

Allan, Stuart (2006) *Online news*. Maidenhead and New York: Open University Press.
Business Wire (2004) "Monster Worldwide announces strategic interactive acquisition." *Business Wire*, 16 March.
Carne, Lucy (2006) "Defence silences diggers' war blogs." *The Sunday Mail*, 10 December.
Department of Defense (2007) "Opening remarks for RDML Mark Fox teleconference with bloggers." *Department of Defense*, 1 February.

Emanuel, Jeff (2006) "Biography." *Jeff Emanuel Online.*

Federal News Service (2008) "Hearing of the Senate Foreign Relations Committee." *Federal News Service*, 30 January.

Jardin, Xeni (2006) "Under fire, soldiers kill blogs." Wired, 29 October.

Johnson, Thomas J., & Kaye, Barbara (2006) "Blog day afternoon: are blogs stealing audiences away from traditional media sources?" In Ralph Berenger (Ed.), *Cybermedia go to war; role of converging media during and after the 2003 Iraq War.* Spokane: Marquette Books.

Jones, K.C. (2007) "Soldiers' blogs monitored; group sues for more info." *Information Week*, 7 February.

Junnarkar, Sandeep (2007) "Interviews: Sarah Szalavitz." Alive in Baghdad (KCET).

Kinniburgh, James, & Denning, Dorothy (2006) "Blogs and military information strategy." *Joint Special Operations University.*

Lowrey, Wilson (2006) "Mapping the journalism-blogging relationship." *Journalism*, 7(4), 477–500.

OpenNet Initiative (2007) "Key indicators." OpenNet Initiative.

Pincus, Walter (2007) "State Department tries blog diplomacy." *The Washington Post*, 19 November, Lexis-Nexis database.

Reese, Stephen, Rutigliano, Lou, Hyun, Kideuk, & Jeong, Jaekwan (2007) "Mapping the blogosphere; professional and citizen-based media in the global news arena." *Journalism*, 8(3), 235–261.

Robbins, Elizabeth (2007) "Muddy boots IO; the rise of solider blogs." *Military Review*, September–October.

Shachtman, Noah (2007) "Army squeezes soldier blogs, maybe to death." Wired, 2 May.

Shachtman, Noah (2008a) "Top general: let soldiers blog." Wired, 31 January.

Shachtman, Noah (2008b) "Air Force blocks access to many blogs." Wired, 27 February.

Shachtman, Noah (2008c) "Military report: secretly 'Recruit or Hire Bloggers.'" Wired, 31 March.

Sherman, Jason (2006) "CENTCOM eyes blogs to shape opinion." InsideDefense.com, 3 March.

Silverstein, Ken (2008) "Return of the Pentagon's media surrogates." *Harpers Magazine*, 11 April.

Singer, Jane (2005) "The political J-blogger; 'normalizing' a New Media form to fit old norms and practices." *Journalism*, 6(2), 173–198.

CHAPTER THREE

Citizen Photojournalism during Crisis Events

SOPHIA B. LIU, LEYSIA PALEN, JEANNETTE SUTTON, AMANDA L. HUGHES, AND SARAH VIEWEG

INTRODUCTION

During times of crisis, some people feel compelled to take photos to document events as they unfold. Sharing photos in such situations can be informative, newsworthy, and even therapeutic. Though it is fair to say that such activity has taken place since the invention of cameras, today's digital cameras and photo-sharing websites mean that the arena for sharing photographic-based information has expanded its reach to a remarkable extent.

Digital cameras, including cell or mobile telephones equipped with cameras, make opportunistic eyewitness photography easier than it has ever been. In assessing the significance of what may be characterized as "citizen photojournalism," this chapter draws upon our current research in an area called *crisis informatics* (Palen et al., forthcoming), which considers the role of technology in emergency events. The chapter aims to help elaborate the ways in which members of the public participate during times of crisis by closely examining the evolving role of the prominent photo-sharing website Flickr with regard to a range of crisis events that have occurred since its launch in February 2004.

Online Photo Sharing

Everyday citizen photography is becoming a social and cultural documentary practice among diverse publics (Harrison, 2004). Photographs, as visual artifacts, have the power to open up new vistas for understanding and expressing the intricacies of human life in relation to situated experiences (Martin & Martin, 2004; Rosen, 2005). Now with digital photography and online photo sharing, people can easily store, display, manipulate, and share their pictorial experiences. This is achievable, in part, because the automatic and manually generated metadata (like tags) associated with digital photos provide contextual cues for organizing and searching for images within a website's archive.

Flickr allows its members to store, sort, search, and share photos and images easily and efficiently. Social organization around photos and topics of interest is evident through the creation of dedicated groups. According to one Flickr user, "the photographs themselves can be seen as facilitators of community building... [in that]... each photo is like a landmark or a virtual space where people can meet and have a conversation" (quoted in Giles, 2006, p. 15). The capabilities of Flickr support online documentary practice through "photoblogging," where real-world accounts are quickly recorded often with less effort than text-based blogs.

In this chapter, we describe the evolution of Flickr's role during emergency response and recovery efforts. We discuss features of its emerging evolutionary growth as a community forum for crisis-related grassroots activity based on the findings from our qualitative study of 29 groups across six crises over recent years.

Social Media and the Rise of Citizen Journalism

Members of the public regularly seek out accurate, relevant, and reliable information during emergencies—activities that are expanding because of pervasive information and communication technology (Palen & Liu, 2007). "Media convergence," where information flows across multiple old and new media, is also "reshaping the relationship between media producers and consumers" (Jenkins, 2006, p. 19). Consumers are learning how to become producers by using these different media technologies to have better control over media flow. In an increasingly digitally connected society, we see the rise of a participatory culture that facilitates, over a broader reach and in new forms, activities of collective sensemaking.

Social media technology—mobile and web applications that support easy, ad hoc ways to communicate—are increasingly testing conventionally understood boundaries between informal and formal crisis response activities (Palen & Liu, 2007; Sutton, Palen, & Shklovski, 2008) through grassroots organization and "citizen journalism" information reporting (Gillmor, 2006). As we become a more networked society, Allan (2007) explains that "journalism is being decisively reconfigured across an emergent communication field supported by digital platforms" (p. 2), and that "instant reporters" go beyond traditional journalistic boundaries by situating it through personal experience.

THE STUDY

We conducted a longitudinal qualitative study to investigate how crisis-related Flickr activity evolved for six notable crises between December 2004 and November 2007. These emergency events—natural, human-induced, and technological—do not account for all crisis-related Flickr activity but were significant and widely publicized events useful as analytical landmarks (see timeline in Figure 1). The December 2004 Indian Ocean earthquake and tsunami event was chosen because it was the first major crisis that exhibited a widespread humanitarian response after Flickr's launch in February of that year. The July 7, 2005, London bombings led to notable forms of citizen journalism, especially through the use of cameraphones, and was a key turning point in professional journalists' assessments of its transformative potential for news-gathering processes (Allan, 2007). In August 2005, Hurricane Katrina was a major US disaster that led to prolonged emergency response and recovery efforts and resulted in significant changes in emergency management practice and policy. Immediately after the shootings at Virginia Tech in April 2007, students innovatively used social media to facilitate critical information generation and sharing activities (Palen et al., forthcoming). Following the Minneapolis bridge collapse in August 2007, photojournalism activity was high across multiple photo-sharing sites including Flickr. And finally, the Southern California wildfires in October 2007 were chosen because they generated a large range of Flickr groups in response.

Within the context of each crisis event, we analyzed those Flickr groups that showed some form of significant participation based on their membership, discussion posts, and/or the number of photos in their pool (29 groups in total; see Figure 2). We analyzed each group's accompanying *About* description, discussions, activity of the top five contributors, and the group administrators' roles. We also analyzed the title, captions, tags, number of views, comments, and other metadata of significant crisis-related Flickr photos. We conducted email-based interviews with nine Flickr users who uploaded significant or unusual photos, were group administrators, or were top contributors. For each interview, questions were individually tailored to each participant to understand what motivated them to join their respective groups and/or upload their particular photos. Our

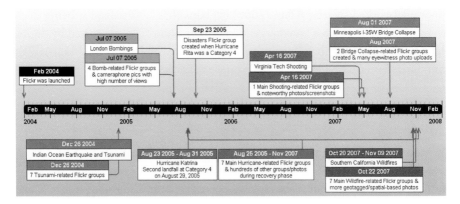

Figure 1. Timeline of Crisis-Related Flickr Activity

analysis considered content as well as the social context for how these images were produced and shared.

CRISIS-RELATED FLICKR ACTIVITY

Since its launch in 2004, different types of crisis-related activity have appeared in Flickr. Countless photos by individual contributors have been uploaded, a subset of which have been attached to particular Flickr groups. Figure 2 broadly describes overall levels of group-based activity by number of members, photos, and discussions, and is intended to give a sense of the amount and nature of activity across the groups that were a part of our investigation. In the following findings section, we first discuss the development of the two norms emerging around crisis-related Flickr activity and then describe certain types of crisis-related photographic content.

Norm Development

Norms emerge from "private citizens working together in the pursuit of collective goals" (Stallings & Quarantelli, 1985, p. 94) to guide participation and interaction. The establishment of normative behavior also helps legitimate a collective's existence and presence. We see some early evidence for attempts at self-realization and legitimation in the "response milieu" (Kendra & Wachtendorf, 2003) by crisis-related Flickr groups in the attention members pay to the stated purpose of the groups. Attempts to formalize a crisis-related tagging nomenclature suggest

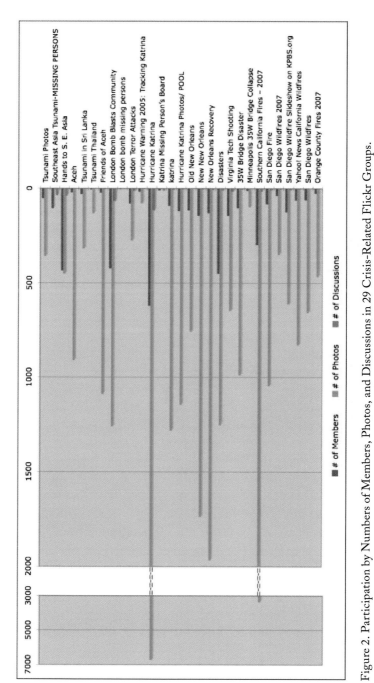

Figure 2. Participation by Numbers of Members, Photos, and Discussions in 29 Crisis-Related Flickr Groups.

another area for normative development that might emerge over time. We discuss each in turn.

Finding Purpose with Crisis-Related Flickr Groups

Each time a Flickr group is created, its group administrator (the "group admin") has the option to state the group's purpose, which at least initially defines the boundaries of the content that is to be posted. Oftentimes, group admins will solicit membership to their groups by finding independently posted photos (public photos that exist outside of the Flickr groups) and posting an invitation to join in each photo's comment box.

For groups created in the aftermath of the December 2004 Indian Ocean Tsunami (the first instance of crisis-related Flickr activity), their stated purpose favored themes about newsworthiness, solidarity, historical value, and global education. The Tsunami Photos group consisted of "pictures, which will show the extent of devastation & other info about the Tsunami waves." The Hands to S.E. Asia group created a place to "gather images of our hands and send the power of our urge to help the people of S.E. Asia whose lives, families, homes and environment were damaged." The admin for the Aceh group thought it would be "a good time to get to know this historic region of Southeast Asia at the northern tip of Sumatra island [sic]."

Seven months later, groups created in the wake of the July 2005 London bombings again organized around themes of newsworthiness and global awareness. The group admin of London Bomb Blast Community initially requested that users "post all your personal photo's of the turmoil in London 07 & 21.07.2005 and the days thereafter so that the world can be informed [sic]."

For Hurricane Katrina in 2005, which hit the US Gulf Coast region six weeks later, we begin to see the start of some formalization around the role that Flickr groups might be able to serve around crises. This is in part because we also see the emergence of a particular user as a leader in creating crisis-related Flickr groups. "Kefira," the group administrator for the Hurricane Katrina group, posted that this was an "image aggregator group." In an email interview, she expanded on this designation:

> I wanted people who were still on-line or were afterwards able to get their personal experience out there into a localized location (the group). What followed though was that MANY people from across the world joined and we all posted a variety of news photos during the event which helped global viewers understand and also people in the thick of things understand if they didn't have a good source of news (A huge frustration for me during 9-11.... I wished I had Flickr then).

Following this foray into the topic of crisis, Kefira created the Hurricane Rita group "for the collection of images related to Hurricane Rita in 2005." Similarly, we noticed an emerging trend in group administration, where a Flickr user directly affected by the crisis would often become an additional group admin to support localized requests and activities.

Hurricane Rita, which occurred in the midst of the 2005 Hurricane Katrina aftermath, prompted the start of a meta-disaster group called Disasters, indicating what we believe to be another step in Flickr's evolution of crisis-related activities among members of the public. Although the fledgling practice had been organized around specific events, the rapid succession of crisis events in an already hard-hit region and the rising occurrence of crises around the world were the catalysts for formalizing a bigger-picture proposition for the role that Flickr might play in future crisis events. The Disasters admin posted the following statement:

> We've seen new Flickr groups pop up for specific disasters including 9-11, the S.E. Asian tsunami of December 2004, Hurricane Katrina, Hurricane Rita, various earthquakes and volcanic eruptions, and other disasters around the world. This group is to serve as a general forum for photos and discussions of all major disasters. Whenever a disaster occurs, all people who are concerned are welcome to join.

Whereas previous group creation was instigated in *response* to an event, the act of creating this catch-all or meta-group was looking to the *future*, and an attempt to establish a recognized destination for Flickr-based, crisis-related communication. However, it became clear to the admin that this would not be the only group to contribute to, since his latest announcement posting on the main group page about the August 2007 Minneapolis bridge collapse states, "There is a Flickr group dedicated to the August 1, 2007 bridge collapse in Minneapolis: 35W Bridge Disaster and Minneapolis 35W Bridge Collapse. Please post your images and stories both there and here in the Disasters group." Although photos and discussions of major crises around the world continue to populate this group, other crisis-related groups continue to appear, and so the role of the Disasters group with its meta-purpose in the world of Flickr remains unclear.

The Virginia Tech Shooting group in April 2007 was the third crisis-related group created by Kefira with the purpose of being "an image aggregator" as well as a "way for us to cope with this nightmare." She elaborated in the interview that "the community aspects of Flickr makes it a caring place so its not just photos, not just news, but a personal context and place to come and give condolences and prayers/thoughts." The purpose and intent of this group was to reach beyond photos and news to become an "experience aggregator" as well. Ever since this crisis, news organizations began contacting the admins of crisis-related Flickr

FLICKR PHOTOS: CALIFORNIA WILDFIRES

» More California wildfire photos on Flickr

Figure 3. Yahoo! News Link to Flickr Group

Photo Credit: The Notorious T.D.P.; Alex Miroshnichenko (Miro-Foto.com); and Dan's Sordid & saundry pictures

groups and seeking permission to use the photos in these groups for their news coverage.

By the time of the Minneapolis bridge collapse in August 2007 and the 2007 Southern California fires two months later, it became a regular practice to institute Flickr groups as events unfolded. The 35W Bridge Disaster group had the express purpose of collecting photos related to the collapse; however, the admin also posted that the Disasters group provided a link to this group suggesting people reciprocate by cross-posting photos on the two groups.

Furthermore, the 35W Bridge Disaster group provided links to other online resources relevant to the collapse (e.g., the local chapter of the American Red Cross and the I-35W Mississippi River bridge Wikipedia article). We suggest that the inclusion of these links demonstrates a recognition that such a group *could* grow to serve a larger role in the greater response milieu space by pointing people to relevant resources and information outlets. These are the kinds of participative activities that direct and attract social involvement, and serve to coordinate the elicitation and generation of information.

The Southern California Fires—2007 group provided links to five other Flickr groups created in response to the fires. In addition, Yahoo! News (Figure 3), KPBS, and News 8 created Flickr groups themselves, enabling them to use a collective set of eyewitness photos on their official news sites. These activities are ways of legitimating Flickr—its services *and* its members and their activities—as an authoritative source that is growing to serve an important societal function in crisis situations.

Attempts to Create Tagging Nomenclatures

Tags are keywords associated with some object of information in the arena of social media: photos, in the case of Flickr. Tags can serve as indicators of collective interests and activities (Morville, 2005) when they are aggregated across many people. They allow users "to gather, sort, catalog and share collections of resources or metadata" (Fox, 2006, p. 169). However, research has shown that the naming of tags varies greatly by people and even within a person's own practice, depending on their perception of the future use of tagged objects (Sen et al., 2006).

Some Flickr users have attempted to propel self-organization by providing instructions for tagging photos for specific crises. Immediately after the 2005 Hurricane Katrina, one blogger asked Flickr users to streamline tagging by using tags like "katrinamissing" for missing persons, "katrinafound" for those found, and "katrinaokay" for all evacuees. Similarly, after the 2007 Minneapolis bridge collapse, an E-Democracy.org wiki author explicitly requested that people upload their photos to Flickr and tag them with "mpls35W." The admin for the San Diego Fire Flickr group suggested that users should agree to use a set of tags like "SanDiego" and "Fire"—although we hypothesize that these are common terms that might not have specific enough meaning at a future time.

Although some Flickr users have attempted to formalize the tagging of photos for Katrina and the bridge collapse, few appear to have followed these suggestions. This could be attributable to any number of reasons, including a limited audience, poor marketing, requiring too much effort, poorly designed tags, and so on. Our investigation reveals little evidence that the practice has taken hold, though we predict that this issue will continue to be a point of organizational activity, as the role of photo-sharing sites in crisis contexts continues to emerge.

Photographic Content

The photographic content in the groups of study captures physical features of the crisis over time. Within these photos, we also see features of social convergence that occurred at the geographical site of the crisis as well as sites online.

Images of the Hazard

The activity surrounding the 2007 Southern California fires captures the kind of behaviors that can only occur in crises that have protracted hazard agents. In the case of wildfires, the hazard lends itself to being photographed and in fact builds on a tradition among wildfire fighters who have a shared interest in fire photography.

Between October 22 and 24, 2007, seven of the most active Southern California fires Flickr groups were created with photos showing the smoke and fire at a distance where it might be interpreted as a "threat" (Figure 4) and up close

Ready for evacuation

Figure 4. Fire Threat on October 23
Photo Credit: boiani

FHR_Fire(125)

Foothill Ranch, Orange County, CA. Santiago Canyon Fire. View from backyard of a
Tessera Ave home. Flames are extremely close. First time all day I actually felt the heat of
the fire and was concerned if the winds shifted towards my direction.

Figure 5. Fire Impact on October 29
Photo Credit: Alex Miroshnichenko (Miro-Foto.com)

London tube bombing

Figure 6. London Tube Bomb on July 7
Photo Credit: Adam Stacey uploaded by qwghlm

showing immediate "impact" (Figure 5). In contrast, hazard agents with sudden onset and short impact like bombings and earthquakes can be difficult or impossible to photograph; photos that document such events are often post-impact images of the aftermath. Many cameraphone photos were taken immediately after the 2005 London bombings and uploaded to photo-sharing websites. One of the most notable images that appeared across the internet and was broadcast by mainstream news is the cameraphone photo of people escaping a smoke-filled train, which has now received over 89,000 views on Flickr (Figure 6).

Images of Post-Impact Response

A majority of the photos in these Flickr groups illustrate post-impact response and recovery efforts. Immediately after the Minneapolis bridge collapse, some photos were posted to Flickr (Figure 7). Other photos documented rescue activities by emergency responders and members of the public (Figure 8). Across all the crisis events analyzed here, many photos were taken post-rescue and during the process of recovery, when focused formal and informal relief efforts take place. Many of the photos were of places where people converged on-site to perform relief services, to memorialize, or to witness the devastation (Figure 9).

r_1487317_1

I- 35W Bridge Collapse; Minneapolis, MN.

08/01/2007 6:37pm (cell phone pic)
1.3M Pixel, f/1:2.8, 5.28mm

Interstate 35W Collapse

Figure 7. Images Taken Immediately After the Minneapolis Bridge Collapse
Photo Credits: Rocketalk; david_wetzel2; and Noah Kunin uploaded by Aaron Landry

I-35W Bridge Collapse(6)

Rescuers search the Mississippi River for victims after the collapse of the 35W bridge in Minneapolis.

35W

View of collapsed bridge and rescue operations.I-35W Bridge before and after collapse photos on WorldFlicks

HPIM0199

Citizens helped carry stretchers.

Figure 8. Images of the Rescue Efforts After the Minneapolis Bridge Collapse
Photo Credits: Poppyseed Bandits; spiderleggreen; and TJ Ryan

050101 - Phuket 014 (Mark)

Corpse processing teams at work

IMG_2779

Evacuees at Qualcomm Lining Up for Food

Nobody will be hungry at Qualcomm..

Figure 9. Physical Sites of Convergence during the Post-Impact Stages
Photo Credits (top to bottom): paul_ark; enteroneness; and Nick Carlson

Continued

08072005(013).jpg

Flowers being left at Kings Cross station, London.

Virginia Tech Shooting memorial

Onlookers on Bridge 9

Figure 9. *Continued*

Photo Credits (top to bottom): robinhamman; panchosebas and Jana Stow

Images of Other Online Social Convergence Activity

We see evidence of users cross-referencing to other online activity by uploading screenshots of other social media sites and map mashups—sites that combine data from different online sources to create new information visualizations. Screenshots of Google Maps mashups provided spatial information about the location of the hazard agent and relief resources. After the London bombings, some Flickr photos were screenshots of maps indicating the location of the London bombings. Similar cross-referencing behavior through maps appeared most recently during the Southern California wildfires, with more extensive annotations of relief resources and eyewitness accounts (Figure 10).

In the wake of the 2007 Virginia Tech shooting tragedy, the Flickr user who took a screenshot of Facebook search results (Figure 11) wanted "to track how information traveled much faster than conventional media." Screenshots from Second Life (Figure 12) were also uploaded to Flickr to illustrate the memorialization activities in this virtual world. Such cross-referencing of other forums places Flickr in the web of online activity, thus attracting additional viewers and participants to images that instill more value than what we conventionally associate with photographs.

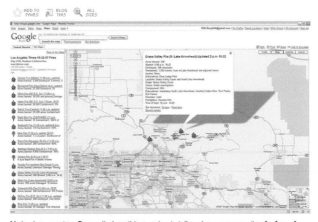

Figure 10. Google Map Mashup Screenshots during the Wildfires

Photo Credit: Will Merydith

Continued

Fire perimeters and evacuation areas as of 9pm 10/22

These are rough estimates from several maps I have seen online. The satellite imagery is from earlier today of course. The smoke plumes are greater now.

For some reason making maps about this helps me cope with not knowing how my friends are doing...

Updating the Google Map

Heather Despol compares the county map to update fire movements online

Figure 10. *Continued*

Photo Credits: nalini asha and Nathan Gibbs

Figure 11. Screenshot of Facebook Group Search
Photo Credit: ArvinSinghKang

VT Memorial

Figure 12. Screenshots from SecondLife of VT Memorials
Photo Credit: scotheadley

Images of Personal Belongings

In Southern California Fires—2007, the admin created the "Strange Pictures" discussion to point out how people were uploading photos of their possessions by using Flickr as a personal repository, and then tagging them with "fire." Having these photos of personal belongings turn up in the results of her searches on the fires was initially "strange" and unanticipated, but the advantages of efficiency and safekeeping within Flickr for these types of photos immediately became clear. As she explained in this discussion post, people were "quickly taking pictures to inventory their houses for insurance purposes and then uploading them to Flickr before they evacuate."

Photo documentation during the warning and threat stages is no longer just motivated by personal reasons but may also be requested explicitly by formal agencies to facilitate recovery. Because Flickr is a repository both for personal use (though these photos are often publicly available) as well as group-based interaction, the features of Flickr—because they cannot discriminate between these two uses—produce curious points of convergence between different stakeholders in disaster settings.

CONCLUSION

Sharing eyewitness photography through social media sites has made citizen journalism more visible, particularly through the cross-referencing and convergence of different media sources. Cameraphones have also made citizen journalism even more significant to emergency response efforts, as they are no longer seen as mere personal accounts but also as evidential documents. Indeed, it is now common for eyewitness photos to be requested by formal emergency response agencies. Mainstream media are already starting to use this information to their advantage with services like Yahoo!'s You Witness News and CNN's iReport. No matter how good professional photojournalists are in crisis situations, "the sheer number of people with cameras and internet access makes it inevitable that many of the best pics will come from normal people," as one Flickr user commented.

Of course, what we see in Flickr and other citizen media venues represents only the beginnings of such possibilities. This is an organic process of innovation that nevertheless has significant elements of self-organization. New, important questions thus arise about how we can shape technological development to adapt to this emerging phenomenon of citizen photojournalism into avenues that help in crisis response, recovery, and education.

ACKNOWLEDGMENTS

This chapter is based upon our paper "In Search of the Bigger Picture: The Emergent Role of On-Line Photo Sharing in Times of Disaster," presented at the 5ᵗʰ International Information Systems for Crisis Response and Management (ISCRAM) Conference, Washington, DC (see Liu et al., 2008). We are deeply appreciative of those who participated and assisted in our studies. Any opinions, findings, and conclusions or recommendations expressed in this material are those of the authors and do not necessarily reflect the views of the National Science Foundation. This research has been supported by the National Science Foundation: NSF CAREER Grant IIS-0546315 awarded to Palen; NSF Graduate Fellowship awarded to Liu; and NSF grant CMMI-074304 awarded to the Natural Hazards Center.

REFERENCES

Allan, S. (2007) "Citizen journalism and the rise of 'mass self-communication': reporting the London bombings." *Global Media Journal: Australian Edition, 1*(1), 1–20.

Fox, R. (2006) "Cataloging for the masses." *OCLC Systems & Services: International Digital Library Perspectives, 22*(3), 166–172.

Giles, R. (2006) *How to use Flickr: the digital photography revolution.* Boston, MA: Thomson Course Technology.

Gillmor, D. (2006) *We the media: grassroots journalism by the people, for the people.* Sebastopol, CA: O'Reilly Media, Inc.

Harrison, B. (2004) "Snap happy: toward a sociology of 'everyday' photography." In C.J. Pole (Ed.), *Seeing is believing? approaches to visual research* (Vol. 7, pp. 23–39). Amsterdam: Elsevier.

Jenkins, H. (2006) *Convergence culture: where old and new media collide.* New York: NYU Press.

Kendra, J., & Wachtendorf, T. (2003) "Reconsidering convergence and converger legitimacy in response to the World Trade Center disaster." In *Terrorism and disaster: new threats, new ideas.* New York: Elsevier.

Liu, S.B., Palen, L., Sutton, J., Hughes, A.L., & Vieweg, S. (2008) "In search of the bigger picture: the emergent role of on-line photo sharing in times of disaster." *Proceedings of the 5th International Information Systems for Crisis Response and Management (ISCRAM) Conference,* May 5–7, 2008, Washington, DC, 140–149.

Martin, J., & Martin, R. (2004) "History through the lens: every picture tells a story." In C. Pole (Ed.), *Seeing is believing? approaches to visual research* (Vol. 7, pp. 9–22). Amsterdam: Elsevier.

Morville, P. (2005) *Ambient findability.* Sebastopol, CA: O'Reilly Media Inc.

Palen, L., & Liu, S.B. (2007) "Citizen communications in disaster: anticipating a future of ICT-supported public participation." *Proceedings of the SIGCHI Conference on Human Factors in Computing Systems,* 727–736.

Palen, L., Vieweg, S., Liu, S.B., Hughes, A., & Sutton, J. (forthcoming) "Crisis in a networked world: features of computer-mediated communication in the April 16, 2007 Virginia Tech event." *Social Science Computer Review (Special Issues on e-Social Science),* Sage.

Rosen, C. (2005) "The image culture." *The New Atlantis: A Journal of Technology & Society, 10* (Fall), 27–46.

Sen, S., Lam, S., Cosley, D., Frankowski, D., Osterhouse, J., Harper, F., & Riedl, J. (2006) "Tagging, communities, vocabulary, evolution." *Proceedings of the 2006 20th Anniversary Conference on Computer Supported Cooperative Work*, 181–190.

Stallings, R., & Quarantelli, E. (1985) "Emergent citizen groups and emergency management." *Public Administration Review, 45*, 93–100.

Sutton, J., Palen, L., & Shlovski, I. (2008) "Back-channels on the front lines: emerging use of social media in the 2007 Southern California wildfires." *Proceedings of the 5th International ISCRAM Conference*, May 5–7, 2008, Washington, DC, 624–632.

CHAPTER FOUR

Wikinews Reporting OF Hurricane Katrina

FARIDA VIS

When Hurricane Katrina hit the American Gulf Coast in the summer of 2005, more than 1,800 people lost their lives as a result of the storm. Mainstream news media in the country were quick to criticize the slow rate at which the government was responding to the disaster and getting aid to its victims, and rightly so. Intermingled in many reports, however, were accusations of blame directed at the mostly African-American storm victims themselves. Such insensitivity, commentators observed, made the victims' tragic predicament even worse (Giroux, 2006; Harris & Carbado, 2007; Sommers, Apfelbaum, Dukes, Toosi, & Wang, 2006).

With most of New Orleans underwater and difficult to reach, communication networks were gravely affected. Major news media, unable to gain sufficient access, severely compromised normal journalistic routines of fact checking. Unsubstantiated claims were all too frequently reported without adequate checking and later found to be either grossly exaggerated or false (Barsky, Trainor, & Torres, 2006). Some of the more extreme reports mobilized racial stereotypes, focusing on allegations of looting, rape, and murder within a narrative frame of urban uprising (Entman & Rojecki, 2000), rather than that of a natural disaster, where such behavior is extremely rare (Sommers et al., 2006). Even the (relatively) more balanced news reports routinely framed the city as being lawless, New Orleans being characterized as a war zone (Giroux, 2006).

For those on the ground, the collapse of the communication network meant that coordinating a response was severely hampered. Local media provided a vital resource for those able to connect to the internet, creating "virtual spaces for people to connect with one another, posing questions and sharing information" (Allan, 2006, p. 158). Comparing three crisis situations in 2005 including Hurricane Katrina, Thelwall and Stuart (2007) examined which, if any, new technologies were used during these events. For Katrina, echoing Allan's observations, they noted that the local media (such as *The Times Picayune* and its affiliated website NOLA) played a significant part alongside the mainstream media, CNN in particular. New communication forms were seen to be especially useful for sharing information and fact finding in the initial stages of the event. Examples included online forums and discussion boards such as those provided by some local television stations; missing persons registers such as Katrinacheck-in.org, Craigslist New Orleans, and Hurricane Katrina Survivor Forums; the use of Google Maps' API to power the Katrina Information Map website, which contained markers and written entries about conditions in their respective neighborhoods; the photo-sharing website Flickr.com, which contained collections of photographs taken by ordinary citizens; not to mention the syndication of content by Wikipedia, the successful online encyclopedia (see Allan, 2006, pp. 158–159).

This chapter discusses how news of the hurricane and its immediate aftermath was reported on Wikipedia's sister project, Wikinews. It analyzes the news reports, focusing on a selection of stories and, furthermore, the transparent wiki production process rendered visible through the talk and history pages linked to every article. The qualitative findings presented here are thus drawn from a combination of textual analysis with an assessment of the production process through retracing and examining all electronically documented steps. Of particular interest, in my view, was the extent to which Wikinews succeeded in offering alternative perspectives to the prevailing framing of the event in the mainstream media.

WIKINEWS: A BRIEF OVERVIEW

Wikinews emerged as a sister project to Wikipedia, with users voting to accept the proposal for the news site, in October 2004. Its structure was adopted from Wikipedia, including a hierarchy where elected administrators could block/delete stories and/or users, with bureaucrats above them afforded additional powers. Regular users, proving their dedication to the project through hard work, can request to advance in this hierarchy, and users vote on all such requests (Bruns, 2006; Lih, 2004; McIntosh, 2008; Thorsen, 2008).

Key to this new endeavor was that news should be written from a Neutral Point of View (NPOV)—a policy inherited from Wikipedia, which extends to all news articles (but not their associated talk pages). Wikipedia founder Jimmy D. Wales argued that the NPOV "attempts to present ideas and facts in such a fashion that both supporters and opponents can agree" (Wikinews, 2005a). The policy is similar in principle to the ideals of impartiality and objectivity, though neutrality is further perceived as pluralistic and only achievable through a *collective* process of mediation (Allan, 2006). While a laudable ideal, Thorsen (2008) demonstrates how "the implementation of the neutral point of view policy is inconsistent" across Wikinews articles and as such is "more likely to reflect the individual contributors' interpretation than a unified concept" (p. 949).

Two types of articles can be found on Wikinews: synthesis articles and those containing original reporting (OR). The first type, by far the most common, is reliant on media reports from other sources. The second, relatively infrequent, revolves around first-hand news items written by Wikinews contributors reporting news events on the spot (Wikinews, 2004). These latter reports carry an identifying textbox with the Wikinews logo and a message stating that it relies on "first-hand reporting." Furthermore, the policy on original reporting stipulates that "adequate notes" must be accessible on the discussion page along with the article, and information should be from "qualified sources"—that is, essentially elite or expert sources that are "taken seriously by the general public when commenting on a particular area of expertise" (Wikinews, 2004). In contrast to Wikipedia, when major developments take place, these require new stories and not simply updates to existing articles.

In essence, then, Wikinews is about news "written from a neutral point of view" that is "factual," "relevant," and, of course, "collaborative" (Wikinews, 2004, 2005b). Significantly, it "is not an encyclopedia; that is, not an in-depth collection of non-newsworthy information," and it "is not a dumping ground for failed Wikipedia articles" (Wikinews, 2005c). Despite this distinction, a comparison between the two websites is frequently drawn. *The New York Times*, for instance, published a story in July 2007 highlighting how Wikinews produced "only" 8–10 articles a day on a "grab bag of topics" (Dee, 2007). This was in strong contrast to Wikipedia, which was identified as increasingly having become "a go-to source not just for reference material but for real-time breaking news," particularly in large, national news events such as the mass murder at Virginia Tech (Dee, 2007). In one of many responses from the Wikinews community, Edbrown asserted that while Wikipedia "does not do news.... Sadly, Wikinews is not doing news" either, adding that "original reporting cannot be performed until the community comes to accept new users, insists on notes (I guess) and accept on good faith that the report is respectable" (Wikinews, 2007). This highlights issues of trust among the core community of users and its suspicion of newcomers, who may just file for one event, thus hindering efforts to embrace plurality on the site and make it fully inclusive.

McIntosh (2008) posits that the English Wikinews sits at the crossroads of three journalistic fields: collaborative journalism, "with its tendency toward techno-geek interests, non-market operating principles, and culture of collaboration and consensus"; citizen journalism, "with its heritage in alternative media and ideals regarding participatory democracy and an engaged citizenry"; and finally mainstream journalism—arguing that it does not completely fit into any one of these, nor does it easily fit into all three (p. 197).

This chapter will now turn to examine how Wikinews responded to Hurricane Katrina and its aftermath, focusing first on the tension between original reporting and eyewitness reports, and second on the reporting of lawlessness.

REPORTING HURRICANE KATRINA ON WIKINEWS

In order to identify the Wikinews articles dealing with Katrina and its aftermath, two search terms were used in the Wikinews archive: "Hurricane Katrina" and its shorthand term "Katrina." The latter of these produced the most results, 147 stories with Katrina either in the headline or the main body of text. Two stories were discarded, as they involved people named Katrina and were unrelated to the hurricane. Of the remaining 145 stories, 109 (75.2%) appeared in 2005, but further stories appeared every year since (18 in 2006, 14 in 2007, and 4 in 2008).[1] These often involved updates on issues directly linked to the aftermath of the hurricane, such as funding (or lack thereof) for evacuees and their ongoing displacement, the reappointment of New Orleans Mayor Clarence Ray Nagin, threat of other storms, and comparisons between these and Katrina.

This chapter concentrates on the stories that appeared within 20 days of the first reports of the storm on August 26, 2005. It was felt that this accurately depicted the time frame within which news of the hurricane and its aftermath was most prominent. In this period, 78 stories were published, which represents the majority (71.6%) of the stories for 2005, and more than half (53.8%) of the total stories to date. Based on information in their respective headlines, these stories were subdivided into a number of categories to better understand what types of stories were being written.[2]

ORIGINAL REPORTING AND EYEWITNESS ACCOUNTS

Within 20 days of Katrina striking New Orleans, Wikinews had published six stories containing original reporting of some sort. A further two stories were labelled as "eyewitness accounts." If we include such accounts as part of original news material produced, then 8 stories out of 78, representing 8.9%, contained original coverage. Although the two eyewitness reports had been highlighted and flagged as valuable source material by regular contributor and professional journalist Clare White, they were not used in any story. Responding to one eyewitness account, contributor Borofkin asked for clarity about "the difference between a Wikinewsie doing original reporting, and an eyewitness who posts a report directly to the site" (Wikinews, 2005d). Edbrown commented that the "one-person writing approach is not the wiki way…an eyewitness report is a sole person contribution" (Wikinews, 2005d). Respondents thus agreed that this material should be treated as "source material" alongside other sources, and—because of its perceived bias—clearly marked as "eyewitness account," so that these stories could be moved to the right place on the site rather than deleted.

An important example of an unused eyewitness account is from September 6 and written by two visitors to the city caught up in Katrina's aftermath. They wrote a detailed and eloquent report commenting on the "callous and hostile" law enforcement, inept relief effort, and role of the media. Left to their own devices, they and others had camped outside a central police station to be "plainly visible to the media" and a "highly visible embarrassment to the City's officials." They left only when it was promised that buses were waiting at the city limits. When met by police fire instead, it became clear to them that the "poor and black" were "not getting out of New Orleans" and that the police broke up groups like theirs because "in every congregation of 'victims' they saw 'mobs' or 'riot,'" concluding that "lives were lost that did not need to be lost" (Wikinews, 2005e).

One further report, labeled as original reporting, that did not quite fit Wikinews's own strict OR guidelines warrants closer inspection here. The story, "Colleges offering admission to displaced New Orleans students," first published on September 2, included a list of colleges in the United States and elsewhere to which people affected by the storm could transfer. At the same time it included messages from individuals willing to take students into their homes as well as instructions to new users on how to add more information. Dan100 commented: "It's not what Wikinews would normally consider a 'story'…but if we can't make exceptions at times like these, we'd be a bunch of assholes" (Wikinews, 2005f). Furthermore, Clare White observed: "This is a remarkable piece of work: the sort of collaborative reporting that gives people the chance to do something useful in response to the news and Wikinews is the place to come for new information, *the purest sort of news*" (Wikinews, 2005f; emphasis added). While this is the only such list tagged as containing original reporting, a further five information lists containing similar collated material were produced, collectively responsible for a staggering 65% of the total words produced during the first 20 days of coverage under discussion here.

REPORTING LAWLESSNESS

During the first 20 days of coverage, a total of six articles centered on crime or looting, or both, two of which will be analyzed below. It is worth noting that these six stories were collectively written by 51 different users, seven[3] of whom made contributions to more than one story—all of whom are active Wikinewsies. Moreover, 37.3% of the contributors to these six stories are unregistered users, this typically being their first contribution.

The first story, "Crime in New Orleans sharply increases after Hurricane Katrina," was first published on September 1 by Paulrevere2005 and contained one source (AP). It consisted essentially of an opening sentence and a quote from Chief of Police Eddie Compass, stating that people were being raped and getting beaten, and further highlighting that up to 20,000 people waiting at the Superdome were growing increasingly hostile.

The opening sentence of this article warrants further examination so as to demonstrate how various users made key changes in order to reduce its seemingly unverified sensationalism: "Victims of hurricane [sic] Katrina are being raped and beaten, fights and fires are out of control and corpses lay out in the open as New Orleans resembles a scene straight out of Dante's 'Inferno'" (Wikinews, 2005g). Before Brian "fixed" the story, freezing it from further edits (on June 3, 2007) after two automated changes by Craig's bot,[4] the story had been changed 13 times, most notably by Yarvin and unregistered user 204.96.170.74, identified only through their IP address. Yarvin commented on the talk page that he "updated the article to make it past tense and make the first paragraph *less sensational* and have *less implication of authority*" (Wikinews, 2005g; emphasis added). Yarvin thus changed allusions to Dante's *Inferno* and the ending of the first paragraph to: "the city descended into anarchy" (Wikinews, 2005g), which is how it stayed as the story was edited. The second, unregistered, user made significant changes to the story, adding two further sources to the two listed at that point, 12 days after the story was first released. Most crucially, the poster added the following statement: "Reports of rampant violence though, may have been overblown, even by New Orleans standards, as many reports of sensational violence have not been verified" (Wikinews, 2005g). Through adding two sources—a piece by Gary Young from the UK paper *The Guardian* on separating fact from fiction in New Orleans and an item from *Slate* on examining rumors that martial law had been declared—the story now offered some counterweight to the seemingly unquestioned remarks by the New Orleans police chief and the earlier sentiment of the piece.

The second story, "Widespread looting blamed for disrupted rescue efforts in New Orleans," first published on September 1, contained 28 changes written by 20 different users, of which half were not registered. This story highlighted FEMA's reported halting of aid shipments to the city due to perceived danger from looters. The article discussed various acts of looting, including information coming through blogs and grassroots organizations that claimed police officers were looting cars and stores, which slowly came to the attention of the mainstream media.

During the development of this story, the NPOV policy was raised twice, once by Wikinews regular Paulrevere2005 and once by an unregistered user. Paulrevere2005 made significant changes to the fifth sentence of the article, which claimed a rescue helicopter was shot at and as a result had aborted the operation. The sentence was changed to: "A rescue helicopter attempting to retrieve stranded people from New Orleans's Superdome stadium was *reportedly* shot at; *but this has not been confirmed*" [additions by Paulrevere2005 in italics]. Highlighting the issue on the talk pages, he stated: "In our reporting we must be careful. CNN reported earlier that it is unclear whether a helicopter was even shot at or whether the transportation of refugees was even delayed" (Wikinews, 2005h). The unregistered user changed the opening sentence by altering the claim that Mayor Nagin had given orders to stop "saving lives" to deal with civil unrest—which was deemed value laden—to stopping "the rescue effort"—which is arguably less so. On the associated talk page, one anonymous user posted comments attacking both the slowness of Wikinews as well as the NPOV policy, commenting (under the headline "WIKINEWS, WHERE ARE YOU?"):

> **Where the hell are you?** Every other media org is covering how incredibly late the Federal govt.'s response was to this disaster. But not a peep out of WIKINEWS. By now, EVEN Bush has admitted the response was inadequate. WIKINEWS seems to be very late in the game on things like this.... **I have to wonder if there is a lot of conservatives here who rabidly delete/edit factual news and headlines and hide behind a bullsh|t NPOV to promote their agenda here?** (Wikinews, 2005h; boldface in original)

While the comment did not receive a response here, it also appeared on the much more elaborate talk pages of another Katrina article, "Louisiana officials accused of blocking rescue volunteers," which first appeared on September 2. Containing original reporting, it was based on an email received by a local attorney who forwarded it to Wikinews as possible source material.[5] In response to the anonymous comments, Wikinews contributor Robert Horning observed: "There is definitely an agenda right now among some reporters and media outlets to use this as an opportunity to try and burn Bush once and for all. *That is not the role of Wikinews*" (2005g; emphasis added).

CONCLUSION

Robert Entman (2003) has highlighted how difficult it is to counter dominant media frames once they have been reported for several days. Particularly so, I would argue, when they are so heavily wrapped in ingrained racial stereotypes (see also Entman & Rojecki, 2000). While there was some evidence in the selected crime and looting stories that Wikinewsies urged care in reporting and also sought additional sources to balance more sensational claims, this was a fairly slow process. Although promising eyewitness accounts were available, these were not used, and the site, struggling to produce original reports, continued to rely on a syndication of other news media—though including a mix of international, national, and local online and offline sources in its reporting. Where the site excelled was in producing collated lists of information, though it was not the purpose of this study to determine the accuracy and usefulness of these. However, returning to Wikinews's own ideas on freely accessible public knowledge, and Thelwall and Stuart's (2007) findings on crisis communication, such collated information can be of vital importance. Indeed, those produced by *The Times Picayune*'s website NOLA.com made a significant difference to rescue efforts, attracting international attention and heralding a watershed moment in participant journalism.

There seems to be a genuine drive and desire among Wikinews contributors to produce original material. However, there is also frequent discussion of the practical difficulties of doing so and the inevitability of having to rely on the mainstream media for information. Two years after Katrina, contributor DragonFire1024 summarized the bottom line: "If we had news that was just OR we would have *no news*" (Wikinews, 2007; emphasis added). Indeed, the reluctance of Wikinews in embracing raw eyewitness reports and the requirement for a pluralistic interpretation of the Neutral Point of View in each article appear in the case of Hurricane Katrina to have hindered the website in publishing the plethora of accounts seen on other citizen journalism sites. This is not to suggest, however, that Wikinews as a citizen journalism project is futile. Rather, it indicates that the community is still in the process of developing their unique form of journalistic practice. Indeed, just as their neutral point of view is described as an ongoing process (Thorsen, 2008, p. 939), the Wikinews model is a process that requires time to mature in order to reach the level of success that Wikipedia is experiencing.

NOTES

1. The stated figure for 2008 was accurate in June 2008. Data accessed June 12, 2008.
2. The ten categories used for this simple division, choosing a category based on its prime topic, were: "weather/meteorological," "economy," "survivors/evacuees," "critique/blame of

the government," "fundraising/donations," "crime/looting," "eyewitness accounts," "state aid," "rescue effort," "other."

3. These seven users were Paulrevere2005, McCart42, NGerda, CmWhite, Craig's bot, Brian, and Cspurrier.

4. Craig's bot is a software program that performs automated tasks and is owned by keen Wikinews user Cspurrier, who joined after having tried to set up a similar site before discovering Wikinews and making his first edit on March 15, 2005, swiftly climbing to the status of administrator and bureaucrat (October 3, 2005). Furthermore, Lih (2004, p. 9) highlights the use of such bots on Wikipedia, one in particular: software robot RAMBOT. Between October 18 and 26, 2002, it was responsible for creating 30,000 articles on the US cities from census data.

5. It is worth noting that this email is not one of the two eyewitness accounts highlighted earlier.

REFERENCES

Allan, S. (2006) *Online news: journalism and the internet.* Maidenhead and New York: Open University Press.

Barsky, L., Trainor, J., & Torres, M. (2006) "Disaster realities in the aftermath of Hurricane Katrina: revisiting the looting myth." *Natural Hazards Center Quick Response Report, 84,* 1–4.

Bruns, A. (2006) "Wikinews: the next generation of online news?" *Scan Journal* (1).

Dee, J. (2007) "All the news that's fit to print out." *The New York Times,* 1 July.

Entman, R.M. (2003) *Projections of power: framing news, public opinion, and U.S. foreign policy.* Chicago: University of Chicago Press.

Entman, R.M., & Rojecki, A. (2000) *The black image in the white mind: media and race in America.* Chicago: University of Chicago Press.

Giroux, H. (2006) *Stormy weather: Katrina and the politics of disposability.* Boulder, CO: Paradigm Publishers.

Harris, C.I., & Carbado, D.W. (2007) "Loot or find: fact or frame?" In D. Trout (Ed.), *After the storm: black intellectuals explore the meaning of Hurricane Katrina.* New York: The New Press.

Lih, A. (2004) "The foundations of participatory journalism and the Wikipedia project." Paper presented at the Association for Education in Journalism and Mass Communications, Toronto, Canada, 7 August.

McIntosh, S. (2008) "Collaboration, consensus, and conflict: negotiating news the wiki way." *Journalism Practice, 2*(2), 197–211.

Sommers, S.R., Apfelbaum, E.P., Dukes, K.N., Toosi, N., & Wang, E.J. (2006) "Race and media coverage of Hurricane Katrina: analysis, implications, and future research questions." *Analyses of Social Issues and Public Policy, 6*(1), 39–55.

Thelwall, M., & Stuart, D. (2007) "RUOK? Blogging communication technologies during crises." *Journal of Computer Mediated Communication, 12,* 523–548.

Thorsen, E. (2008) "Journalistic objectivity redefined? Wikinews and the neutral point of view." *New Media and Society, 10*(6), 935–954.

Wikinews (2004) "Wikinews: content guide." *Wikinews*.

Wikinews (2005a) "Wikinews: neutral point of view." *Wikinews*.

Wikinews (2005b) "Wikinews: what Wikinews is." *Wikinews*.

Wikinews (2005c) "Wikinews: what Wikinews is not." *Wikinews*.

Wikinews (2005d) "Wikinews: Water cooler/miscellaneous/Archive/8." *Wikinews*.

Wikinews (2005e) "User:Cmwhite/Disasters and accidents/Eyewitness accounts/Katrina aftermath Bradshaw and Slonsky." *Wikinews*.

Wikinews (2005f) "Colleges offering admission to displaced New Orleans students." *Wikinews*.

Wikinews (2005g) "Crime in New Orleans sharply increases after Hurricane Katrina." *Wikinews*.

Wikinews (2005h) "Widespread looting blamed for disrupted rescue efforts in New Orleans." *Wikinews*.

Wikinews (2007) "Wikinews: Water cooler/proposals/Archive/15." *Wikinews*.

CHAPTER FIVE

Citizen Journalism IN India: The Politics OF Recognition

PRASUN SONWALKAR

These are early days for citizen journalism in India, where the chiaroscuro of cultures, politics, and geography is slowly and steadily breaking through the limitations of mainstream media and providing new forms of expression and empowerment. The country is frequently heralded in Western press accounts as the next economic success story due to factors such as its commitment to democracy, the prevalence of the English language, the growing prosperity underpinning a burgeoning middle class, the prestige of its information technology sector, and the relative proportion of young people making up its population. India is seen as a challenge and a land of opportunity; an investor in Western nations and a taker of Western jobs.

The evolution of citizen journalism in India needs to be situated within these and related contexts. It is useful to look at India on three levels: global India, developing India, and the poorest India—all three existing at the same time. It is true that India's economic base has grown since it accelerated reforms in the early 1990s, but this does not conceal the larger reality of deprivation and poverty for the majority of its one billion-plus population. Beyond gushing news accounts and glitzy television shows, serious problems continue to challenge policy-makers dealing with "developing India" and the "poorest India." There are several segments of Indian society—in Bhargava's (2002) words, "the isolated and shunned India"—that are struggling for the basics of human existence, including recognition as normal and equal citizens.

This conundrum of everyday contradictions intersects with the world of news media and citizen journalism in several ways. The "global India" seems to have taken off with breathtaking speed: the country is now the second largest newspaper market in the world, hundreds of local television channels have emerged, Bollywood rivals Hollywood, the number of mobile telephone users increases by millions every month, and internet connectivity is spreading at a remarkable rate. In addition, television growth has added a visual dimension to India's public sphere. Together, the new media and nascent citizen-driven journalism have increased interaction and integration among peoples, institutions, local economies, regions, and cultures that do not have much in common, let alone sharing a singular conception of national identity.

This technologically deterministic good-news story has an equally valid part and counterpart: quantity is not the same as quality. News media output has been widely criticized for its focus on cricket, crime, celebrities, and the occult, as the quality of journalism and ethics suffer at the altar of fierce competition and ratings. The constant breach of journalism's professional ideals has called into question the reputations, if not integrity, of the mainstream news media and their capacity to create and sustain public discussion and debate over pressing social issues in positive, responsible ways. It is against this backdrop that the empowering potential of citizen journalism has generated hope that the hitherto insular "global India" will not only enjoy its newfound prosperity, but will also focus attention on the serious difficulties of everyday life facing the majority of people in the country.

This chapter looks at some unique ways in which citizen journalism is being used to recognize minorities, influence public discourse, seek justice, cut corruption, and raise awareness among people about their rights. In a media-rich, poor country where the basic infrastructure required to practice citizen journalism—electricity, computers, phones, internet service—is still limited to a small segment of the population, the effects may not be immediately apparent. Citizen journalism has yet to achieve the same status here as it has in the United States, the United Kingdom, or even South Korea, but there are several indications that it is beginning to take root and realize its potential. Across the country, alternative spaces are opening up for otherwise marginalized voices to be heard.

THE POLITICS OF RECOGNITION AND CITIZEN JOURNALISM

Citizen journalism, which is predicated on the ability of citizens to contribute to mainstream and alternative news discourse, has the potential of enriching the public sphere and enabling the expression of a wider range of opinions necessary to function as aware and responsible citizens in a democracy. This is particularly important in a society as diverse as India, where the benefits of modernity and democracy have been asymmetrically dispersed.

Sixty years after independence in 1947, there are large sections of Indian society clamoring to be recognized, that is, to be acknowledged as equals of other citizens, entitled to all the rights and privileges duly accorded in a democracy. This politics of recognition includes different minorities (gender, religion, caste, ethnic) who are sometimes also located in peripheral regions such as the northeast, thereby further accentuating their distance from national consciousness (Sonwalkar, 2004).

Reporting for *The Times of India* from the insurgency-ridden north-east region, I often travelled to remote areas through difficult terrain and hostile circumstances. Often, the datelines of my news reports were names of villages and small towns that had never figured in national newspaper discourse before. Copies of the newspaper would reach the region a few days after publication. On several occasions, readers would write to the editor that "even if India has not recognized us and our village, at least *The Times of India* has." The very sight of the village or town name as the dateline in a prestigious newspaper (often identified with the New Delhi-based establishment, which people in the region regarded with some hostility at times), became cause for much comment and satisfaction, irrespective of the contents of the actual news item.

Citizen journalism's potential to extend such forms of recognition is becoming increasingly evident. Blogs and news websites have been set up in large numbers, catering to the issues, events, and everyday life of such groups and regions (Sonwalkar & Allan, 2007). They not only provide a form of recognition but also inspire some privileged citizens to highlight issues that are of concern to minorities and, in the process, seek to influence and enrich the Indian public sphere.

Macro-perspectives of citizen journalism by scholars such as Bruns (2008) and Atton (2008) attest to the fact that citizen journalists can, and often do, empower themselves and their communities. As Atton (2008) noted, "This journalism is less focused on the journalist as a professional; instead, it proposes a relationship between writer and reader that reimagines the status of journalism and its audiences" (p. 216). New technologies have, in essence, led to new ways of thinking, practicing, and producing journalism content in India, even if it continues to be limited to a small section of the "global India." This was evident during the Boxing Day tsunami in South Asia (Srinivas, 2005) and later during the earthquakes in Gujarat, Kashmir, and the torrential rains in Mumbai in 2005.

CITIZEN JOURNALISM IN INDIA

The first websites devoted to news—Samachar.com and Rediff.com—were set up in the mid-1990s by entrepreneurs Rajesh Jain and Ajit Balakrishnan. Traditional English and Indian-language newspapers soon went online, and several other news websites unrelated to media groups were set up. Hundreds of thousands of Indians have since created their own personal blogs to debate a range of topics. Blogging has yet to reach Western levels, but there are indications that it is rapidly gaining in popularity. Citizen journalism has since influenced the reporting of crises, intervened in social and human rights issues, exposed political corruption (e.g., Tehelka.com), highlighted malpractices in mainstream media (e.g., the Pen Pricks blog), and voiced issues of concern to women in a male-dominated society. The internet has enabled civic society groups to enhance awareness of events and issues, evoke reactions, and coordinate protests in different parts of India.

The reporting of the Mumbai rains in July 2005 was a high-water mark, as commentators remarked that it signaled the beginning of internet-based citizen journalism in the country. Several websites published eyewitness accounts of the incessant rains, updating them regularly with information and advice for help. The news portal Rediff.com, which registers a large number of hits from within India as well as outside, also became a crucial link for rescue acts. One of the many emails the website received was:

> Please help!
> July 26, 2005 23:45 IST
> rediff.com received this mail from a reader last night.
> Subject: URGENT: 100 LIVES AT RISK IN KURLA, NEAR BKC BUS DEPOT, IT IS A DOUBLE DECKER BUS, PLEASE HELP!!!
> Date: 26 Jul 2005 17:12:02 -0000
> From: "gopa chakrabarti"
> Hi please do something. my younger sister and more than 100 people are in a double decker BEST BUS near BKC bus depot. they are unable to call from their mobiles, i called my sister with great difficulty. the water has filled the first floor of the bus and they are all stuck.is there no one that can help, fire brigade, helicopters, even if someone could pass them a rope from some height their lives can be saved. they are unable to come out as the water is flowing with force and is above 15 feet. i tried calling police 100 and 101 but no reply. u r my only help as i know u can reach to many people. I am in nagpur and am helpless.
> please help.
> gopa

The key source of breaking news on the rains was no longer the radio, television, or the press. Rediff.com not only reported the news; its journalists also tried to help by telephoning officials and passing on information received from citizens' postings on the website. It received information through email and bulletin boards from citizens not only within India, but also from the large number of Indians working or settled in the United States and the United Kingdom. For the Indian diaspora, the internet was the main source of communicating and seeking information about the developing situation in Mumbai. During the downpour, the movement of television crews was severely hampered by waterlogged streets, which prompted citizens stranded in their homes to use video cameras to record the devastation around them. Such citizen-gathered footage was aired extensively on television news channels such as Aj Tak and STAR News, making them the most widely watched channels during the rains.

In 2006 the first Indian website wholly devoted to citizen journalism was set up, named merinews (meri news = my news) and with the motto: "Power to People." It hails itself as "India's First Citizen Journalism News Portal." Six months into its operation, it won the Manthan Award for publishing the best e-news content in India for the year, and in 2007 it was an Official Honoree at the Webby Awards. Upadhyay (2008), the site's founder and editor, calls merinews a "product with a mission: a people's news platform of the people, by the people, for the people, providing power to the people and empowering democracy." It also runs a campaign to create a citizens' manifesto for India's next 60 years—a blueprint for the future of the nation—which is also meant to reinvigorate citizens' participation in the political process.

The idea is to provide a platform for issues and opinions of people who may not find space in the mainstream news media and, in the process, further democratize India's public sphere. The website publishes news content that is written by citizens as well as journalists keen to highlight issues that are neglected in the mainstream news media. Since the early 1990s, when a focus on profit led to a perceived "dumbing down" of news content and "Murdochization" entrenched itself (Sonwalkar, 2002), several socially relevant beats—such as education, health, rural development, and agriculture—have been abolished in the newsrooms of the mainstream news media. Websites such as merinews have taken up reporting such beats to highlight the plight and problems of "developing" India and the "poorest India," even though its impact is not as yet clear.

The most visible dimension of citizen journalism is the participation of citizens in the news production of news channels that invite contributions from within India and South Asia, as well as the Indian diaspora across the globe. Most channels have citizen-produced content as an essential element of their output. CNN-IBN, a joint-venture news channel between CNN and India Business News, has hoardings across major Indian towns with the catch-line: "You see it. You report it." Viewers of NDTV, a widely watched news channel, regularly use text messaging to force courts to re-open longstanding, unresolved criminal cases and to expedite the delivery of justice. The channel broadcasts a daily bulletin called "My News," for which the running-order is voted on by viewers. Channels broadcasting in Hindi, English, and several other Indian languages use such strategies to highlight the ways in which ordinary people are actively engaged in the collating and presenting of news. As Singh (2008) observed,

> The new trend of including video clips sent by the common man in the news content has resulted in substantial changes in television news. As the handy cameras have become a common electronic device in Indian urban middle class homes, now common viewer can also shoot and share it with the world. This possibility has explored completely new kind of public space which is more democratic in nature…in many cases common people use camera as a tool for fighting corruption and other kind of anti-social activities. (Singh, 2008, p. 4)

In a society that was until the early 1990s served by the relatively staid and mostly officially driven print media, citizen participation is gradually transforming traditional—top-down, official-led—definitions of journalism.

In the next section, three recent examples point to the growing use of new media by citizens to highlight public issues.

Blogathon India

One of the first interventions by citizen journalists to influence India's political process was called "Blogathon India, April 2008." It was inspired by the community of Bangalore-based bloggers called "Blogalorean," and was held from April 20 to 26 during the elections to the Karnataka Assembly. (Bangalore is the capital of the state of Karnataka.) The event was supported by bloggers from cities such as New Delhi, Kolkata, Chennai, Pune, Hyderabad, and Mumbai. According to the organizers, the objectives of the blogathon were:

- Instil a mass awakening amongst citizens and bloggers alike towards issues of social importance that affect our day to day lives.
- Building an interesting and close-knit community of bloggers to learn, share and socialize with a larger purpose.
- Motivate NGOs and other experts to embrace the net and start blogging with their invaluable ideas.
- To provide a platform for thought leadership for ideas to emerge, to get discussed, improved and implemented.
- Introduce citizens to blogging and help them to adopt blogging platforms and tools to express their views.

- Encourage people to blog in regional languages including Hindi, Urdu, Kannada, Tamil, Malayalam, Telugu and Bengali among others. (Citizen Matters, 2008)

Such an organized, online endeavor during a closely contested election, with citizens seeking to talk back to politicians, marks a new development in Indian political communication. The intention was not only to highlight issues of concern to Bangalore, India's IT hub, and other cities in Karnataka, but to also draw in bloggers from different parts of the country.

The event was widely covered by the mainstream news media. The impact of Blogathon India on the elections was not immediately evident, but politicians and political parties are increasingly aware of such websites. There is evidence that political parties are becoming net savvy and often communicate their messages to voters via texts and emails. In constituencies with high numbers of bloggers, politicians are inclined to take citizen journalists seriously. In recent years, journalists writing for news websites have been accredited by the government and also invited to join foreign tours by the president, prime minister, and other representatives.

Blogging on Mobile Phones

Using internet-based SMS services as news broadcasting tools has further enriched citizen journalism in India. Blogging through a mobile telephone is the latest news dissemination format that provides local news "you can use." After decades of enduring a technology deficit, the recent proliferation of telephone (roadside PCOs) and mobile technology has resulted in what can only be described as a communications revolution in India. This is particularly evident in rural areas and in regions where surface communication is slowed by difficult terrain and inclement weather. As of January 2008, there were 241.6 million mobile phones in India, and every month 7.8 million new mobile connections (on average) are added. According to Internet World Stats, in 2007 there were 42 million internet users in India, comprising 3.7% of India's population.

Services such as SMS GupShup and Vakow allow users to send common SMS messages to all members of their groups. Twitter, a US-based micro-blogging service, recently introduced an India gateway to tap into the vast pool of text users in the country. Enterprising individuals have set up groups comprising hundreds of thousands of mobile numbers belonging to particular communities, including language or regional groups. News updates and developments are sent to members several times a day. For example, New Delhi-based Lalchung Siem, a 33-year-old government employee, uses his mobile phone a few times a day to blog in Hmar, a tribal language spoken in north-east India. Hmar is one of many smaller tribes seeking greater recognition and autonomy. Siem's posts are sent free of cost to over 6,000 readers by the SMS GupShup platform. In a widely reported incident, Siem received an SOS call when two boys fell into a river in the Saidan village in Manipur, 2,400 km away from New Delhi. He flashed an SMS, and within minutes a hundred people reached the spot and rescued one of the boys.

Some local journalists have also started their own news services through mobile blogging. A reporter in the north-east offers breaking news from his small town on SMS GupShup.com. A news site in the eastern state of Orissa offers breaking news via the same site and is one of the largest, with over 26,000 subscribers.

"I Never Ask for It"

In the myths and mists of Indian culture, women are accorded a privileged and exalted status. However, the reality of everyday life for most women is very different. In a deeply male-dominated society, women are seen as "items" of pleasure and entertainment or as house-bound individuals, whose sole purpose in life is to look after the family. Women are also seen as inferior and, in many cases, are subjected to domestic violence. On the streets and in public transport in New Delhi and several other towns across India, women are subjected by men to what is popularly called "eve-teasing," which means sexual harassment on the streets, verbally and/ or physically.

Faced with such behavior, a women's group launched an online project called Blank Noise that invites victims to express their experiences in text and video, and in the process engage the "perpetrator, survivor and the mute spectator" of "eve-teasing." Many of Blank Noise's interventions are based on the idea of women physically occupying public spaces—and doing nothing but being alert. The spaces targeted include the South Extension Subway in New Delhi, Brigade Road in Bangalore, Victoria Terminus in Mumbai, Marina Beach in Chennai, and Eat Street in Hyderabad.

The project was set up in January 2005, and accounts of harassment on the blog have triggered debates about women's modesty, dress codes, and definitions of "eve-teasing." Its first blogathon, which invited bloggers to share their experiences, attracted more than 300 bloggers over 10 days, some sharing their experiences for the first time and speaking of incidents that had occurred decades ago. "It was almost as if women in the blogosphere were experiencing a mass catharsis" (Patheja, 2008). The event led to considerable interest in the mainstream media at both national and international levels. As a result, it received contributions from people who were new to blogging. The project evoked much interest from neighboring regions, where women in similar situations wanted to initiate Blank Noise chapters.

Blank Noise also runs a campaign called "I Never Ask for It" that invites women to send in one garment they were wearing when they were sexually harassed in public. Each garment becomes a living testimonial, a witness to the incident. Dress items collected have included salwars, short skirts, jeans, t-shirts, dupattas, and sarees. The organizers of the blog plan to display the items in various cities to highlight the issue. As the blog states:

> When women experience sexual violence/harassment/ or are "teased" they are made to feel guilty for experiencing it. We are taught to blame ourselves for being "dressed provocatively," for being in the wrong location, at the wrong time. Public perception and blame also assumes that a certain female stereotype gets assaulted for the "right reasons".... No matter what you wear, a no means NO. There is no such thing as "asking for it." Blank Noise challenges notions of time, place, dress and person. With I never asked for it—we challenge the notion that women actually "ask to be sexually assaulted."

Indian women have often been blamed, even by senior politicians, for inviting sexual attacks by dressing indecently or provocatively. The blog, supported by a growing number of men and women, has highlighted the scourge of "eve-teasing" in a way that the mainstream news media have never done.

CONCLUSION

So far, citizen journalism in India has had an impact mainly in situations of crisis (tsunami, earthquake, rains), but it is slowly exerting influence in politics by exposing corruption, and in society by highlighting issues such as sexual harassment of women and the problems of people on the margins. It is most visible on television channels where viewers contribute substantially to news content in the form of SMS messages and opinion polls, first-person blogs, video footage, critical commentary, and even via studio discussions about citizen journalism. While its impact has been uneven, the rapid take-up of internet technology by a middle class that is nearly 500 million strong is likely to exert growing influence in reshaping India's public sphere.

POSTSCRIPT

By December 2008, it became increasingly clear that in urban areas such as Mumbai, Bangalore, Chennai, and New Delhi, blogging and participation by citizens in the news-production process was increasing, particularly during crises. If a tipping point of sorts was reached by the online reporting of the incessant rains in Mumbai in 2005, the terror attacks in Mumbai in November 2008 saw citizen journalism playing a more active role. During the 60-hour standoff between terrorists and commandos, there was far more information, support, and pictures provided by citizen journalists on blogs and sites such as Twitter and Flickr than on news channels, which were reporting the events live. Footage captured on mobile phones by guests trapped in the hotels was shown on news channels even while commandos were neutralizing the challenge. While television coverage of the crisis was soon criticized in print and online for its lack of distance, jingoism, sensationalism, and for giving out locations of security forces when the terrorists were being challenged, the online coverage of the crisis saw Mumbai emerging as the "capital of citizen journalism" in India.

REFERENCES

Atton, C. (2008) "Alternative media theory and journalism practice." In M. Boler (Ed.), *Digital media and democracy: tactics in hard times*. Cambridge, MA: MIT Press.

Bhargava, R. (2002) "On the majority-minority syndrome." *The Hindu*, 9 July.

Bruns, A. (2008) *Blogs, Wikipedia, Second Life, and beyond: from production to produsage*. New York: Peter Lang.

Citizen Matters (2008) "Blogathon in April." *Citizen Matters.in*.

Patheja, J. (2008) "Blog to fight back." Tehelka, 16 June.

Singh, D.V. (2008) "Citizen journalists: democratizing news coverage: a new experience of Indian television journalism." Paper delivered at conference on "Convergence, Citizen Journalism & Social Change: Building Capacity," University of Queensland, 26–28 March.

Sonwalkar, P. (2002) "Murdochization of the Indian press: from by-line to bottom-line." *Media, Culture & Society*, *24*(6), 821–834.

Sonwalkar, P. (2004) "Mediating otherness: the English-language national press and Northeast India." *Contemporary South Asia*, *13*(4), 389–402.

Sonwalkar, P., & Allan, S. (2007) "Citizen journalism and human rights in North-East India." *Media Development*, *54*(3), 31–35.

Srinivas, S. (2005) "Online citizen journalists respond to South Asian disaster." *Online Journalism Review*, 7 January.

Upadhyay, V.K. (2008) "Keynote speech" at conference on "Convergence, Citizen Journalism & Social Change: Building Capacity," University of Queensland, 26–28 March.

CHAPTER SIX

Human Rights AND Wrongs: Blogging News OF Everyday Life IN Palestine

HEBA ZAYYAN AND CYNTHIA CARTER

Citizen journalism has only very recently begun to develop in the Arab World. Its growth has been particularly slow in the Occupied Palestinian Territories (OPTs), where access to the internet has been severely limited due to declining economic conditions since the beginning of the al-Aqsa Intifada in 2000. Exacerbating this situation was the election of a Hamas-led Palestinian National Authority (PNA) government in 2006 (and Hamas's success in regional elections in Gaza in 2007). Some members of the international community proceeded to impose a number of restrictions on the newly elected government, the most serious of which was cutting off certain financial aid. The EU cut $600 million per year and the US $460 million (Pan, 2006). Life in the OPTs, especially in Gaza, where the popularity of Hamas was highest, quickly began to deteriorate, affecting the economic, political, and social infrastructure. By the end of 2006, the official unemployment level stood at 30%, while unofficial figures suggest that a mere 31% of working-age people have some form of employment (Hever, 2007).

Despite such political and economic obstacles, citizen journalism is now experiencing extraordinary growth that is being driven, in part, by a rising desire, especially among young people, to engage in public debate across a wide range of political and social issues (Beckerman, 2007; Talaat, 2006). Also significant in this, according to Hani Jabsheh of the Arab news service Al Bawaba, is the fact that mainstream Palestinian news media are widely perceived to be politically biased (cited in Glaser, 2005). Across the Arab world, most local newspapers and broadcast news programs are either directly or indirectly state controlled, and thus often subject to strict censorship. In this context, it is often difficult for mainstream journalists to challenge prevailing political and religious orthodoxies.

To better understand the current state of Palestinian citizen journalism, we begin by briefly exploring the cultural context within which bloggers operate. We focus specifically on Palestine's high literacy levels and how they are linked to increases in internet use. Given the fact that mainstream, predominantly Arabic media appear to have little influence outside the region, we turn our attention to an examination of the influential English-language alternative news website Electronic Intifada (EI) and, more specifically, citizen journalism provided through its section "Diaries: Live from Palestine." From there, we briefly consider the contribution of two citizen journalism sites created by bloggers living in different parts of the West Bank—Bethlehem Bloggers and Stranger than Fiction. Each represents a different form of citizen journalism, as we outline later in this chapter. We then turn to Heba Zayyan's citizen journalist blog, Contemplating from Gaza. Departing from the usual conventions of academic writing, we include Zayyan's views about her work as a citizen journalist in her own words. The chapter concludes by assessing the role of citizen journalism in widening public debates on the Middle East conflict and in highlighting the ways in which such reporting bears witness to its human consequences.

LITERACY LEVELS AND INTERNET USE

While only 60% of adults across the Arab countries are literate, in Palestine this figure is 92% (UNICEF, 2007). The importance of education is widely recognized among the Palestinian population, and there is a determination to make the most of new information technologies for this purpose. The cost of internet access in the OPTs, about US $25 per month according to Arabic Network for Human Rights Information (HRinfo, 2006), is extremely high in relation to the average monthly household income of about $300 (Global Policy Network, 2006). Even so, the internet market is growing rapidly. At the same time, the Palestinian Authority government is exceptionally weak, and as such it is unable to impose tight controls over personal internet use. On this point, human rights representatives from the Arabic Network for Human Rights Information note:

> There are no Palestinian laws covering the dissemination of information on the Internet, or to [organize] the workings of Internet cafés. In addition, there are no reports about any kind of official control over web content or rules declaring what

constitutes legitimate activities on the Internet. It seems that this remarkable freedom perhaps has more to do with technical reasons than respect for freedom of expression. (HRinfo, 2006)

In contrast, an Egyptian court gave the so-called Egyptian blogger, a 22-year-old former law student by the name of Abdel Karim Suleiman (known online as "KarimAmer"), a four-year jail sentence in February 2007 "for insulting Islam and the president." Hafiz Abour Saada, who represents the Egyptian Human Rights Organization, has stated that this verdict sent a "strong message to all bloggers who are put under strong surveillance" (cited in BBC News Online, February 22, 2007).

Internet access and use across the Middle East currently stands at approximately 10% of the population (Internet World Stats, 2007). The OPTs compare favorably with a figure of 7.9%. In 2004, a Palestinian Central Bureau of Statistics (PCBS) report affirmed that 9.2% of Palestinian households had access to the internet. The following year, the Alternative Information Center (Palestine/Israel) polled 1,040 adults across the West Bank, East Jerusalem, and Gaza, reporting that 37.6% of those surveyed claimed to use the internet, out of which 23.7% do so on a daily basis (AIC, 2005). Internet access is now growing at a steady pace. Perhaps unsurprisingly, given the high levels of literacy in the region, one of the key types of usage is knowledge acquisition for education, discussion, and news.

NEWS WEBSITES AND CITIZEN JOURNALISM BLOGS

One of the most influential English-language news websites reporting on the situation in the OPTs is the EI—claiming to be "Palestine's Weapon of Mass Instruction." Based in the United States and the OPTs, it was launched on March 8, 2001, as a non-profit venture. EI was set up by four activists: Ali Abunimah, Arjan el Fassed, Laurie King-Irani, and Nigel Parry, whose paths crossed in 1998 on a Palestinian email list. As King-Irani (2001) recalls,

> We quickly became cyber-friends…writing to each other regularly to express our dismay at the continuing lack of critical media coverage of the Israeli-Palestinian conflict and the persistence of US and Israeli efforts to achieve "peace" while bypassing any question of justice and all instruments of international law.

Shortly after the al-Aqsa Intifada began in September 2000, Parry suggested to the others that what was urgently needed was a website (in English) that would centralize information about what was happening in Palestine to counter what they saw as a strongly pro-Israel slant in US and other Western news coverage. To do so, it would be essential to have fact sheets providing information that activists needed to challenge mainstream representations of the conflict, locally, nationally, and internationally. The four also decided that the site should become a "cyber-clearinghouse" of links to relevant international legal documents, human rights reports, UN resolutions, maps of settlement building, verifiable statistics on deaths and injuries, to support activists (King-Irani, 2001).

To further support alternative media reporting, the EI team established a citizen journalism section on the website called "Diaries: Live from Palestine," launched in April 2002. Developed partly as a response to Israel's "Operation Defensive Shield," a large-scale military intervention that began that month in Ramallah (the most extensive since the Six Day War in 1967) that was accompanied by barring journalists' entry to the city, the "Diaries" offered "continually updated and dramatic accounts from local residents detailing life under a punishing curfew and military invasion. For a period of two weeks, these were literally the only voices heard from Ramallah" (EI, 2006). Since then, the section has become a regular feature, offering almost daily citizen journalist reports (professional journalists occasionally contribute to the section as well), written by people living in or visiting the OPTs. Frequently they are the personal reports of NGO workers such as those by Anna Balzter, a volunteer with the International Women's Peace Service in the West Bank. Balzter's diaries from Nablus during the week of March 12, 2007, for example, are moving accounts that help to humanize the suffering felt by those directly affected by Israel's operation "Hot Winter," which began a fortnight earlier (Katz, 2007). In her diaries from Nablus, posted in installments over a number of days, Balzter talks about the difficulties she has been facing in going into the Old City to deliver food and medical supplies to families living under strict curfew and thus unable to leave their homes. In her entry of March 14, entitled "Nablus invasion diary III: Resistance, hypocrisy and dead men walking," Balzter reports:

> Once when the army stopped me and Firas from UPMRC from entering part of the OldCity with bread, Firas waited ten minutes and then said, "Anna, come with me." He grabbed as many bags as he could carry, and began walking past the jeeps. I grabbed 12 pounds of bread and scrambled after him past the soldiers, who had come out of their jeeps and were yelling, "Hey! Stop! What are you doing? We said you can't enter!" Firas kept walking steadily and I turned around to the soldiers. "We're delivering bread to hungry people. What are you going to do, shoot us?" They were speechless and held their fire. (Baltzer, 2007)

Further forms of citizen journalism are made available through the EI website, including blogs written by citizens living in the West Bank and Gaza, as well as by Palestinians and supporters of Palestine living in other countries. Authors often declare that, by writing in English, it is their hope that their reporting will prove to have a greater international impact on global public opinion about Palestine.

The importance of reaching a global audience is stated in the "So, who are we? And what is the point of a Bethlehem Blog?" section on the Bethlehem Bloggers site, launched on March 20, 2005. Specifically, these bloggers are "Palestinians and internationals who are living in the Bethlehem region, and who want to tell the world what it is like to be living in occupied territory, under an economic siege, encircled by a wall and military checkpoints: what it is like to live in a Palestinian Ghetto" (BethlehemGhetto.blogspot.com). The site is a vital window for outsiders to look in, so that they might "see past the walls, barbed-wire fences, and the media distortions; to hear from the people in Bethlehem themselves." Citizen journalists on the site are identified by cyber pseudonyms to protect themselves from harassment or harm, and stress that they are not affiliated with any political party or NGO. Instead, they define themselves simply as a group of concerned citizens living in Bethlehem who have come together to "show the world the effects of the Israeli occupation of Palestine and in particular, Bethlehem." Explicitly political news reports include a discussion of Israeli democracy in crisis, settlement expansion, a report on the trial of an activist protesting against the "apartheid wall," the Israeli Army invasion of a village near Bethlehem, and the killing of a Palestinian worker by an Israeli border guard. The site also provides a long list of links, to Bethlehem human rights, research, cultural, and peace centers, to Palestine/Israel blogs, Middle East blogs, news and information, human rights and activism, international activism, world news, and art and music.

Stranger than Fiction is a citizen journalism blog launched on February 21, 2006, written by Dana Shalash. Shalash lives in Ramallah and teaches at Birzeit University in the West Bank. Much of her blog discusses the struggle of teaching students in Palestine who have no hope of a better future. She tends to address a wide array of political issues, often from a gender perspective and from a personal and local perspective, to show how they affect people around her. Issues have included female identity in the Arab World, the Palestinian economy, the politics of the headscarf, public worker strikes, rights to education, motherhood, International Women's Day, and the Palestinian unity government. Perhaps one of the most telling entries is one Shalash posted on January 20, 2007, which effectively pinpoints the restrictions imposed upon Palestinians' everyday lives. The entry is entitled: "A Palestinian counting his/her blessings!" Instead of Shalash's usual analysis of a political issue, we are presented with a simple, long, and demoralizing list of "Standing prohibitions," "Periodic prohibitions," and "Checkpoints and barriers" with which all Palestinians live. Included in the 16 "Standing pro-hibitions" are rules such as:

- Palestinians from the Gaza Strip are forbidden from staying in the West Bank;
- Palestinians are not able to enter the area around Israeli settlements (even if their lands are inside the settlements' built area);
- Palestinians are not allowed to enter Nablus in a vehicle;
- Palestinians cannot travel abroad via Ben-Gurion Airport;
- Gaza residents are forbidden from establishing residency in the West Bank.

(Shalash, 2007)

Shalash's citizen journalism provides much more than information about the types of restrictions being invoked. It also conveys something about how living with them might feel—that is, how heavily they weigh upon people on the receiving end of state power. Not only are their physical movements severely curtailed, in effect turning the West Bank and Gaza into large, open prisons, but such restrictions also work to limit psychological and intellectual freedoms in profound ways. This is where citizen journalism can play a crucial role. It provides virtual spaces where Palestinians are making efforts to maintain a sense of intellectual openness, and reach out to others beyond the physical restrictions of everyday life. In the next section of this chapter, we turn to Heba Zayyan's blog, Contemplating from Gaza. It is a typical example of the politically engaged form of personalized citizen journalism that has developed in the OPTs in recent years.

CONTEMPLATING FROM GAZA: A CITIZEN JOURNALISM STORY

Unlike most mainstream journalism, citizen journalism blogs are unedited and uncensored channels of communication offering Palestinians platforms from which they may express ideas and reflect on their troubled environment (see also Hofheinz, 2007). Many Palestinian bloggers, most of whom are in their 20s and 30s, see themselves as free speech and human rights activists (Dheere, 2008). As such, they believe that they have a social responsibility to openly engage with global audiences in order to tell them how ordinary Palestinians are experiencing the conflict. As Friedman (2007) notes, "A reoccurring trend seems to be stirring through the Palestinian blogs: their longing to be heard and recognized as a people, rather than objects that can afford to be misplaced."

Beirut-based journalist and citizen journalism lecturer Jessica Dheere (2008) argues that many bloggers in Palestine and across the Arab World feel that even though others might regard them as citizen journalists, they understand that role as something quite different to the traditional journalist. As citizen journalists, they tend to see themselves as playing a "more active role in the news than simply reporting it. They are often instigators of change in the first place" (Dheere, 2008).

Citizen journalism blogs have helped to tell a truth different from the one frequently related in the mainstream media in many countries. The more globally influential ones are in English and use an array of citizen journalism approaches. As Bruns (2008, pp. 180–181) notes, some citizen journalists only obliquely discuss news and current affairs in their blogs, while others are regular reporters on their own blogs or on alternative news websites such as EI, Slashdot, and Kuro5hin (see also Allan, 2006). Beckerman (2007, p. 19) reminds us that most citizen journalists in Arab countries come from privileged backgrounds, having high levels of education, income, and leisure time in which to blog. Syrian blogger Ammar Abdulhamid does not see this as a problem, however, insisting that Arab citizen journalism often "cross[es] the bridge between the elite and the grass roots" in reporting on human rights abuses and in helping to organize public campaigns to end them (Beckerman, 2007, p. 19).

In the Palestinian context there seems to be another type of citizen journalism that regularly engages with the news, but which does so in a way that intimately connects political events to the experiences of ordinary people. Heba Zayyan's Contemplating from Gaza, launched in November 2006, is an exemplar of this type of citizen journalism. It was chosen for further exploration here, as it provides one of the richest examples of independent citizen journalism in the region, by someone who has no background in journalism. (There are similar blogs, such as Laila El-Hadad's Raising Yousuf and Noor, but Hadad works as a professional journalist.) She has also been an occasional contributor to Islamonline.net, which bills itself as an online forum for open discussion and free thinking, and a two-time guest author on the online website of the *Independent* in its "Open House" forum.

Zayyan is a university-educated, 29-year-old married woman with two young daughters, working for an international women's organization. She makes no claim to journalistic objectivity in her writing, but instead offers independent observations as one who is living and bearing witness to everyday life in Gaza. Her citizen journalism talks about how restrictions and sanctions are affecting her life and that of those around her. She also engages with broader issues such as honor killings, reflecting upon the fact that laws made to protect women that were weak in relatively stable times have now become largely unenforceable. Other entries refer to events in the news. For example, in August 2008, she wrote a story on the "freedom ships" that came to Gaza from Cyprus hoping to open the port to Palestinians living in the area so that they might export agricultural goods and gain control from the Israelis over imports. She had to watch this event on television, even though it was happening only a short distance from her home, for fear that the ships might be detained by the Israelis.

My blog

I am an ardent reader of Laila Haddad's citizen journalism blog Raising Yousef and Noor. I found reference to it by chance reading an English magazine entitled *Palestine this Week* in October 2006. Before that, I was unaware of the blog phenomenon that was sweeping the globe. I admire Laila's honesty and the straightforward way she presents her daily struggles as a Palestinian mother who lives between Gaza and the United States.

Citizen journalism offers an opportunity where anyone can publish on any topic that s/he thinks is significant or interesting, without censorship or editing—that is, if they are lucky enough to have the time and money to do so. I realized very early that blogging could provide me with a platform for political and personal liberation. Before I started my blog in late 2006 I felt caged, both intellectually and physically, so the chance to present my ideas and experiences felt wonderful. From the beginning its focus was socio-political, written in a way that would help shed light on how politics is affecting individual and collective life in Gaza.

I decided to write in English because I thought that it was important that the wider world should know what is happening in Gaza. It was no use writing in Arabic where I would be talking to fellow Palestinians and other Arabs about what we already know. My citizen journalism was to be about reaching the "Other." I wanted to advance international awareness that Palestinians do not just exist as images in the news. The more I write about Palestinians, the more I will help change worldwide misconceptions and stereotypes in the media that label us as "terrorists."

Many Palestinian citizen journalism blogs emphasize exposing how Israeli actions directly lead to human suffering, assessments of current peace negotiations, issues surrounding refugees and right of return, checkpoints, and Israeli incursions into the OPTs. I prefer to put more emphasis on people; their joys and hopes; their sadness and disappointments; and first and foremost, their daily struggle to survive. I initially thought about my blogging as an opportunity to write a Gazan people's journal of events. My post ideas have become increasingly focused on giving people I meet a voice. Simple, everyday experiences, like a woman who told me that she was happy that she finally got her medicine; a barefooted girl from a poor family who could not afford to provide a warm coat and shoes for her, whom I met sitting in a cold hospital reception area; or a man waiting for hours to fill a gas cylinder so that he could cook his food and heat his home, all matter. I believe that I should keep my political beliefs out of my blogging to maintain its social humanitarian touch. I am determined not to fall into the trap of stimulating political and personal prejudices. This has not prevented me from talking about political events that have caused people to suffer such as various Israeli military incursions into Gaza, the denial of movement for pilgrims, and factional fighting amongst different Palestinian groups.

Being a Gaza resident and experiencing, along with everyone else, deprivations such as power cuts, scarcity of gas for transportation, cooking and heating, food shortages, and limited access to good quality health care and medicines, I feel I have a certain responsibility to explain how people suffer and yet at the same time show courage and maintain a sense of humor. What I hope a reader will find in my blog is a picture very different from media created stereotypes.

CONCLUSION

Across the Arab World, citizen journalism is making an increasingly important contribution to widening public participation. In sharp contrast with those Arab countries where mainstream journalism is state censored and journalists and their editors routinely face harassment, even jail, for criticizing the government, in the OPTs alternative forms of online citizen-based reporting are experiencing few formalized restrictions.

Palestinian citizen journalism is shifting the terms of debate on the conflict in the Middle East. In assuming the role of journalists, ordinary people are bearing witness, and blogging their own stories about everyday life under conflict. These blogs offer deeply personal insights into lives lived in extraordinarily difficult circumstances, and how those on the wrong end of state power endure the consequences of political decisions taken elsewhere. In attending to the everyday, in all of its heart-rending travails, blogs such as Heba Zayyan's and others like it represent important political interventions in their own right. They embody a simple hope, namely that by raising awareness of the depth and scale of suffering, pressure will be brought to bear on politicians around the world to help end it.

REFERENCES

Allan, S. (2006) *Online news: journalism and the internet*. Maidenhead and New York: Open University Press.

Allan, S., Sonwalkar, P., & Carter, C. (2007) "Bearing witness: citizen journalism and human rights issues." *Globalisation, Societies and Education*, 5(3), 373–389.

Alternative Information Center (2005) *Poll: internet use and reading habits in Palestine*.

Baltzer, A. (2007) "Nablus invasion diary III: resistance, hypocrisy and dead men walking: diaries: live from Palestine." *electronicintifada.net*, 14 March.

BBC News (2007) "Egypt blogger jailed for 'insult.'" *news.bbc.co.uk*, 22 February.

Beckerman, G. (2007) "The new Arab conversation." *Columbia Journalism Review*, January/February, 17–23.

Bruns, A. (2008) "The active audience: transforming journalism from gatekeeping to gate-watching." In C. Patterson & D. Domingo (Eds), *Making online news: the ethnography of new media production* (pp. 171–184). New York: Peter Lang.

Dheere, Jessica (2008) "Arab bloggers meet to discuss free speech, reject 'journalist' label.'" *PBS MediaShift*, 12 September.

Electronic Intifada (2000) "Introduction: the Electronic Intifada." *electronicintifada.net*, 1 January.

Electronic Intifada (2006) "Six years of Electronic Intifada: selected milestones 2001–2006" *electronicintifada.net*

Friedman, J. (2007) "Discovering the accuracy of US media through Israeli-Palestinian blogs." *Philip Metres.*

Glaser, M. (2005) "Gaza disengagement coverage splintered by factional views online." *Online Journalism Review.*

Global Policy Network (2006) *Overview of current economic conditions in Palestine.* www.gpn.org

Hever, S. (2007) "Occupation and aid." *electronicintifada.net*

Hofheinz, A. (2007) "Arab internet: popular trends and public impact." In Naomi Sakr (Ed.), *Arab media and political renewal: community, legitimacy and public life* (pp. 56–79). London: I.B. Taurus.

HRinfo (Arabic Network for Human Rights Information) (2006) "The initiative for an open Arab internet: Palestine report." Implacable adversaries: Arab governments and the internet. *openarab.net*

Internet World Stats (2007) *Internet usage statistics: the big picture.*

Katz, Y. (2007) "'Hot winter' continues in Nablus." *jpost.com*

King-Irani, L. (2001) "The Electronic Intifada." *electronicintifada.net*

Palestinian Central Bureau of Statistics (2004) "Computer, internet and mobile phone survey." *pcbs.gov.ps*

Palestinian Central Bureau of Statistics (2007) "Households survey on information and communications technology, 2006." *pcbs.gov.ps*

Pan, E. (2006) "Hamas and the shrinking PA budget." *Council on Foreign Relations.*

Shalash, D. (2007) "A Palestinian counting her/his blessings!" *palestiniandana.blogspot.com*, 20 January.

Talaat, S. (2006) "Bloggers or journalists, news perspective in the Arab media." Paper prepared for International Association of Mass Communication Research, American University in Cairo, Egypt, 23–29 July.

UNICEF (2007) "At a glance: occupied Palestinian territory." *unicef.org*

CHAPTER SEVEN

Citizen Journalism IN China: The Case OF THE Wenchuan Earthquake

JOYCE Y. M. NIP

The Wenchuan earthquake in southwestern China in May 2008 saw a seismic shift in the way the Chinese government handled the news media. For the first time in the Communist regime that began in 1949, the media has enjoyed freedom to access and report a disaster. For decades, a multi-faceted news control mechanism that relies on trusted personnel implementing story guidelines from above and censoring stories deemed undesirable has strived to fabricate a dream nation untainted by negative events (see also Chapter 18, this volume). Reports about the destruction caused by a comparable earthquake in northeast China in July 1976, for example, were suppressed. It was not until three years later that the death toll of 240,000 was reported (Xu, 2006). Similarly, the government tried to cover up the infection figures during the SARS epidemic in 2003. A press conference was called by the Guangzhou government only when panic occurred after news spread via mobile phone messages, but still the government kept a tight rein on news reporting of the outbreak (Nip, 2005). This process was again visible only two months prior to the Wenchuan earthquake, when reporters were evicted and news access was blocked during the Tibet uprising (Bell, 2008; Choi, 2008).

In the aftermath of the Wenchuan earthquake, in a rare moment of openness, citizen journalists shed light on the tragic events by being the first to report the earthquake and, more importantly, to question the government's culpability. While Twitter may have been the first citizen journalism website to report the quake to the international community (Cellan-Jones, 2008), the Chinese-language citizen sites preempted this and the professional media in first reporting the news to the Chinese audience. This chapter focuses on these Chinese citizen media sites and their performance in the immediate aftermath of the earthquake. Specifically, this study relies on four main sources of data: observations of Tianya and Sina; texts from the Wisenews database, which contains stories produced by professional news organizations in mainland China and Hong Kong; and personal interviews.[1]

The chapter will begin by examining various online publishing initiatives of citizen-content in China. The reporting and commentary roles of citizen journalism in the Wenchuan earthquake are then discussed with respect to its vital contribution to the mainstream news coverage. The chapter concludes with a discussion of the limitations of citizen journalism in the context of China.

LANDSCAPE OF CITIZEN JOURNALISM IN CHINA

In China, the overwhelming majority of citizen content on the web is published as individual blogs or on forums (bulletin boards or text chat groups). These are hosted via online community forums, portals, and blog service sites (some featuring videos, audio files, or digital photographs with captions), as well as more traditional sites associated with mainstream news organizations.

Short messages (SMS) between mobile phones, although usually considered interpersonal communications, play critical roles in public information dissemination through one-to-many forwarding and reforwarding. This practice attracted much press attention during the SARS epidemic in 2003, although it was not described as "citizen journalism" at the time. Here it is worth noting that SMS and text chat content is not recorded systematically and is therefore difficult to analyze.

Tianya Club is the biggest national online community and regularly draws over 200,000 of the 253 million internet users in China (CNNIC, 2008). The huge community site builds its reputation on tolerance of liberal ideas. It contains more than 280 bulletin boards started by the administrators, as well as dozens of blogs, chat groups, and photo albums created by users. Of the bulletin boards, more than 120 are local in scope, targeting users of various provinces and cities. Trailing behind Tianya are the national community sites Cat898 (cat898.com), which draws around 40,000 browsers at any time, and Mop (mop.com). Besides the national sites, there are numerous regional and local community sites.

The major national portal sites are Sina (sina.com.cn), Sohu (sohu.com), NetEase (163.com), and QQ (qq.com). They produce little original content, but mainly aggregate content from multiple sources, which, among others, include professional news outlets. Registered users are free to publish by starting their own blogs or posting on the site's bulletin boards.

Sites run by professional news organizations could be national, provincial, or municipal in scope. They mainly publish content produced by their staffers but do provide opportunities for registered users to blog and post on forums. Some forums on the professional news sites focus on specific topics that echo the organization's editorial policy. National examples are the "Strong Nation Forum" on the official *People's Daily* website, and the "Development Forum" on the site of the Xinhua news agency, Xinhuanet. These forums contain a number of bulletin boards and usually include a "Cream of the cream" section, showcasing politically correct posts written in official style. For example, one of the topics treated in this section of the "Strong Nation Forum" since the Tibet protests in March 2008 was "Counter separatists; Protect Olympic torch." Although these forums appear to be open to any contributor, content posted on them is more appropriately considered participatory journalism, published under guidelines and conditions set by the professionals (Nip, 2006). Citizen-generated content has also become a source of news for the professional media. Some newspapers (e.g., *Wuxi Daily*, *Ram City Evening Post*) report it regularly in specially created sections. Topics raised provide leads for follow-up by professional journalists.

CITIZEN JOURNALISTS FIRST TO REPORT QUAKE

As soon as the first main quake occurred in Wenchuan, Sichuan, at 14:28 on May 12, 2008, citizen journalism sites in China were overwhelmed. Administrators of the citizen publishing platforms, including the government-run professional media outlets, called on users to submit content, which was then aggregated under special sections.

My observation of the earthquake on Tianya started in the "Mixed Talk" bulletin board on the day of the tremor, before moving to the "Wenchuan Earthquake" bulletin board created the following day. An aggregation of Tianya blog posts that contained the word "earthquake" was started at 15:22:59 the same day (Record of the Big Earthquake, 2008).

On Sina, at 16:15:36, less than two hours after the first quake, a special collection was created by a Sina member to consolidate blogger videos about the quake (Littlepee, 2008). By 19:00 on May 13, 170 blogger videos had been collected. By 16:40 on May 31, the number had grown to 1,070, Together they had been watched 6,588,986 times. Many were watched more than 100,000 times each. Text blogs written by authors based in the affected Sichuan province were also collected on one page, which showed more than 485,000 by May 28, 2008.

The first mention of the quake was on a post seemingly published one minute after the official time announced for the quake. The post on the "Tianya Mixed Talk" bulletin board, marked as published at 14:29:00, read: "Very urgent!!!! Where has a massive earthquake occurred???" (Don't be too TMD cctv/Niu Ben, 2008). YouKu (youku.com), the Chinese equivalent of YouTube, claimed to have the first video of the quake uploaded at 14:30 (*Yangtze Evening Post*, 2008). But the Chinese media widely reported that an eight-character post, "Earthquake happens in Sichuan region" (IP address 61.161.76, 2008), running under a three-character headline "earthquake" on the Baidu bulletin board that appeared at 14:35, was the first text report of the quake. These citizen journalist reports were published before any of the professional Chinese news reports, the first of which was dispatched by Xinhuanet at 14:46. However, the Xinhua report gave more information—including the location of the epicenter, Wenchuan, and the magnitude of the quake, 7.6 (which was later officially amended as 7.8 and then 8.0) on the Richter Scale.

One of the first video clips uploaded to multiple sites—one recorded by a student using his mobile phone in his dormitory at the Sichuan University, Chengdu—was later shown on news broadcasts of the official China Central Television (CCTV) and on television in Hong Kong. A video taken of Beichuan, located right next to Wenchuan, and first disseminated in QQ chat groups, was also shown on CCTV (Chao, 2008).

In the early stage of the aftermath, before professional journalists arrived, and before official information was released, citizen journalists filled the vacuum of information. On the night of May 12, when no news was yet available about the Wenchuan county at the epicenter (Xinhuanet, 2008a)—except the little information from one eyewitness who happened to be driving out of the area (Xinhuanet, 2008b)—a citizen journalist who claimed to have escaped from the heavily destroyed Yingxiu town of Wenchuan disseminated the first photographs of the town's destruction in an online chat group. The photographs taken on his mobile phone were later verified to be authentic (*News Morning Post*, May 14, 2008). On May 14, the *Beijing Daily News* reported that no news or telephone call had come from Yingxiu or Xuankau, but at 19:02:00 the previous day, a citizen journalist had posted on Tianya a series of photographs taken on the way from Xuankau to Dujiangyan while traveling on foot (Sicilyd, 2008).

Some of the most sought-after information was the extent of casualties. A thread on the "Tianya Mixed Talk" bulletin board that updated the figure had attracted 977,571 visitors by 10:32 on May 13. Tianya administrators tried to aggregate updated information by starting a thread at 11:36 for visitors to report what they knew and post photographs that they took. They also included links to the bulletin boards of the affected localities. In response to the call were a series of reply posts. Most of them were short and simple, but they provided valuable hyper-local information not always found in professional news. A post uploaded at 12:12:12 on May 13 by Little Orchid is typical:

> I am from Dujiangyan. I am now in Hangzhou. I contacted my family at around 10 o'clock. Up to now what I learned from my family is:
>
> In town: Massive collapse of buildings in Xinjian Primary School, the Chinese medical hospital, the row of old houses in the lower section of Jianshe Road, the whole building of the Internet café on the upper section of Xujia Road, [and] half of the street on Kuiguang Road.
>
> The School of Light Industries also has some collapsed buildings. It has been raining. Most people did not sleep at home, and were gathering in the streets. ("Throughtrain to earthquake damages," 2008)

A few exceptional posts cited multiple sources. One uploaded at 12:56:18 on May 13 by Fen Ya cited his family, two friends, and one company in reporting the situation in Mianzhu in 1,050 characters ("Throughtrain to earthquake damages"). In just over two hours, between 11:36:00 and 13:50:56 on May 13, the equivalent of 25 A4 pages of citizen contributions had been posted. Not all of them provided facts, of course. Many merely offered best wishes and exclamations of horror.

Of the observed citizen videos on Sina, very few were shot in the devastated areas. Those uploaded on May 12, for example, mainly showed shaking objects inside buildings, or people running around in the streets of cities. A few exceptions were observed. One was the "Post-quake visit to Yingxiu town," uploaded on May 22, which captured images of destruction in the area, including the collapsed primary and secondary schools, with textbooks and student photographs buried in debris, as well as the tents of the rescuers. Subtitles were used to indicate the objects shown. Natural sound was absent; instead a song played throughout. Another video, uploaded on May 23, claimed to show the exclusive pictures of the Dujiangyan hospital during the quake. It started with an official-looking man speaking at a conference table, who was then interrupted by violent movement accompanied by the sound of heavy falling objects, with the subtitle "earthquake." When the subtitle showed the time as 14:50, people were sent to the hospital, and medics were seen attending to the injured on the streets. At 17:00, a helicopter was shown flying past. On May 14, one box of aid was seen dropped off at the location. The entire clip was accompanied by natural sound (Yang, 2008). However, these were exceptions. The majority of the videos did not carry subtitles. And none of the ones that I played, except those that were recorded from news broadcasts, carried narration. This limited the amount of information provided.

In terms of accessing official information, citizen journalists could not match professionals, either. Such information would be decisive in showing a comprehensive view of the disaster, which required the total number of casualties and damages, the progress of rescues, the condition of communication and electricity facilities, the supply of drinking water, the safety of nuclear and chemical plants, and so on.

CITIZEN COMMENTARIES SET MEDIA AGENDA

By June 1, citizen posts were more likely than not to be asking two key questions about the earthquake. One was whether the government had covered up the forecast of the quake. The other was whether the government was responsible for the extensive collapse of school buildings. The first question emerged on the first night of the quake on the "Tianya Mixed Talk" bulletin board. An 892-word post, "Some questions and reflections about this earthquake," uploaded at 23:19:00 (Airconditioner virus, 2008), responded to a looming debate about why the Seismological Bureau had not given any warning: "If earthquakes cannot be forecast, what is the point of spending so much money on the Seismological Bureau?" This question of "why" led to a search for facts about whether the government was covering up the prediction of the earthquake, a search in which both citizen and professional journalists alike were to follow. At a press conference on May 13, reporters from Singapore's *Lianhe Zaobao* interrogated the spokesperson of the China Seismological Bureau about a complaint they had received from the bureau workers that they were forbidden to speak about signs of the earthquake observed beforehand, in consideration of the upcoming Olympics. The question was reported with the official's denial the following day (ifeng.com, 2008; *Shantou SAR Evening News*, 2008; Zong, 2008).

Citizen journalists threw a few bombshells into the mix. One post, uploaded at 23:21:00 on May 12, onto the "Tianya Mixed Talk" bulletin board, contained a news report published on the site of the Sichuan provincial government a few days before, positively denying that an earthquake was about to happen (Snow in June, 2008). Google searches for the news report at 13:30 on May 13 indicated that it had been deleted, as were the citizen posts on other spaces that referred to it. Nevertheless, a captured screenshot of the page remained live, linked to from a Tianya blog post. This post, under the name Airconditioner virus, also disappeared soon after.

Citizen commentary was reinforced by leaks from experts. On the first night, a researcher of the Chinese Academy of Sciences, Li Shihhui, posted on his Sina blog that a seismologist friend of his, Geng Qingguo, had predicted the earthquake since 2006. A report made by the Natural Disaster Forecasting Professional Committee of the Chinese Geophysical Society, of which Geng was vice-chair, had narrowed down the prediction in a report written on April 26 and 27, 2008, that earthquakes of magnitude 6–7 were likely to occur in the region south of Lanzhou, where the borders of Sichuan, Ganxu, and Qinghai met. The report, which was sent to the China Seismological Bureau on April 30, also specifically said that the critical period for earthquakes of magnitude above 7 in the region would be the 10 days prior to and after May 8. This post was widely referred to and cross-posted on other citizen publishing spaces. The story was picked up by the professional media (Jian, 2008). But by then Li's post on his blog had been deleted. A copy of it pasted on one of the Tianya blog posts (Shock2, 2008) was still accessible at 23:20 on June 2, 2008.

The Chinese government insisted that earthquakes could not be predicted scientifically. Rebuking this claim, a Tianya blogger (luotal) re-posted on May 15 an academic paper published in 2006, which, after going through complicated calculations, concluded that within one to two years before or after 2008, earthquakes of 6.7 magnitude or above were likely to occur in the Sichuan and Yunnan region. A 633-character Tianya blogger post (Person without place, 2008), which appeared first on May 15 and which was re-posted every day until my last observation at 00:14 on June 2, succinctly summed up the gist of the debate:

> I do not believe the country's seismological department really was not able to forecast the earthquake. Yes, even the most advanced countries cannot forecast earthquakes precisely. But the focus of this sentence should not be on the "cannot," but rather on "precisely." I do not expect them to forecast precisely as to what minute, which hour, and on which date.... [H]ow could such a massive earthquake not give any sign beforehand?....

Similarly, the issue of collapsed schools was first raised by citizen journalists (melody2006lgs, 2008) before professional media followed up on it (Smith, 2008; Szema, 2008). By the end of May, a government official eventually acknowledged responsibility for the collapses caused by a combination of factors in site selection, structural design, materials, and construction standards (*New Zealand Herald*, 2008; Spencer, 2008).

LIMITATIONS OF CITIZEN JOURNALISM

Although citizen journalists were the first to report China's Wenchuan earthquake, and the first to supply hyperlocal accounts of the epicenter, the amount of information provided was small. They certainly fell far short of providing a comprehensive picture of the events in which more than 85,000 people perished.

It seems fair to say that the value of citizen journalism is the greatest when and where the professional media fail.

The quality of citizen reporting has long drawn criticism from professionals. The lack of details in many of the reports reaffirmed this concern. Tianya administrators tried to enhance the veracity of information by requiring informational posts to provide links to the sources cited, after one post that predicted the earthquake precisely for May 12 was found to be fake. Aggravating the quality problem was the lack of access to official sources and government-controlled areas, which could be overcome if citizen journalists were accredited. Yet accreditation seems far-fetched if citizen journalists work in an ad hoc, individual manner without affiliation to any identifiable entity.

The individual mode of operation of citizen journalists also made coordination of the reporting efforts difficult. The Tianya administrators did make some attempt to match the needs of the news audience and the citizen reporters. While calling for submission of reports, they also called on people to submit requests for information. However, the effect was doubtful.

The chronological displays made it difficult for potential users to identify what information was available and where it could be located. On Tianya, the casualties figure was updated in the title of the thread that consolidated reports submitted. Color and boldface were used for the title. Irrelevant posts were cleared away. But still, trying to identify information among a sea of posts pouring out at 50 per minute on a bulletin board was a daunting task. The difficulty, of course, was multiplied many times over when all the publishing spaces were considered. Cross-posting and reposting were attempts to overcome the difficulty. I suspect that search engines are likely to become a more important vehicle of news delivery, given the proliferation of citizen sites and the 24/7 operation of professional news media.

The quality and display problems both point to the potential advantage of dedicated collective citizen journalism operations such as OhmyNews and Merinews. Yet, how an identifiable news operation in China, albeit a non-professional one, could escape official control is difficult to imagine.

Even in its "guerrilla" form, citizen journalism in China appears to be turning into the new battleground of control over public opinion. My observation is that some of the posts were official in content and tone. These posts were plentiful after the brief opening of news freedom closed on May 23, when mainstream news organizations received a directive to focus on positive aspects of the events, and then on May 27 when major portal sites received instruction that prohibited topics including shoddy construction of the collapsed schools, prior forecasts of the earthquake made by experts, complaints about the progress of rescue, and problems about the distribution of aid (Zhang, 2008). On June 4 and 5, some videos taken by reporters who were sent by Sina had been uploaded onto the blogger collection. Some of the blogger videos seem to have been displaced. The song-accompanied "Post-quake visit to Yingxiu town," for example, was no longer found by 14:00 on June 4. Similarly, on YouKu, many new video channels containing official-style clips were created in the latter period of my observation. Many were clips from newscasts of professional news organizations.

This observation was consistent with news reports that the Chinese government paid people to contribute content on the web (Bandurski, 2008; Lee Ping, 2007). Government infiltration of citizen publishing spaces, in addition to outright censorship, could become a new strategy aimed at controlling citizen-generated content. Censorship is a fact of life in China, so much so that sometimes posters on bulletin boards try to evade keyword filtering by inserting symbols between words in a search term, or writing in an oblique way. Sometimes they directly challenge the administrator of the bulletin board not to delete their posts. These efforts at fighting censorship were widely observed in this study, despite the relative openness shown by the government to news media access, and despite Tianya's reputation for tolerance.

The above discussion of the practice of citizen journalism has focused on its role in providing information and monitoring public life through commentary. These two roles were played out in conjunction with two other roles: sharing and mobilizing. While some citizens reported the goings-on, many more expressed their grief, anger, and sympathy. The sharing of feelings and sentiment set off a large-scale drive for donating and volunteering. The convergence of these roles in citizen journalism is in stark contrast to the emphasis on objectivity in professional journalism.

NOTE

1. Interviews were conducted with: Lam Oiwan, Director of InMedia (www.inmediahk. net)—a Hong Kong-based citizen journalism site—and Chinese editor of Global Voices, on April 22, 2008; Li Yongfeng, a researcher who specializes in the Internet in China, at *Yazhou Zhoukan*, the Chinese edition of *Asia Week*, on April 11, 2008; and Ran Yunfei, well-known mainland Chinese blogger, on May 3, 2008.

REFERENCES

Airconditioner virus (2008) "Some questions and reflections about this earthquake." Re-post on Jingmen Club.

Bandurski, David (2008) "China's guerrilla war for the web." *Far Eastern Economic Review*, July.

Bell, Thomas (2008) "China acts to stop news of riots reaching citizens." *The Daily Telegraph* (London), 17 March, p. 17.

Cellan-Jones, Rory. (2008) "Twitter and the China earthquake." *BBC* blog, 12 May.

Ceng Yu (2008) "Photos from disaster centre." *News Morning Post*, 14 May.

Chao Xiao (2008) "700 million QQ users donate for disaster." *Information Times*, 15 May.

China Internet Network Information Center (CNNIC) (2008) "CNNIC releases the 22nd statistical report on the Internet development in China." 31 July.

Choi, Chi-yuk (2008) "HK print, TV journalists ejected from Lhasa hotel after night raid." *South China Morning Post*, 18 March.

Chongqing Commercial News (2008) "National Seismological Bureau denies earthquake forecast coverup." 14 May.

Don't be too TMD cctv/Niu Ben (2008) "Very urgent!!!! Where has a big earthquake occurred???" Tianya "Mixed Talk" bulletin board, 14:29:00, 12 May.

ifeng.com (2008) "Foreign media: Seismological Bureau workers forecast signs of quake. Government: rumour ungrounded," citing China.com.cn, 16:32, 13 May.

[IP] 61.161.76 (2008) "Earthquake happens in Sichuan region." Baidu, 14:35, 12 May.

Jian Xun (2008) "The bigger an earthquake, the easier to predict." *Yazhou Zhoukan*, 1 June.

Lee Ping (2007) "Beijing speeds up training of 50-cent party." *Apple Daily*, 25 September, p. A27.

Littlepee (2008) "Sina video bloggers' record of the 8.0-magniture earthquake in Wenchuan, Sichuan."

Luotal (2008) [Reply post without subject] 19:39:00, 15 May.

Melody2006lgs (2008) [Reply post without subject] 18:58:00, 13 May. "Record of the big earthquake," Tianya.

New Zealand Herald (2008) "Govt admits quake blame." 2 June.

Nip, Joyce (2005) "Changing connections: the news media, the government and the people in China's SARS epidemic." In Angela Romano & Michael Bromley (Eds.), *Journalism and democracy in Asia* (pp. 28–40). London: Routledge.

Nip, Joyce (2006) "Exploring the second phase of public journalism." *Journalism Studies*, 7(2), 212–236.

Person without place (2008) [Reply post without subject] 19:21:00, 15 May.

"Record of the Big Earthquake," (2008). Tianya.

Shantou SAR Evening News (2008) "Cover up forecast results for Olympics? Unreasonable." 14 May.

Shock2 (2008) "Seismological expert dry with tear. 5.12 earthquake was forecast." 8:39:00, 14 May.

[Sichuan] Provincial Seismological Bureau (2008) "Sichuan Aba Earthquake Disaster Mitigation Authority successfully quells earthquake rumour." 9 May.

Sicilyd (2008) "Photos on walk from Xuankau, Wenchuan to Dujiangyan." http://cache.tianya. cn/publicforum/content/free/1/1229311.shtml, accessed 3 June 2008.

Smith, Peter (2008) "China's quake: why did so many schools collapse?" *Christian Science Monitor*, 14 May.

Snow in June (2008) "News on 9 May: Sichuan Aba Earthquake Disaster Mitigation Authority successfully quells earthquake rumour." 13 May. Tianya.

Spencer, Richard (2008) "China's guilt over lost children rare admission of responsibility for school collapses as soldiers race against time to drain earthquake lake." *Daily Telegraph*, 31 May.

Szema Shing (2008) "Military and politicians: thorough investigation of military and civilian buildings." *Oriental Daily*, 14 May, p. A40.

"Throughtrain to earthquake damages" (2008). Tianya.

Xinhuanet (2008a) "Rush: communication to Wenchuan country still broken 6 hours after quake." 21:16:01, 12 May.

Xinhuanet (2008b) "Wenchuan earthquake: witness account near the epicenter." 21:12:07, 12 May.

Xu, Xuejiang (2006) "Late news: behind the reporting of Tangshan earthquake's death toll." Xinhuanet, 28 July.

Yang Fei (2008) "Exclusive: never-revealed real-life quake moments at Dujiangyan People's Hospital." 23 May.

Yangtze Evening Post (2008) "We upload warmth." 14 May.

Zhang Jieping (2008) "Media reporting storm." *Yazhou Zhoukan*, 8 June, 24–31.

Zong He (2008) "State Information Office press conference on Wenchuan earthquake: cover-up for Olympics unreasonable." *Southern Daily News*, 14 May.

CHAPTER EIGHT

Blogging THE Climate Change Crisis FROM Antarctica

EINAR THORSEN

If every kid has a blog, why not every scientist?

(BREANA SIMMONS, ANTARCTIC BLOGGER)

Mainstream news organizations have traditionally struggled to report the process of climate change, or indeed science more generally, since it tends to be perceived by journalists to be lacking in spectacle or tangible events that can be easily recast in their news coverage (see Allan, 2009; Carvalho, 2007; Carvalho & Burgess, 2005; Russell, 2008). It is "one of the most complicated stories of our time," Wilson (2000) argues, which "is also affected by a number of journalistic constraints, such as deadlines, space, one-source stories, complexity and reporter education" (p. 206). Reporting of the climate change crisis, therefore, is often visualized through events staged by political figures, some of whom travel to remote areas of the world so that they can be seen to be bearing witness to a crisis otherwise imperceptible to the human eye.

The climate change crisis has been steadily making its way up the news agenda due to what Neverla (2008) describes as a "climatic turn." In highlighting recent research that indicates there have been both quantitative and qualitative shifts in media coverage on climate change, she argues that this has been driven in part by global warming increasingly being associated with a negative framing (e.g., "climate catastrophe") and elite-political figures (e.g., Al Gore, the IPCC, the British prime minister, or the German Parliamentary Commission), thus fulfilling some of traditional media's news values (p. 5). However, the science that maps the process of global warming remains largely underreported. Certainly in the case of the British popular press, as Gavin (2007) observes, the crisis has been denied in-depth treatment. More dramatically, in relation to the US press and television, Boykoff and Boykoff (2007) argue that "the mass media can adversely affect the interactions between science, policy, and the public" (p. 1201). Adherence to "the norms of dramatization, personalization, novelty, balance, and authority-order," they contend, has led to "informationally deficient coverage" of global warming and "has helped to create space for the US government to defray responsibility and delay action regarding climate change" (p. 1201).

Scientists working in Antarctica have recognized the need to counteract the problems associated with the mainstream media's treatment of the climate-change crisis. For this reason, several of them have assumed the role of citizen journalist in order to report on the effects of global warming first-hand. More specifically, they have chosen to communicate directly with the general public through official or personal blogs. In so doing they are capitalizing on the way the internet is changing science news and journalism (see Allan, 2009; Trench, 2007).[1]

This approach to citizen journalism has become a central part of an educational outreach strategy aimed at connecting Antarctic scientists with members of the public around the globe, including schoolchildren. The ensuing form of dialogue, where they respond to questions put to them on the blog, helps to bridge a perceived disconnect between scientific experts and lay people. This chapter draws on an analysis of these blogs, as well as data from e-interviews with the bloggers themselves, in order to examine how scientists "on the ice" act as citizen journalists.

PEOPLE AND COMMUNICATIONS IN ANTARCTICA

Antarctica is a hostile, frozen continent without an indigenous population or even national sovereignty—the continent being effectively controlled by the Antarctic Treaty System. While there are no permanent inhabitants in Antarctica, 28 countries maintain research bases through their respective National Antarctic Programs. There are 38 year-round bases, with the South Pole Station and the McMurdo Station, both run by the US Antarctic Program, being the largest. Seasonal-only stations operate during the austral summer months and consist of permanent and temporary facilities, including tent camps and mobile traverses in support of research. The number of scientists and support staff across these stations peaks at approximately 4,000 during summer and falls to around 1,000 during winter. Some 30 nationalities were represented in 2007–2008, with the majority of the population stemming from the United States, Argentina, Russia, Chile, Australia, and the United Kingdom.

The history of Antarctic communication is rich with technological innovation, engendered in part by the extreme weather and distance from other continents. Satellite communication was introduced initially through the Inmarsat system in the mid-1980s. The world's first dedicated Antarctic satellite communication system was the Australian ANARESAT launched in 1986–1987, which was closely followed by similar systems deployed by other national Antarctic programs. Used in combination with the internet, it became possible to communicate more frequently, sharing richer content, and with a greater degree of interaction than had previously been possible.

By way of example, the continent was host to some of the very first online journals, precursors to what are now commonly referred to as blogs. Appearing in the latter months of 1993, Dr. Stokers Project Status Reports and the more chatty, informal Dale's Dive Diary (written by Dale Anderson) were online, interactive companions for the *Live From... Other Worlds* television series. The team of scientists answered questions via email until February 1994, responding to more than 100 questions—including several on "global climate change" and "global warming"—put to them by schoolchildren back in the United States. The websites exemplify early experimentation with the internet as a way of reporting on the daily activities of scientists in Antarctica and engaging lay audiences with their research.

BLOGGING ON THE ICE

By the time of the International Polar Year (IPY) of 2007–2008, internet access had evolved to become an integral resource for the scientific community in Antarctica. It is increasingly available in high bandwidth, both on permanent bases and on temporary field bases. While the primary purpose of the internet has been to coordinate logistics and the collection of research data, it has also provided scientists with a new way of keeping in touch with distant family members and friends.

Through various forms of citizen journalism—blogs, podcasts, and live webcasts—scientists have been able to share their experiences on a daily basis. Indeed, widespread internet access has created something of an Antarctic blogosphere, reflecting the diversity of people active in supporting and carrying out research on the continent. Dispatches are published to blogs from most Antarctic bases, with people from a wide range of nationalities and research disciplines contributing.[2]

An example of one of the more avid writers is Ross Hofmeyr of the AntarcticDoctor blog. Based in the South African SANAE IV base, he has published extensive posts containing text, images, and sometimes videos uploaded to YouTube. Alessia Maggi and JJL maintain the sismordia blog, reporting on their seismologic research at the Concordia base, run by France and Italy. Atle Coward Markussen publishes a personal photoblog from the Norwegian Troll Station, each post containing an incredible range of images and typically accompanied by a single line of commentary. Sudhir Khandelwal became the first Indian to blog from Antarctica when he began publishing Himalayan Adventurer from the Indian Maitri Station. Unlike many other bases, though, Maitri Station has no direct access to the internet, which has meant that it has to be updated via a shared email address accessible over a slow satellite link.

Antarctic bloggers seem to be self-consciously aware of their (potential) global audience. This leads most of them to write in English, which they perceive to be a more international language than their own, reflecting for some their aspirations to act as citizen journalists or "amateur" science writers. However, there are also numerous blogs in other languages, including French, German, Norwegian, and Spanish. The choice is not always straightforward, though, and depends on the intended audience. Berts Iceposts, penned by Bert from the German base Neumayer Station, epitomizes this politics of language. Having started the blog in English, he switched to German after just two posts "due to severe protests from my german [sic] friends" sent via email. This pressure was also evident on the blog itself, where one comment to his second entry read: "BITTE SCHREIB DEUTSCH!...vergiss nicht deine wurzeln im eis! [PLEASE WRITE GERMAN! Do not forget your roots on the ice!]"

Antarctic blogs document a remarkable amount of detail about the extreme conditions in which scientists and support staff operate. Some trivia about life "on the ice" posted in blogs has even been picked up by mainstream news organizations. For instance, a story about some 16,488 condoms being ordered for the McMurdo base was picked up by a New Zealand newspaper in June 2008 and subsequently reported as a curiosity internationally. Blogs also provide a continuation of stories in the news, such as that of Sigurd Sande, a Norwegian mechanic who broke his leg while at the top of Mount Buddamagen in October 2008, which was a prominent news story in Norway at the time. His online diary, siggiantarktis.com, although very brief and basic (single HTML page with no comment facility), revealed his personal thoughts on the ordeal. This included an entry on the day of the accident—ending "Glad eg lever [Pleased I am alive]"—and then continued to report updates about his transfer from Antarctica to a Norwegian hospital.

The most prominent use of Antarctic blogs, regardless of whether they are published in an official or personal capacity, seems to be in connection with educational outreach. This chapter will now turn to look specifically at how citizen journalism facilitates science education, with particular emphasis on how it provides relatively direct access to scientists who are recording the effects of climate change first hand.

CITIZEN JOURNALISM AS EDUCATION

Educational outreach is seen as an integral part of scientific programs operating in the Antarctic and is also strongly encouraged by institutions such as the US National Science Foundation. Traditionally this would involve scientists visiting schools, writing educational books, and possibly appearing on television. However, citizen journalism has increasingly been adopted to complement these activities as it provides a more immediate and interactive form of communication.

In many instances, the scientists interviewed for this study were actively blogging for private reasons before the practice was picked up and promoted in a more official capacity. Sarah Fortner, who publishes the blog Crampons and Cornfields, explained that when she first started reporting from the Antarctic, she "did so unaware that this was encouraged":

> I have never been directly approached to blog from the Antarctic, but feel that I am in a community that supports communicating with the public. (Sarah Fortner)

Indeed, many of the blogs that are overtly educational in nature are published and maintained in a personal capacity, which reflects the commitment many scientists have to educating and promoting their research to a wider audience. Becky Ball's Polar Soils Blog exemplifies this intricate relationship between Antarctic blogging and education. She describes how it was actually a polar science section of the US second-grade science curriculum that "initially inspired the blog." This collaborative blog has been closely followed by science classes across the United States, with the team actively encouraging teachers to shape how its contributors report on day-to-day activities.

> Before leaving for the field, we communicate with school teachers to get an idea of the material that they would find useful to have covered. This helps me choose what topics to blog about throughout the 2-month field season. (Becky Ball)

Beyond reporting daily events, topics are also chosen "in response to questions asked by the classes and the general public" on the blog itself, according to Bell. The first season they blogged from Antarctica, however, "the schools were not very communicative." Instead, she comments, it was "the general public that picked up the blog (the non-target audience)" who were most interactive during this period, with the blog receiving "a lot of questions and comments from a variety of people."

This demonstrates that, despite the close connection many of these educational blogs have with school classes, they also have a broader journalistic function for other members of the public.

During the IPY there were several new projects aimed specifically at raising awareness of the climate-change crisis, such as *IGLO* (International action on GLObal warming), *Inuit Voices: Observations of Environmental Change*, and *IntSchool* (International School Education on Polar issues). These projects were also concerned with finding new ways of communicating science and extending educational outreach. The IPY website, for instance, contained a section with a series of IPY blogs. The blogs were categorized into six different focus areas (atmosphere, ice, land, oceans, people, and space), but could also be filtered by target audiences (educators, participants, and press) or by the approximately 50 different contributors. While people were able to read full entries and submit comments to blogs on the IPY website, they appear not to have been as frequently updated as the main project websites or personal blogs.

For instance, the Norwegian-US Scientific Traverse of East Antarctica—a high-profile, collaborative project to measure climate indicators in the least-explored section of the continent—had at time of writing published 66 entries to the IPY blog compared to 135 entries to their online diary on the official project website. The project was aimed at investigating the response of East Antarctica to anthropogenic activity and climate change. This is reflected in many of the blog entries where scientists report not only the mechanisms of their research, but also the relevance of samples and data collected for understanding climate change. Several members of the traverse team also contributed articles to personal blogs, while Norwegian public service broadcaster NRK embedded a dedicated reporter and photographer who filed reports on the NRK website, Traversen.

The Norwegian-US traverse was perhaps the one IPY activity that gained the most attention in mainstream media, though the most significant new initiative in terms of coordinating science writing from the polar regions was undoubtedly the Ice Stories website run by the Exploratorium science museum in San Francisco, California. The project was intended to provide "a public face for IPY by using the power of contemporary media to bring current research to mass audiences with unprecedented intimacy and immediacy" (Exploratorium, 2008). Ice Stories featured seven citizen journalists from Antarctica in the 2007–2008 season and 12 in the 2008–2009 season, with 10 scientists reporting from the Arctic in 2008. The website combines scientists' dispatches with stunning photographs, podcasts, video content (including a series of live webcasts from the polar regions), and special feature articles providing background on anything from penguins to climate change.

The Ice Stories website's chief scientist co-ordinator, Mary Miller, describes the project as having been "successful beyond my wildest imagination." She continues, pointing out that there "are many scientists who are eager to communicate with the public," and the Ice Stories website helps to facilitate their storytelling. Miller explains how the Exploratorium "conducted a six-day workshop with 12–18 scientists in each and trained them in video production, digital photography, audio production, writing and story telling." Media producers and educators from the museum acted as instructors, together with "outside professionals from PBS, NPR, and the San Francisco Chronicle." The training was an important aspect of the Ice Stories project to maximize the impact and to further encourage the scientists to continue with their citizen journalism efforts in the future.

Cassandra Brooks, one of the Ice Stories contributors researching Antarctic toothfish, started with a personal blog from Antarctica in 2006 and then moved to Ice Stories when she returned in 2008. "Science writing appealed to me very much," she explains:

> Through writing dispatches I truly grasped the powerful tool that writing is for educating the public.... Once you get people to care about a place, then they will want to protect it and given how the climate is changing most rapidly at the poles, its a critical time for people to take interest. (Cassandra Brooks)

Howard Koss, who studies climate variability in historical terms so as to better anticipate future climate change, contributes to three blogs—hosted at Ice Stories, Reach the World, and the dedicated project website—each written with a different target audience in mind so as to engage as many people as possible. Koss views his blogging as a way of bypassing the limitations of more traditional forms of communicating research, thereby helping to reconnect ordinary people with the science behind climate change.

> This is my motivation, to make people, from young school children to adults, aware of the need to understand how our global climate will change into the future, and how we as a scientific community are going about it. There has long been a disconnect between the sciences and lay people. I hope to bridge that gap through my blogging efforts. (Howard Koss)

Breana Simmons, who contributes to *The World of Nematodes*, also stresses the need to connect directly with distant publics. She comments that the way traditional media frame scientific research, and indeed Antarctica itself, can be problematic:

> Teaching young people about Antarctic science, from Antarctica, makes the frozen southern continent a real place, instead of an abstract concept shaped by popular media. Students are incredibly tech-savvy, and publishing a blog seemed like an excellent way to connect with them, and to hold their attention. (Breana Simmons)

The extent to which blogs are successful in achieving these laudable ambitions is difficult to measure by web statistics or online comments alone. Indeed, Becky Ball felt uncertain about how well they were connecting with the schools they were linked to, "until after we returned to the US, when we received drawings and reports about what they learned." Similarly, Mary Miller believes the Ice Stories website has been very successful, with the public having "responded, both on our website through blog comments and our in-person audience for webcasts in the museums."

UNMEDIATED REPORTING?

Scientists interviewed as part of this project frequently expressed a desire to connect with ordinary members of the public, often bemoaning the role of mainstream media in providing an unsatisfactory portrayal of their research. Citizen journalism was seen as a way in which they could bypass this mediated process and communicate directly with the public, reporting their research, life on the ice, and—crucially—their first-hand experience of the dramatic climatic changes taking place. David Ainley, a leading expert on how Adéle penguins respond to environmental change and contributor to Ice Stories and Penguinscience.com, explains:

> My motivation is to include a wider audience in our research than just the scientists we would reach by publication or presentation at scientific meetings. Very few scientists, other than the very few James Hansen's, are going to change the world, but "regular" people just might if given some information first hand, rather than filtered through professional journalists. (David Ainley)

Antarctic bloggers operate in very challenging conditions, however. Perhaps most obviously the scientists are necessarily affiliated with research institutes or science programs and thus are present in Antarctica in a representative capacity. Scientists have no choice but to use the internet connection provided (no alternatives are available) and are subsequently bound by guidelines that govern what can or cannot be reported, regardless of the platform it is being published to. One communications manager, who wished to remain anonymous, explained how their organization monitors "all personal blogs by going to them on the internet and reading them," which "has been highlighted by comments and action taken when blog entries have not pleased . . . management." Several of the bloggers interviewed described an element of self-restraint in the way they publish as a direct consequence of such guidelines or a perceived duty to avoid negative publicity.

Official or coordinated blogging projects may also have an additional level of editorial control. "We serve as the mediators between the public and the world of research," explains Mary Miller of Ice Stories, "but we let the individual voices of scientists come through without alteration for the most part." They provide feedback on initial story ideas and guide the scientists to provide "content suitable for a public audience."

> After a few rounds, the scientists generally get it and their work improves so that we do very little editing (grammar, spelling, and some minor video production or photo sizing is about all we do). (Mary Miller)

The editorial role of sites such as Ice Stories thus contravenes the familiar sense of blogs being raw, impressionistic, and—most important—unedited. However, none of the scientists interviewed who were affected by this level of mediation felt that it posed a serious problem in and by itself. On the contrary, they were grateful for what they thought helped to sharpen their message, enabling them to be better placed to report on their research and life on the ice.

CONCLUSION

The climate-change crisis resonates throughout the Antarctic blogosphere as the bloggers strive to bear witness to the dramatic impact of global warming unfolding around them. Even scientists whose research is not directly related to climate change frequently publish accounts describing how they are observing the transformation first-hand. This emergent form of science reporting provides an important contrast to traditional forms of journalism, where the process of climate change is a difficult fit for conventional, event-led news agendas.

Indeed, even blog posts about day-to-day scientific activities attract a sizeable audience, with readers evidently mesmerized by the exotic and extreme nature of this remote location. Such personal narratives help to further personalize the scientists and their work. For the lay reader, the style of writing adopted by the majority of these citizen journalists makes the scientific arguments more accessible, not to mention more interesting. Readers' comments, posted to the blogs, frequently make statements of admiration and support, while also asking questions about the entries themselves. As highlighted in this chapter, scientists often respond to such feedback directly, either as follow-up comments or in new posts published at a later stage. The blogs therefore facilitate a dialogic interaction that goes some distance to bridge the gap between scientists and the public.

While this new form of citizen journalism helps to raise people's awareness of the climate-change crisis, it also signals an important way in which mainstream environmental reporting can be reinvigorated. Scientists' blogs, with their interactive forms of storytelling providing relatively direct access to expert knowledge, represent a remarkable resource, the potential of which is only now being recognized.

ACKNOWLEDGMENT

The author wishes to thank the many Antarctic bloggers, including those not cited here, who took part in e-interviews and provided background information for this chapter.

NOTES

1. The Pew Internet Project and Exploratorium (2006) found that the internet was a primary source of science news for 20% of the US population (second only to television), with 59% of the respondents saying they would turn first to the internet to find more information about climate change. The figure is likely even higher now as Horrigan (2008), the chief researcher behind the report, points out, given the increase in broadband connectivity.
2. Official blogs associated with specific projects are usually hosted on dedicated websites. Personal blogs, however, predominantly use free services such as Blogger, WordPress, LiveJournal, or TypePad, with only a minority maintaining traditionally styled websites.

REFERENCES

Allan, S. (2009) "Making science newsworthy: exploring the conventions of science journalism." In R. Holliman, J. Thomas, S. Smidt, E. Scanlon, & L. Whitelegg (Eds.), *Investigating science communication in the information age: implications for public engagement and popular media*. Oxford: Oxford University Press.

Boykoff, M.T., & Boykoff, J.M. (2007) "Climate change and journalistic norms: a case-study of US mass-media coverage." *Geoforum, 38*(6), 1190–1204.

Carvalho, A. (2007) "Ideological cultures and media discourses on scientific knowledge: re-reading the news on climate change." *Public Understanding of Science, 16*(2), 223–243.

Carvalho, A., & Burgess, J. (2005) "Cultural circuits of climate change in U.K. broadsheet newspapers, 1985–2003." *Risk Analysis, 25*(6), 1457–1469.

Exploratorium (2008) "Exploratorium's ice stories: dispatches from polar scientists." *International Polar Year*.

Gavin, N.T. (2007) "Global warming and the British press: the emergence of an issue and its political implications." *Elections, Public Opinion and Parties*. University of the West of England, Bristol: Political Studies Association.

Horrigan, J.B. (2008) "Science & cyberspace: what user behavior means for science educators." *Leadership Initiative in Science Education Conference*. Philadelphia, PA: Chemical Heritage Foundation.

Neverla, I. (2008) "The IPCC-reports 1990–2007 in the media. A case-study on the dialectics between journalism and natural sciences." ICA-Conference, "Global Communication and Social Change." Montreal: International Communications Association.

Pew Internet Project/Exploratorium (2006) *The Internet as a resource for news and information about science*. Washington, DC: Pew Internet & American Life Project.

Russell, C. (2008) "Climate change: now what? A big beat grows more challenging and complex." *Columbia Journalism Review*, July/August, n.p.

Trench, B. (2007) "How the internet changed science journalism." In M.W. Bauer & M. Bucchi (Eds.), *Journalism, science and society: science communication between news and public relations*. New York and London: Routledge.

Wilson, K.M. (2000) "Communicating climate change through the media: predictions, politics and perceptions of risk." In S. Allan, B. Adam, & C. Carter (Eds.), *Environmental risks and the media* (pp. 201–217). London: Routledge.

SECTION TWO: CITIZEN JOURNALISM AND
DEMOCRATIC CULTURES

CHAPTER NINE

The Iranian Story: What Citizens? What Journalism?

GHOLAM KHIABANY AND ANNABELLE SREBERNY

The notion of citizen journalism has spread rapidly in many contemporary media systems, especially in the United States and Europe, over the past few years. The practice is often seen to challenge central aspects of the classic paradigm of journalistic activity. This includes professional training and recognition, paid work, unionized labor, and behavior that is often politically neutral and unaffiliated, at least in the claim if not in the actuality. Citizen journalists, by contrast, are often untrained, unpaid, non-unionized, and highly politicized. However, even in Western mediacracies, the boundaries and practices are blurring. Fine lines are becoming harder to draw.

When such a neologism is applied to a very different setting, some interesting questions are triggered. These include a critique of the export of such notions to different contexts; that is to say, do conceptualizations developed in particular locations necessarily travel and travel well? But the opposite kind of critique is also important: what kind of questions does this new concept raise about the assumptions underlying both journalism and citizenship elsewhere?

Our focus here is on media practices inside the Islamic Republic of Iran. Broadcast media have always been centralized under the jurisdiction of the state, so the focus in this chapter is on the press. We ask: what purchase does the notion of "citizen journalism" possess, both in terms of citizenship and journalistic practice? Both elements in the term have significance, and each is very differently configured in contemporary Iran in comparison, say, with contemporary Britain, where the present authors are both based.

CITIZENSHIP AND JOURNALISM IN IRAN

Citizenship is a problematic concept in Iran, but it is creeping into public discourse, as indicated by the establishment of a new weekly magazine under that name. Until the 1979 revolution, however, the simplest analysis would have put all Iranians as subjects of a centralized monarchical system. While there was some pretense of formal politics—even women were granted the vote in the 1960s—by the 1970s Mohammad Reza Pahlavi, the last shah, had dissolved all political parties in favor of his own party, Rastakhiz. Independent unions were disallowed, and any gathering of over three people was subject to investigation by SAVAK, the secret police. One of the many strands that mobilized Iranians in revolution was the lack of political freedom to organize and to articulate concerns.

The system that emerged after 1979 is hardly more democratic. The Islamic Republic is based on a constitution that is a contradictory and compromised body of legislation that combines some democratic principles with theocratic arguments and institutions. It is important to note that the constitution is ambivalent about its source of legitimacy and sovereignty. On the one hand the constitution recognizes the people and their right to choose who will govern them by direct vote, including members of Parliament (*Majlis*) as well as the president. However, on the other hand it subordinates the people's will to the clerical establishment via institutions of *velayat-e faqih* (rule of supreme jurist) and *Shura-ye Negahban* (The Guardians Council). The latter body is a powerful second chamber that has to approve all bills passed by the Parliament and ensure that they conform to the constitution and Shari'a.

In Iran's modern history the media have never been free, except in times of revolutionary upheaval and in the strong presence of democratic social movements. Thus the history of the Iranian press cannot be separated from the broader history of the struggle for power in Iran. Sreberny-Mohammadi and Mohammadi (1994) rightly suggest that:

> The typical pattern of Iranian political life has been that when the central authority is at its weakest, a dynamic political public sphere emerges with a variety of political groupings and communicative channels. When central authority is strong, an atmosphere of repression exists, with central control over political activity and expression. (p. 54)

Occasions of political and press freedom have been rare. In fact, there are probably only five occasions in which an open press and free political participation have flourished: the Constitutional Revolution (1906–1911); the collapse of Reza Shah in 1941; the premiership of Mossadeq in the early 1950s; the *"spring of freedom"* after the 1979 revolution; and between 1997 and 2000. There is no space here to provide a history of all these moments, so we move directly to an examination of the recent period of Iranian press history and the movement from print to the internet. Our argument is that the history of the Iranian press cannot be separated from the wider history of the country and that these shifts have less to do with technology per se and far more to do with the parlous state of democratic politics inside Iran.

REFORM AND THE MEDIA AFTER 1997

The new movement for democratization in Iran, defining itself under the banners of "civil society" and the press as a "fourth estate," resulted in two landslide victories for the reformist presidential candidate Khatami in 1997 and 2001. The press, in the absence of an independent system of political parties, became a key milieu wherein the debates about political participation and the contours of the public sphere could be articulated. Khatami was elected on the promise of greater press freedom and more diversity. He was also aware that since conservatives controlled the national broadcasting organization, *Islamic Republic of Iran Broadcasting* (IRIB), he would need a sympathetic press to gather support for his policies.

The new cultural and political atmosphere was reflected in newspaper titles. In contrast to conservative dailies such as *Resalat* (Prophetic Mission) and *Jumhouri-e Eslami* (Islamic Republic), new, colorful titles emerged such as *Jameh* (Society), *Neshat* (Joy), *Mellat* (Nation), *Azad* (Free), *Mosharekat* (Participation), *Fath* (Victory), *Hughugh-e Zanan* (Women's Rights), *Rah-e No* (New Path), *Hayat-e No* (New Life), *Bahar* (Spring), and *Goonagun* (Variety). Many were regional and local titles, ensuring that the movements were not limited to capital and major cities (Tarock, 2001, p. 590). They offered little space for religious and "official" stories, instead publishing hard-hitting investigative reports on corruption, inefficiencies, and abuses of power by significant institutions in the Islamic Republic, including the Ministry of Intelligence and the Islamic Republic Revolutionary Guards.

Yet the Khatami period was contradictory, with many new titles flourishing immediately after his victory, but followed by a vehement campaign against the press. The censoring and closing of newspapers and harassment and arrest of journalists marked his last few years. Advocacy of "civil society" by the pro-Khatami press forced the proponents of conservative policy to retaliate. A new press law passed just before the parliamentary election of 2000 was used to censor publications, raid premises, take equipment, and to harass, fine, and even imprison journalists. By the end of 2002, more than 80 publications in Iran had been banned by the judiciary, although many reemerged in online form (Khiabany & Sreberny, 2001). Furthermore, by labeling the reformist and independent press as enemies of Islam and the Islamic Republic, the regime continued the tradition of mobilizing supporters of the dominant faction to intimidate dissident voices and journalists. Certain elements of the "fourth estate," namely IRIB and daily *Keyhan*, were used to discredit and humiliate those not considered "sympathetic" to Islam, the Islamic Republic, and its Supreme Leader.

The Iranian press market reflects the broader picture of the Iranian political economy, marked by the presence of massive and large-scale, state-owned corporations on the one hand and petty production and small enterprises on the other. Large-scale media enterprises include the firm of *Keyhan* (13 titles, including three dailies in Persian, Arabic, and English); *Ettelaat* (eight titles, including two dailies catering to national and international readers); and Islamic Republic of Iran Broadcasting (IRIB) and its publishing arm, *Soroush* (seven titles including the daily *Jame-Jam*). Other major firms with direct links to the state are Iranian News Agency (seven titles, including the daily *Iran*), *Hamshahri* (a bestselling daily published by the Tehran mayor's office), and *Quds* (published by the estate of Imam Reza in the holy city of Mashhad). With massive financial resources and generous subsidies by the state, these all have state-of-the-art printing presses and facilities (Khiabany, 2007).

The other model of ownership, wrongly perceived as merely *private*, is the *individual* ownership of newspapers. Many of these individuals, however, are ex-ministers, MPs, and officials who have turned to the press market to promote themselves and their policies through some of the best-known dailies. *Salam* was owned by Khoeini'ha (ex-district attorney); *Khordad* was owned by Nouri (exInterior minister); *Jameh* was owned by Jalaipour (ex-commander of the Revolutionary Guards), and so on. If the dominance of petty production has provided a platform for the emergence and revival of many titles and has contributed to some extent to the existing diversity in the press market, it also has made the survival of such publications difficult. In addition to economic difficulties, the judiciary managed to suspend many of these papers by simply targeting the individual owners. *Salam*, *Khordad*, and many others ran into difficulties as soon as their owners found themselves on the wrong side of the judiciary. Such dynamics continue to the present day. For example, in the fall of 2008 the newspaper *Sharvand* was shut down because it published an article revealing that Ayatollah Khomeini had authorized the murder of a critical Ayatollah, Lahouti.

JOURNALISM TRAINING

In many countries, citizen journalism is seen to challenge the long-established profession of journalism. In Iran, it is legitimate to ask how professional was and is journalism, indeed what would make it so.

At various times politics impacted the development of the press. But other elements of a professional press were also weak. Professional training, one criterion of professionalism, arrived quite late in Iran. Most of those involved in journalism came from the worlds of politics and literature and were learned and practiced on the job. The first-ever journalism training short course was launched in 1939 by the Law College of Tehran University, ending abruptly with the Allied invasion in September 1941 (Shahidi, 2007, Ghandi, 1998). After the 1953 CIA coup, Mesbahzadeh—the publisher of daily *Kayhan*—recommended that the University of Tehran establish a College of Journalism. US scholars came to teach journalism, and some Iranians went abroad for training (Ghandi, 1998). In 1964 a two-year training course in journalism was established. After the revolution, the program re-emerged in the 1990s as part of Allameh Tabatabaee University, with MA courses and a PhD program.

Another program, established in 1969, was the College of Voice and Vision, offering specialized courses in broadcasting, media management, and advertising and now run by IRIB (Shahidi, 2007, p. 116). Other institutions teach journalism, including the Centre for Media Studies Research of the Ministry of Culture and Islamic Guidance. The non-governmental Islamic Azad University has courses in online journalism, television journalism, and media management. The School of Media Studies (News College), affiliated with IRNA, the national news agency, offers a BA in News Reporting and a BA in News Translation (Arabic and English).

More recently, international broadcasters have also started to offer training. In 2006, the BBC World Service Trust (2008) "provided training in the principles and practice of fair, balanced and independent journalism to 31 journalists and 26 young aspiring journalists from Iran. Trainees were selected from over 1,000 applicants and came from all over the country." The Trust has also launched a Persian online magazine called *Zig Zag*, for which trainees write stories and practice their skills.

However, the lack of job security, poor pay and working conditions, and the state's control of broadcasting and the press all play a role in the weak professionalization of Iranian journalism. The emergence of a semi-independent press and the internet, and above all the renewed struggles for a more open and democratic society by workers, students, women, and minority ethnic groups (all struggling for spaces to communicate their critique, ideas, and aspirations) have created a renewed interest in media training.

Professional bodies and associations for journalists have also had a checkered history. Media workers have always been at the forefront of the struggle for democracy, including the right to form independent associations and unions. Prior to the revolution, the only organization "representing" media workers was the Syndicate of Newspaper Writers and Reporters established in 1962 and backed by the government. Journalists played a major role during the revolution (see Sreberny-Mohammadi & Mohammadi, 1994), but the new regime announced there was no need for syndicates while allowing the formation of associations. In 1991, a Press Cooperative was established by the publishers of 32 newspapers and magazines. Only in 1997, after the landslide victory of Khatami, was the Association of Iranian Journalists established, which had 2,699 print journalist members in January 2005 (Shahidi, 2007, pp. 111–112).

THE IMPACT OF THE INTERNET POST-KHATAMI

Despite regular attacks upon and censorship of the reform movements, the recent period has seen the communication industries emerge as one of the fastest-growing economic sectors. New media constitute a vibrant politico-cultural space, and popular desire for access to informal channels of communication and for greater cultural consumption are reflected in the increasing use of mobile technology and the internet. The digital divide is real: Iran lags behind its regional neighbors with only 10.6% of its 70 million population online, although its actual numbers constitute 38.7% of all Middle East users. However, limited access and use are part of a more complex story (Khiabany & Sreberny, 2008).

Since broadcasting remains a state monopoly, and as reformist newspapers have been banned, more people—including publishers, writers, journalists, and ordinary readers—have turned to the internet for information, debate, and space for expression. News websites have proliferated, as have sites about technology, music, sports, entertainment, women's issues, and student matters. All major groupings have their own news websites. Sites covering such areas keep appearing, and the number of weblogs continues to grow. The internet has also rekindled links between activists and intellectuals in Iran and the opposition abroad, offering alternative news channels to Iranian activists inside Iran and much-needed international support and solidarity, including from Iranians living in exile.

Weblogs are the most significant area of internet growth in Iran. The publication of Persian-language instructions by a young blogger in September 2000 triggered a massive collective phenomenon, sometimes estimated to include around 700,000 blogs, making Persian one of the leading languages in the blogosphere and increasing the share of Persian material online. The rapid growth of the blogo- sphere was helped by the disabling factionalism of the central Iranian state and the ongoing conflicts between Islamism and Republicanism; by the intense pressure from private capital in Iran that sought a larger share in the expanding and lucra- tive cultural industries; and above all by the existence of an already-dissatisfied young population challenging the Iranian state and actively seeking a new order. As a result, weblog service providers in Iran have emerged as part of the economic liberalization in Iran's communication industries. Companies such as persianblog and blogfa are recognized online brand names in new media and provide a range of services.

Undoubtedly, many Persian blogs express the aspirations, thoughts, and sen- timents of individual bloggers. Blogs present individual lives, with family pho- tos, love poems, laments about failed relationships, whimsy and wit, and all the accoutrements of emergent bourgeois individualism that can be found on British or American blogger sites (see Alavi, 2005). But few blogs are only about the indi- vidual as such, since even the most private and anonymous blogs have become part of a wider community of interests (*halghe*) through the addition of links. There is an evident sense of connectivity among Persian bloggers and pronounced trends toward establishing a sense of solidarity and community. While many blogs remain individualized, private forms of expression in public space, there are visible trends toward collective weblogs. These collective efforts can be seen in the activities of leftist organizations and women, which this chapter will explore in further detail. They show the extent of the networks of reform in Iran and, in a paradoxical man- ner, the existing spaces for debate and dissent within a repressive regime.

The labor movement is active online. *Kargar* (Worker) newsletter critiques capitalism and government changes to the labor law to accommodate private interests; interviews with and updates on arrested and imprisoned workers; and campaigns of solidarity with striking and sacked workers in factories and schools. A significant recent development has been the formation of the Iranian Bus Workers Union, whose leader Mansour Osanloo has been persecuted for devel- oping independent trade union activity to struggle for better wages and working conditions. Osanloo was adopted by Amnesty International's letter-writing cam- paign in 2008.

Workers Action Committee is another collective blog providing news, informa- tion, and analysis of workers' struggles. Its slogan reads: "In preparation for united action against capitalism." Recent posts include news of the arrest of six firefighters who had refused to pour hot water over the striking workers of Albourz Plastics, messages of solidarity with those workers, and news of issues in other factories.

Another blog is dedicated to the Association of Iranian Teachers. The slogan of the blog is "The rights of teachers and students are the rights of the Iranian nation." The aim of the blog is to be a "small medium for the expression of a big pain, a pain which threatens the future of a nation." It says that the foundation of people is based on the education of its children, that teachers are a major source of inspiration, and that the key problem remains "poverty, poverty, poverty. It is poverty which is the source of discrimination and injustice." The union's aim is, therefore, to fight against injustice and poverty. The blog develops the collective efforts of teachers for their rights, closer unity between teachers, the participation of teachers in policy-making, and fights against discrimination in education.

With the advancing wave of strikes and demonstrations across Iran, the concern is how to bring disparate activities and organizations—workers, students, and women—together. Shorayehamkari.com is the blog of *Shoraye Hamkari Tashakolha va F'aaleen Kargari* (Council for Coordinating Workers Organizations and Activists), six different organizations that merged in February 2007. It recognizes and encourages diverse points of view but also aims to coordinate activities, finding common ground for more united efforts, arguing "Our unity is the guarantor of our victory."

Radical students are a significant part of this process, and there are some fascinating secular, occasionally Marxist, student blogs. Abed Tavancheh runs Alaihe Vazeiat Moujod (Against the current condition), an openly Marxist blog, with quotes from Marx and Lenin on the screen. He carries photographs of arrested left-wing students; a poem dedicated to celebrated writer and poet Iraj Janati Ataie; a translated article from Seymour Hersh of *The New Yorker* suggesting that the US excuse for attacking Iran is changing from nuclear weapons to terrorism; and an antiwar announcement by Iranian intellectual Naser Zarafshan with a link to his campaign against war on Iran. The blog provides links to many left-wing sites outside Iran including Monthly Review, Marxist Archives (English and Farsi), as well as his friends and fellow activists.

Among these comrades is Elnaz Ansari, whose blog *Zananeh* (womanly) in turn links to a number of women's sites and blogs. In an original voice, she complains about the obsession with sex in many blogs. She notes that in a society marked by the absence of sexual education, everything is extremely sexualized, and that writing about sex is extremely difficult, since it so quickly becomes politicized. She raises questions about the aims of Persian Television of the Voice of America in propagating US economic policy and the threat of war against Iran , asking why "we" cannot launch a news radio and asks if the movement lacks the trained personnel and financial support for a left-leaning and independent radio or television.

Student publications such as *Militant* don't belong to any political organization but defend the position of radical socialists against the reformist and centrist tendencies in the student movement (*Militant* also has an English site). Socialist Youth Blog publicizes *Militant*, workers' news and critiques of other left-wing organizations, and, like many others, makes Marxist texts available to its readers, including Trotsky's *History of the Russian Revolution*. The *Freedom and Equality Seeking Students* began its activities in 2006 with the two key slogans "No to War!" and "Free Universities from Invading Military Forces!" Developed in response to the threat of war against Iran by the United States and the invasion of campuses by security forces in Tehran, they have organized events including the celebration of March 8, May Day, and Student Day, and they produce a number of blogs/publications including Khak (Earth), Armane No (New Ideal), *Gavaznha* (Deer) magazine, *Shora* (Council) magazine, Toloo (Dawn), and others.

Another highly developed domain of political writing on the net is by and about women, whose print publications were censored (Khiabany & Sreberny, 2004). The struggle for gender equality is evident in various campaigns and demonstrations, supported by a powerful presence in the online environment. The Meydaan-e Zanan (Women's Field) site brings together various activists and campaigns. It is a "focal point where a group of Iranian feminists organize campaigns against gender inequality and challenge different aspects of discrimination." It is open to all "who believe that the road leading from discrimination and equality to freedom and democracy goes by way of women's liberation." Its campaigns include a petition demanding the release of women's rights activists and another campaign for the right to nationality by children of Iranian mothers (but with a non-Iranian father, a situation which affects many with fathers of Iraqi or Afghani origin).[1] "Yes to women sports fans of Iran!" targets the contentious issue of the prevention of Iranian women from attending football matches.[2]

Many of the women's online initiatives try to bridge activism and intellectual debate, practice and theory. The website Maydaan has articles engaging with the issue of the Convention on the Elimination of All Forms of Discrimination against Women (CEDAW): passionate polemics about the need to institutionalize women's rights, including an article by Shadi Sadr, a lawyer and activist, who examines the universal principles in women's conventions across the world while arguing that the solutions are local. Other sites such as Iranian Feminists Tribune, Women in Iran, Focus of Iranian Women, and Zanestan combine news with critical analysis of women's lives and experiences, as well as their concerns and struggles at national and international levels. The Association of Iranian Women wants to be a tribune for all women's activities in Iran, big and small. It says that this online publication wants to write about the demands of "intellectual women as well as ordinary Iranian women", of "women in the centre" as well as those in the "margin", and of "activist women" as well as those in the "shadow."[3] It provides a comprehensive list of 125 women's organizations, including NGOs, charitable foundations, research centers, and local organizations. Womeniniran. org, launched in 2002, has been another key space where significant gender-related issues are raised and debated, including a campaign for the Iranian state to sign the CEDAW. Iran is among eight countries (the others being the United States, Sudan, Somalia, Qatar, Nauru, Palau, and Tonga) that have refused to ratify the 1979 treaty.

In addition to websites, women also produce collective blogs. The Herlandmag. com blog highlights the complexity, aspirations, and multidimensionality of many online initiatives in Iran. The Association of Lively Women (Anjoman-e Zanan-e Zendeh) is the weblog of an Iranian NGO called Women's Cultural Center (*Markaz-e Farhangi-e Zanan*). Launched in 2000, it reflects the concerns of sec-ular feminists. The center immediately celebrated International Women's Day, stating its aim was to "learn from our experience; become aware of the 'perceived natural' situation used and reproduced against women; spread and expand feminist knowledge among ourselves and other women; to look at our issues critically and not from an individual perspective, but as public and social issues; and strengthen ourselves via our collective efforts to transform unequal situation which grip us."[4] It campaigned for Iran to join CEDAW; against violence toward women; and for Afghani and Palestinian women. And it objected to the anti-women policies of IRIB. In 2006 the Center launched a second site, *Zanestan*, to forge stronger links among women activists inside and outside the country, and its online publication has various materials, including a weblog, allowing for quick interactivity. More recently, women's energy has focused on the One Million campaign to make con-stitutional law more gender-sensitive and friendly toward women. Many of the leaders of this new and wider movement have been arrested, imprisoned, or not allowed to leave the country. Their websites are often filtered, creating a complex and expensive cat-and-mouse game of creating new sites, only to find those fil-tered, too. The women's movement is arguably the single most important political mobilization in Iran, and there is considerable evidence of a citizen mobilization on the web promoting gender issues.

CONCLUSION

In Iran, journalism was forced to migrate to the internet because of state censor-ship of the press. There it developed many forms: web-based publications, collec-tive blogs, and individual commentary. State repression appears to be a galvanizing force for political communication.

Journalists were never highly professionalized in the strict sense of the word. Journalism training remains weak and non-standardized. The embryonic journalists' union recently came under severe attack. In June 2008, as part of the general incursion on civil liberties and social movement activities, the Iranian government threatened to dissolve the journalist association and tried to remove the association's executive committee and replace them with conservative journalists. Many in Iran suggested it was a highly political act triggered by the forthcoming presidential election. Through the fall of 2008, many journalists on private newspapers have not been paid for months, and many are being laid off.

If journalism is a form of writing, then the number of (often young) Iranian writers practicing hard is a positive sign for the future. If journalism is a form of economic activity, then times are probably hard for any but the big firms that remain in the good graces of the regime. If journalism is about articulating social and political issues, about investigation and analysis, then the Iranian blogosphere functions as a powerful alternative, free at the point of consumption and relatively free at the point of production—if the mighty hand of the state can be avoided. Both citizenship and journalism are working hard in Iran, in innovative forms that are responses to the political context.

NOTES

1. Under pressure, the Iranian Parliament passed a law in early 2006 granting the children of Iranian mothers the right to apply for Iranian citizenship after they reach 18 years of age. But this doesn't apply to children who were not born in Iran, so the activists are campaigning for further changes
2. Notably depicted in Jafar Panahi's film *Offside*.
3. http://www.irwomen.org/spip.php?article2
4. http://herlandmag.com/about/

REFERENCES

Alavi, N. (2005) *We are Iran*. Washington: Soft Skull Press.

BBC World Service Trust (2008) "How we work: strengthen local media." *BBC World Service Trust*.

Ghandi, H. (1998) "Expert personnel in press." Collection of articles of Second Seminar in *Analysis of Iranian Press* (vol. 2). Tehran: Centre for Media Studies and Research.

Khiabany, G. (2007) "Iranian media: the paradox of modernity." *Social Semiotics, 17*(2), 479–501.

Khiabany, G., & Sreberny, A. (2001) "The Iranian press and the struggle over civil society 1998–2000." *Gazette, 63*(2/3), 203–223.

Khiabany, G., & Sreberny, A. (2004) "The women's press in Iran: engendering the public sphere." In N. Sakr (Ed.), *Women and media in the Middle East*. London: I.B.Tauris.

Khiabany, G., & Sreberny, A. (2007) "The politics of/in blogging in Iran." *Comparative Studies of South Asia, Africa and the Middle East, 27*(2), 563–579.

Khiabany, G., & Sreberny, A. (2008) "Internet in Iran: the battle over an emerging public sphere." In M. Mclelland & G. Goggin (Eds.), *Internationalising internet studies: beyond anglophone paradigms*. New York: Routledge.

Shahidi, H. (2007) *Journalism in Iran: from mission to profession*. London and New York: Routledge.

Sreberny-Mohammadi, A., & Mohammadi, A. (1994) *Small media, big revolution: communication, culture, and the Iranian revolution*. Minneapolis: University of Minnesota Press.

Tarock, A. (2001) "The muzzling of liberal press in Iran." *Third World Quarterly, 22*(4), 585–602.

CHAPTER TEN

Citizen Journalism AND Child Rights IN Brazil

OLGA GUEDES BAILEY

I make newspaper!

(CHILD PARTICIPANT OF THE PROJECT "CLUB OF NEWSPAPERS")

Much of the "conversation" about citizen journalism among professional and non-professional journalists is centered on the web as the central space/place where citizen journalism assumes its familiar shape. Discussions often focus on its interactive nature—the audience and readers becoming producers and/or "co-authors" of mainstream journalism—and how the web has changed the ethos of traditional journalism practice. However, what is of even greater importance, in my view, is the fact that ordinary people are having their say and connecting with the powerful and the privileged, be it by interacting with the "big media," producing blogs, or alternative media.

The web is indeed a fantastic source of information and means of communication, but it needs to be pointed out that many people, particularly in the "developing" world, have no access to computers and have little or no information about, or practice with, communication technologies skills. Accordingly, for most of the world's population, the mass (mainstream) media is still the main source of information. In countries such as Brazil, where part of the population is still illiterate—of a population of 119.5 million, 16.2% were illiterate according to the Census of 2000 (adeanet.org)—broadcast media are the central providers of information and entertainment, even though this content is not always reflective of their needs. More important, for our purposes here, a majority of citizen journalists in Brazil still rely on the traditional media to interact, although gradually some are also acting as an interface between the web and the mass media and/or practicing directly online.

Brazil has a long tradition of alternative media practices for the mobilization and political organization of civil society. In many cases, they are inspired by Freire's (1993) seminal work, *The Pedagogy of the oppressed*, with its focus on a participatory model centered on community engagement and dialogue as a means of individual and community empowerment. A large number of projects focus on the media literacy of children, many of which are designed to challenge an authoritarian political culture. They have come to be seen as significant moments in the process of democratic learning, in the sense of building a new political culture.

The type of citizen journalism practiced in Brazil is characterized primarily by two different but sometimes overlapping features. First is the interaction of the audience with the mainstream news media organizations, where people provide news and images to online sites and broadcast media. Second is the alternative news media journalism produced by both journalists and non-journalists based on a news agenda not always explored by the traditional media. Journalists' debate on citizen journalism centers on a perceived crisis in the ethos of traditional journalism revolving around the latter's apparent decline, in terms of its power to define the public agenda and shape public opinion. This decline is directly linked, in turn, to problems associated with the scale of efforts in mainstream media to reduce costs, which are held to have a decisive impact on the quality and accuracy of news and information being generated. This debate has been important in a number of ways, not least because it has helped to create a space of visibility and public dialogue with positive implications for the practice of democratic communication.

The aspect of citizen journalism discussed here relates to the practices designed for, and experienced by, children to improve their sense of identity and increase their participation in the community, and the possibilities of empowerment for social change. This sort of experience, where children—in addition to adults—are part of the nucleus of development, is paramount for the strength of a democratic Brazilian society that respects its children and fosters their rights to communication and information. In this sense, the capacity for communication becomes a means to enhance children's rights and to strengthen the social, economic, and cultural fabric of their lives within diverse, everyday contexts. Communication becomes a form of citizenship, in other words a way of grasping the notion of belonging and membership in political communities (Waisbord, 2005).

This chapter's discussion of citizen journalism draws upon a case study of a newspaper produced by hundreds of children in the O Clube do Jornal (Newspaper club) in Brazil.[1] The newspaper was conceived as a mechanism for them to voice their views about issues of interest, as a resource to exercise "citizenship-in-the-making." It was also a means to improve morale within the local community by encouraging it "to take pride in its own culture, intellect and environment" (Servaes & Malikao, 2005, p. 98). In the sections to follow, we will discuss the potential of citizen journalism as a practice for facilitating social change in the lives of disenfranchised children who have little or no knowledge of their rights, and a very limited prospect of fulfilling their aspirations. It will be shown how the O Clube do Jornal aims to change the lives of children beyond a "culture of silence" in order for them to become what Freire (1973) might have called "conscious makers of their own culture."

CITIZENS IN THE MAKING

The end of the dictatorship in Brazil in 1985 brought about democracy and a new constitution in 1988, and with it the struggle for the reinstatement of civil liberties, the freedom of the press, and the reorganization of the civil society. With millions of children living on the streets, subjected to all kinds of exploitation and abuse, the new constitution recognized children's rights as an "absolute priority" (Article 227)[2] by families, society, and the state. Soon after, the UN Convention on the Rights of the Child was ratified, and a national "Bill of Rights for Children and Adolescents" was passed.

Two decades later, a great deal has been achieved, but as Godoi (2006) suggests, the legal apparatus is only part of the process of guaranteeing that children's rights are respected in Brazilian society (p. 35; cited in Maropo, 2008). Nongovernmental organizations work to maintain the visibility of children's problems related particularly to forced work, sexual exploitation, and their criminalization in the public—media—agenda, and to develop initiatives to improve their lives. They instigate projects designed to increase the quality of life of poor children at the material and symbolic levels, provide basic services for children, and, in addition, aim to ensure that all rights of children are fulfilled, including the rights to information and to participate in decisions affecting their own lives.

Two examples from a multitude of such initiatives are "Fundação Casa Grande," or "Big House Foundation," in Nova Olinda, Ceará. It is a "communication school" for children that helps them to become active citizens-in-the-making in the community: the children produce videos, newsletters, magazines, and radio programs. And in the Amazonian city of Manaus, project "Uga-Uga" supports a news agency run by children, with the support of local journalists. Here they produce a newsletter distributed to 15,000 students in the state's public schools.

The project is part of the ANDI network—National News Agency for Children's Rights—one of the few in the world that focuses on improving the quality of coverage of children's issues in the mainstream media (Claycomb, 2000).

One of the difficulties of using the "citizens-in-the-making" category for poor Brazilian children is that around 12% have no birth certificate (UNICEF, 2008, p. 13). From the perspective of social inclusion, this is an indicator of their underprivileged socio-economic condition. The concept of "citizen-in-the-making" points to those children who are recognized as citizens in "transition" (Jones & Wallace, 1992), as they are not fully entitled to the "adult" citizen rights. Nevertheless, even though this is of a transitional nature, "citizenship rights are integral to young people as they enter the symbolic and political order of adult life" (Blackman & France 2001, p. 187).

Many of Brazil's young people are thus placed in a position of social exclusion where non-participation is not an option; it is part and parcel of being a child in a country where they are protected but not fully empowered. Participation of the "citizen-in-the-making" needs to be situated in a broader sense of politics not necessarily connected to politicians or the political apparatus of society. As Cullingford (1992) highlights:

> Children develop broadly political concepts at an earlier stage, through their everyday experiences of institutions such as the school and the family: notions of authority, fairness and justice, rules and laws, power and control, are all formed long before children are required to express their views in the form of voting. (cited in Buckingham, 2000, p. 204)

Although for many poor Brazilian children this experience might be different because of their material conditions of existence, an existence that might lead to alienation or harder ways of understanding "politics"—power, exclusion, social prejudice, and so on. This is "politics" beyond the electoral realm, including as it does everyday-life politics. One might argue that experiences of citizen journalism expand the idea of politics, suggesting new forms of participation for children in the community and different forms of participation at different levels.

THE NEWSPAPER CLUB

> The Newspaper club sometimes suffers resistance from the schools' management staff as they are not used to their students expressing their views openly, to freedom of expression. For example, to discuss that the toilets of the school are always dirty might generate a big "mess"! (Daniel Raviolo, director of the NGO and coordinator of the project)

The Newspaper Club is a project conceived and implemented by the Brazilian NGO "Communication and Culture" in partnership with public schools (local and state government). The project started in 1995 and works with schools located on the periphery of cities or in rural areas in several Brazilian states. In 2007, the project was active in 13 schools in the state of Ceara, 17 in Pernambuco, and 10 in the city of São Paulo, and published 82 newspapers with 74,100 copies. During that year the project team developed 46 workshops and seminars on journalism skills and the ethics of the project, and made 177 visits to schools.

The initiative aims to facilitate the exercise of freedom of speech by children at school in order to renew the relationship between the school, students, and community, as well as to strengthen students' participation in organizations such as their "civic clubs" and the school council. The Newspaper Club thus becomes an important element of the management of the school, one where students' freedom of expression and participation are held to be paramount to the political goal of democratizing power relations, which permeates everyday practices.

The ethos of citizen journalism developed by the club is based on dialogical and horizontal communication—to facilitate mutual understanding and to build trust—where children are producers and consumers of information. Freedom of expression, in other words, is extended to include children's voices. In each participating school, students with an interest in communication organize themselves into a "club" where they produce the newspapers that discuss issues of interest to their peers, the local community, and beyond.

Students have open discussions with one another about the project, and together they decide the news agenda, title of the publication, periodicity (no more than nine per year), and design. This deliberative process fuels a sense of both responsibility and ethics. The project's code of ethics perceives the children's freedom of action and expression as a practice of citizenship. The school's staff is not allowed to censor the content of the newspapers. The code of ethics also promotes human rights and nurtures an attitude of tolerance and respect for identity differences such as cultural, ethnic, gender, religious, sexual, disability, and so on. In addition, the newspaper has to abide by the following: it cannot be used for political or personal promotion; all news features are signed by the authors; it has to provide a right of response; all the "opinion groups" active in the school have the right to express their views; the editors cannot censor material or conceal information; and the children responsible for the newspaper have to publish an account of the costs and number of print runs in each newspaper.

Regarding the coordination of the newspapers, there is no direct intervention from the schools' staff. The youngsters may invite teachers to revise texts or to support their campaigns for funds. The teachers can submit texts developed in the classroom or their individual texts as members of the school community. The decision to publish the material is taken solely by the editorial board of the newspaper. Teachers can also develop seminars to discuss the role of the newspaper in the school and the wider community. The supervision of the newspapers (in order to check ethical issues) and mediation of conflict of interest between the newspaper and the school is the responsibility of the "Communication and Culture" mentioned above.

In general, the structure follows the format of a traditional newspaper. However, the agenda, news-values, and process of making news often differ, sometimes in surprising ways, because (following a participatory principle) the stories are constructed according to the children's interests.

The children are responsible for the production and distribution of the newspaper. The standard newspaper has four sheets (A3) printed in black and white, with a print run based on the number of students plus 10% for distribution in the community. Each student gets a copy to take home to their family, which generates new possibilities of social intervention and engages the community with the issues raised by the newspaper.

The organization of the club is defined by the members in accordance with the democratic principles negotiated with the NGO. The initiative is fundamental in building students' capabilities, with training in communication skills such as journalism skills (introduction), computer skills and internet literacy, political literacy, as well as critical skills to understand the importance of information in terms of source, use, and application. As Buckingham (2000) reminds us, the media and education "are public spheres where people represent themselves to each other, and therefore negotiate shared values and priorities" (p. 220). However, the school is in many respects still conservative, authoritarian, and undemocratic, and initiatives such as the Newspaper Club challenge the status quo by suggesting changes in the school's culture of no participation toward a participatory model of democracy.

The production of news engages the children with a politics that is relevant to them, that is, it relates politics to their personal experience, to what is accessible and meaningful in their daily lives. Thus, the discussion about the conditions of the toilets in the school is not only about what is appropriate but becomes a political issue that involves the participation of the children in discussions with the school on rights and obligations in maintaining the cleanliness of the place. In this process the children, citizens-in-the-making, are in charge of the construction of their own knowledge, in which they become active subjects rather than passive ones. The process of news production is a creative way of thinking about citizens-in-the-making as it allows them to explore new possibilities, make choices, and make decisions regarding the news. This enables differing degrees of participation at different ages and thus becomes part of an attitude for facing life and creating the opportunity for young people to forge roles and make identities. The experience also works as a form of community mobilization, which is empowering and motivating for the young participants. For example, in the city of Fortaleza, the young journalists of several Newspaper Clubs have forged contact with professional journalists to exchange information, to learn about and relate to their experiences.

In relation to the newspapers' content, themes may differ from region to region, but there are some similarities in the range of topics associated with these local interests. The more "universal" themes are environmental issues, racism, religion, piracy of music and films, social responsibility, feminism, human rights, sport, problems of poverty, and prostitution. Topical themes are bullying at school, communication between parents and their children, the relationship between men and women/boys and girls, the prevention of sexually transmitted diseases, teenage pregnancy, the importance of voting to combat corrupt politicians and as an exercise of their rights, the well-being and happiness of children, local and school events, information about future professions, and problems in the school and the local community. Most of them have a "message" section where other children send messages to their peers, sometimes romantic messages or poems. They include advertisements ranging from the local shops to the local council. The tone is informative, light, and fun, with a personal touch translated in the illustrations—drawings from the children—or in the editorial.

However, the production of citizen journalism by the children is not the same in every school or indeed always a harmonious process. There are conflicts that they have to face and decisions required to resolve them. Renan Moraes, a student in a school participating in the project, reported an event that took place in his school a few years ago. An edition of the newspaper produced by the students did not arrive from the printing place on the date expected. The parcel, addressed to the young editors of the newspaper, had been intercepted by the schools' managers, who burned the whole edition in a public area of the school while the students watched. Their excuse for this act of wanton destruction and censorship was, they said, because of grammatical errors in the articles. They were not prepared to allow it to circulate in the community, as it would create a poor image of the school. To resolve the impasse, members of other schools' "Clubs" came out in support of the students to demonstrate the importance of freedom of expression and to negotiate a solution to the problem with the school management. It was eventually agreed that a teacher of Portuguese would proof-read the newspaper before publication (Chibli, 2005).

In another case, the mayors of a number of cities took a strong position against local schools because the content of the newspapers opposed their interests. According to Raviolo, "This kind of reaction is inevitable because in the Brazilian political context many aspects of citizenship are still precarious. The work developed in the 'Newspaper Club' points out the need of a cultural shift towards democratic practices" (Chibli, 2005, p. 2). This shift involves creative forms of thinking and practicing education in the schools, in valuing the right to access to information and communication, respect for cultural difference, and a new attitude toward the rights of children as citizens-in-the-making.

Looking to the future, there are plans to have the existing newspapers on the web from 2009, although the printed version will be maintained for the time being. The latest participants in the scheme will be entirely online, however, with a printed version possible only in the event that funds are available. This new online version might alter the dynamic of the newspapers' production and consumption; in terms of text-meaning production, students, parents, and the wider community will have the ability, at least in principle, to interact more with the newspaper. The online version will similarly have the potential to change established practices, such as the teacher's proof-reading of articles. In regard to the readership, it could potentially reach a wider group, although access to the internet in the communities is rather precarious.

CONCLUSION

In more ways than one, the presence of the Newspaper Club in schools has improved the lives of Brazil's poor children. There are at least four positive effects. First of all, it shows the children that they can create and publish a newspaper themselves. In doing so, the practice provides them with an understanding of the contradictions and power of the media and the responsibilities of freedom of expression, as well as giving them a sense of identity and agency. Second, it expands the possibilities of local people being informed about what is happening in their own community through the views of their own people. This might help them articulate their own perceptions of community needs, local knowledge, opportunities, problems, and solutions. Third, it expands the concept of news beyond the mainstream media, the traditional providers of news. Finally, it propels participating schools into an understanding of the important role of the media and communication in the lives of the children. At the very least, this type of citizen journalism adds a much-needed voice to the often authoritarian environment of the school.

In general, the "Newspaper Club" seems to articulate the views of the students and the local community as the product of constantly evolving discourses-in-interaction, offering a conversation not only between them and the school, but many parallel conversations in the community.

The participation and empowerment of the children are the two main aspects of the practices of citizen journalism developed in the schools. It provides an opportunity for them to have an active voice in the school's youth council and in the community, thus participating in decision-making processes. For them, "having a voice" in this process is not only about their ability to express themselves in terms of identity construction—to be more assertive—but also to develop in terms of how they engage with the community, to have their voices taken into account. Along with participation comes a certain level of empowerment that might allow the children to understand their position in the community and the wider society, and to play an active role in defining their reality, priorities, and future biographies.

One may by all means question whether the journalism practiced by the children could be labeled "citizen journalism." What they do is a participative form of journalism close to their own interests and those of the local community. It is a significant experience insofar as it shapes their understanding of public communication, the potential of citizen journalism to challenge legitimized forms of journalism, as well as the meaning of being an active citizen-in-the-making. It might contribute to a necessary shift in the focus of the citizen journalism debate from a media/technology centric perspective to a more social approach, that is, a movement determined by people rather than merely by developments in information and communication technology.

Whether the Newspaper Club project is a channel for empowerment "for life" is unclear. Some of the children at school resist becoming involved in the project, remaining unconvinced that they need to "have a voice." However, many of those who have been involved talk positively about their associations with the newspaper. Undoubtedly, some of the schools' "official" processes of communication and management do not encourage empowerment in the form discussed by Freire (1993). Nevertheless, it is readily apparent to anyone visiting the schools how important it is for children to engage with their creative selves in positive ways, to be alert to the world around them, and to contribute to debates about how their lives could be different. Citizen journalism, it follows, promises to be an important step in this direction.

NOTES

I would like to express my gratitude to Gabriela Reinaldo, Lidia Maropo, Kalu Chavez and Daniel Raviolo for their invaluable help in providing material to inform this chapter.

1. The children participants in the Newspaper Clubs are mostly from low-income families. The children are between 12 and 17 years old and in the secondary level of education.
2. The content of the 227 article of the Brazilian Constitution says, "it is the obligation of the family, the society and the State to guarantee to a child and adolescent, with absolute priority, the right to life, health, food, education, leisure, culture, dignity, respect, freedom, engage with family and community and be safe from negligence, discrimination, exploitation, violence, cruelty and oppression." The new law that came out of this article in the

constitution is the ECA (Estatuto da Crianca e do Adolescente—Statute of the Child and Adolescent) in which the child becomes subject with civil, human, and social rights and obligations defined in the constitution and other laws, becoming *citizens in development* and having their world protected.

REFERENCES

Blackman, S., & France, A. (2001) "Youth marginality under 'Postmodernism.'" In N. Stevenson (Ed.), *Culture & citizenship.* London: Sage.

Buckingham, D. (2000) *The making of citizens: young people, news and politics.* London: Routledge.

Chibli, F. (2005) *Midia na Escola, Revista Educação,* issue 98.

Claycomb, P. (2000) "Networks of children's participation in Brazil." *News from ICCVOS,* 4(2), 17. Unesco.

Cullingford, C. (1992) *Children and society: children's attitudes to politics and power.* London: Cassell.

Freire, P. (1973) *Education: the practice of freedom.* London: Writers and Readers Publishing Cooperative.

Freire, P. (1993) *Pedagogy of the oppressed.* New York: Continuum.

Godoi, G. (2006) "Journalismo, agendamento e construção de uma esfera publica de discussoes sobre a infancia e adolescencia: a experiencia da Agencia de Noticias da Infancia." In I. Sampaio, A. Pinheiro, & A. Alcantra (Eds.), *Midia de chocolate; estudos sobre a relação infancia, adolescencia e comunicação.* Rio de Janeiro: E-papers Press.

Henriques, R., & Ireland, T. (2006) *Brazilian national policy of adult and youth education.* Paris: Association for the Development of Education in Africa.

Jones, G., & Wallace, C. (1992) *Youth, family and citizenship.* Buckingham: Open University Press.

Maropo, L. (2008) *A construção da infancia excluida no Brasil e o nascimento dos movimentos sociais de defesa da crianca.* Paper presented at the Congresso Internacional em Estudos da Criança—Infâncias Possíveis, Mundos Reais. Organized by the Instituto de Estudos da Criança da Universidade do Minho, Braga, Portugal. 2–4 February.

Raviolo, D. (2008) *Projeto do Clube do Jornal.* (Printed material provided by the NGO Comunicacao e Cultura.)

Servaes, J., & Malikhao, P. (2005) "Participatory communication: the new paradigm?" In O. Hemer & T. Tufte (Eds.), *Media and glocal change* (pp. 91–104). Sweden and Argentina: Nordicom and Clacso Books.

UNICEF (2008) Situacao Mundial da Infancia Mundial 2008—*Caderno Brasil.*

Waisbord, S. (2005) "Five key coincidences and challenges in development communication." In O. Hemer & T. Tufte (Eds.), *Media and glocal change* (pp. 77–90). Sweden and Argentina: Nordicom and Clacso Books.

CHAPTER ELEVEN

OhmyNews: Citizen Journalism IN South Korea

CHANG WOO YOUNG

In South Korea in recent years, a new journalistic experiment has been conducted, one based on civil participation in opposition to the capital-based elitist journalism of the conservative press. This highly successful experiment has brought about an innovation in journalism by enabling news consumers to become producers, that is, to participate in the production of news in ways that strongly differ from those of the conventional press. OhmyNews is the epitome of this phenomenon. It has captured the imagination of ordinary citizens striving to transcend the passive freedom of "the right to know" so as to experience the active freedom of "the right to express."

OhmyNews is well known even overseas for its unique motto—"the people's news source"—as well as its innovative reporting concepts, strategies, and practices. Since its foundation in 2000, it has grown into a powerful vessel of citizen journalism (due, in no small part, to its transformative role in the 2002 presidential election when it devoted considerable attention to the campaign of Roh Moo-hyun, a reformist human rights lawyer, who was being virtually ignored by the mainstream—that is to say right-wing—press; he won the election). Over the ensuing years, OhmyNews has firmly held onto its number-one status, enjoying the largest share of readers in the South Korean online newspaper sector. Indeed, it is widely recognized as one of the country's most influential media outlets by any measure.

The rapid proliferation of internet news sites in the country, with OhmyNews leading the way, has been aided by a number of factors. These factors include a state-led development strategy of "informatization" on a national level, the formation of a high-tech information communications environment, public desire for innovation in the established press, and the emergence of popular forms of a multi-participation democratic culture. Two points are especially important in this regard.

First, the financial calamity of 1997, which sparked a major national crisis, accelerated the process of informatization that had been progressing slowly over the previous 10 years. Threatened by the prospect that the country's management would be turned over to the International Monetary Fund (IMF), the government chose the IT industry as one of the core growth industries that would determine the future of the nation (Ministry of Information and Communication, 2000). In the early 2000s, a multi-directional social communication infrastructure, including a national information superhighway and a public network, was completed. It became possible to use the internet in all schools and public organizations without the payment of fees (Chang Woo Young, 2005). The virtuous circle led to the rapid expansion of the information and communication market, facilitating the lowering of internet access fees in the private sector. Unlimited internet access became available in virtually all households for a modest fee, and in internet cafés for an even smaller investment.

Second, and more difficult to discern in some ways, is the emergence of post-Confucian pluralism as a basis of facilitating online communication through the internet. South Korea has been decisively shaped by Confucian culture for more than 1,000 years. The Confucian tradition encourages individuals to internalize community-centered values, a dimension to everyday life that various military, authoritarian governments have exploited in the past in order to govern the population in accordance with their interests. However, recent progress in efforts toward democratization has led to the spread of pluralistic values, a process which has accelerated under the leadership of the younger generation. Members of this younger generation, keenly interested in self-expression, value nonconformity and individualistic participation highly. Taking full advantage of informatization, they have enriched the creative culture of the internet. It is through such personal, often intimate interactions that sites such as OhmyNews have become so popular in cyberspace.

As a result of these and related factors, the internet has precipitated noteworthy changes in communications modes, such as the breakdown of the boundary between producers and consumers of messages, enhanced interactivity in dialogue and debate, and a dissolution of gatekeeping. Online media, in utilizing such advantages of the internet, have been able to create spaces where challenges to the very conservatism of the established journalism can be posed. In this context, OhmyNews is being recognized as the quintessential South Korean internet newspaper and a paradigm of online journalism.

This chapter will focus on OhmyNews in order to explore a range of issues concerning South Korean journalism and the politics of democratization. Particular attention will be devoted to the role of the site's citizen journalists in calling into question the more traditional forms of reporting associated with established news organizations. OhmyNews, I shall argue, is a vessel of counteraction with a significant role to play in the development of democratic culture.

THE EMPOWERED MEDIA AND DEMOCRACY
AFTER DEMOCRATIZATION

Prior to the years of South Korea's democratization, state interference—and accompanying forms of regulation—were the biggest obstacles to achieving freedom of speech. For nearly 30 years, the military government forcefully imposed the Speech Abolition Law, which subjected media organizations to severe restrictions and censorship. The relationship between the government and the press would begin to improve in 1987, when the 6/29 Declaration (Democratic Agreement) fostered democratization. Article 5 of this declaration stipulated that the "government will innovatively improve its system and tradition to guarantee maximum autonomy of the press." In accordance with this article, the new civil governments to emerge would soften governmental regulation of the press and begin to codify greater recognition of freedom of speech as an important civil right (Choi Jang Jip, 2002).

The rapid growth of the press in the years following the democratization saw it become a new type of authoritative institution, however, one that was intent on pursuing a consolidation of its monopolized authority. Instead of acting as a watchdog of the government, the press sought to redefine its role to become a quasi-state agency with similar functions to a governmental institution where managing communication and public opinion were concerned (Cho Hang Je, 2002; Choi Yeong, 2002; Yun Tae Jin & Kang Nae Won, 2001). As a quasi-state agency, the conservative press effectively executed its functions in ways to restrict the development of democracy in order to try to preserve a status quo that benefited wealthy elites. Even though a democratic society should provide a space in which the opinions of ordinary citizens can be freely and rationally communicated, the conservative press attempted to shape public opinion through the logic of a monopolized market (Im Young Ho, 2002). Three conservative newspapers (*Chosun Ilbo*, *Joongang Ilbo*, and *Donga Ilbo*) were particularly influential in this regard, claiming approximately

75% of newspaper readers. Together these newspapers sought to align market profitability with political authority. In short, rather than endeavoring to maintain a neutral or impartial position, the conservative press acted as a king-maker to enable a specific group of elites to acquire centralized power. To a large extent it blocked the expression of diverse opinions and hindered progressive change.

In opposition to the conservative press, the Press Reformation Movement and Progressive Alternative Press Movement emerged in the civil society from the late 1980s onward (Chang Woo-Young, 2005). One of the important dimensions of the reform agenda revolved around the surveillance of legislative improvements, where civil society groups attempted to abolish laws—such as the Regular Publication Law—that had helped to consolidate the monopoly of the conservative press. Furthermore, they pursued regular monitoring of the press's biased reporting. Examples of the latter included efforts to halt the publication *Chosun Ilbo*, so notorious for its right-wing reporting that it was a symbol of the conservative press. A second dimension of the reform agenda was based on the foundation of the alternative journalism. The *Hankyoreh* was founded in 1988 by the journalists who were dismissed under the rule of the military government. The *Hankyoreh* produced and expanded discussions of reformation from a progressive perspective. However, the *Hankyoreh* faced formidable difficulties in securing a foothold in the monopolized newspaper market. Although other alternative journalism outlets were established, they faced overwhelming challenges with regard to the funding necessary for survival, let alone the struggle to gain political influence. Under such circumstances, the rapid informatization and expansion of online spaces provided a crucial opportunity for alternative journalism to be established in South Korea.

ONLINE ALTERNATIVE MEDIA AND CIVIL JOURNALISM

The establishment of OhmyNews presented an innovative model of citizen journalism, one that has succeeded in displaying the social and political influence of the internet newspaper. OhmyNews was established on February 22, 2000, with four special reporters and 727 citizen reporters. Within a year's time, OhmyNews was able to secure 30,000 civil reporters who typically contributed to a total of about 160 to 200 articles on a daily basis. Its development would have been impossible at the time if the formation of a high-tech information communications environment had not been executed in advance. In terms of the penetration of the internet in businesses, government, and households, and with regard to the number of users, South Korea has led the global race for the ushering in of the information society (National Information-Society Agency, 2007).

OhmyNews, from the outset, has sought to overcome barriers to participation in the journalistic community (Hong Seong Goo, 2001). Formative instances of its distinctive approach to news reporting began shortly after its launch. In June 2002, for example, one of its citizen journalists wrote an article about a US Army armored car that hit and killed two schoolgirls near the border with North Korea. The incident was debated in the discussion rooms and rapidly spread to other websites. Netizens were systematically organized. They created websites dealing with the issue and launched an anti-American campaign. Their campaign lasted for several months, culminating in candlelight demonstrations, with hundreds of thousands of protesters participating. A second formative moment, already touched upon above, concerned the 2002 presidential election, when Mong-Joon Jeong of Kookmin Tonghap withdrew his support for Moo-Hyun Roh of the Democratic Party (with whom he was in an election alliance) the night before election day. Progressive cyber community members logged on to key websites, including OhmyNews, in large numbers and instigated a movement to encourage voting, which contributed considerably to the victory of Moo-Hyun Roh. Between December 18 and 19, 2002, the number of people connected to OhmyNews was 6,230,000. The number of viewed pages was over 1,910, which was the highest volume of internet traffic in South Korean history.

In journalistic terms, one of the important characteristics of OhmyNews news article production is that it has deviated from an exclusively professional-based journalistic model in favor of creating a voluntary association of citizen reporters. "My goal was to say farewell to 20th-century Korean journalism, with the concept that every citizen is a reporter," declared Oh Yeon Ho, the site's founder:

> I think citizens like to write their own articles, but simultaneously, they like to be edited by professional reporters.... OhmyNews is a kind of combination of the merits of the blog and the merits of the newspaper. We know what the netizen wants: at the end of every article we have a comment area, and one issue had 85,000 comments. That story began with a suggestion from a citizen reporter, and citizens commented, so it's a unique way to generate a lot of content.... Our main concept is the citizen reporter. Our second concept is: demolish the news-writing formula. We say: "Please communicate in your style: if it is convenient for you, that's fine. Don't just follow the professional reporters." (cited in Allan, 2006, pp. 130–131)

What this reporter system shows is the possibility of a citizen-led communication network developing into an alternative journalistic model. Furthermore, this network has also resulted in the consolidation of a shared political territory by connecting the (typically liberal) aptitude of the citizen reporters with their personal life experiences (Hong Seong Goo, 2001). As of May 2008, OhmyNews employed 60 special reporters while drawing upon the efforts of over 54,900 citizen reporters. My research suggests that the constitution of the citizen reporters is as follows. The gender ratio is 79% male to 21% female. The age ratio is 8.5% teens, 38.4% in their 20s, 34.5% in their 30s, 14.4% in their 40s, 3.2% in their 50s, and 1.0% in their 60s. In terms of their occupations, some 18% are white-collar workers, 17% are university students, 9% are self-employed, 6% are journalists, 6% are freelancers, 5% are professors, 5% are government employees, and 5% are postgraduate students. By virtue of their larger numbers, as well as their positions in all levels of society, these citizen journalists cover a much wider range of news stories than would be reported in the conservative press.

Such development is a result of the strategic implementation of the motto "the citizens are the reporters" and with it a corresponding concept of OhmyNews being "a news regiment of news guerillas." OhmyNews takes seriously its conviction that all citizens can become journalists. Citizen journalists—or "news guerillas" to use the online newspaper's preferred phrase—turn their first-hand life experiences of events they consider to be "news" into articles written from their own fresh perspectives (Oh Yeon Ho, 2003). Some writers are more skilled at identifying and processing news than others, of course. In recognizing this fact, OhmyNews has developed a role distinction between citizen and specialist reporters. Citizen reporters claim their roles by formally registering as members before they are allowed to submit articles (Kim Eun Kyu, 2005). A small, elite group of specialist reporters are employed on a full-time basis by OhmyNews to select and examine news items, checking for a range of factors including the relative news value of the articles composed by citizen reporters.

It is often the case that articles written by citizen reporters show traits of amateurism in quality and formality. For this reason, the editing team of OhmyNews processes these articles in order to maintain the credibility of the organization. Initially, articles written by citizen reporters are registered under the name "Green Wood." Next, in accordance with the decisions made by the editing team, selected articles are registered as formal articles under the name of "Ingeol [lively burning charcoal fire] news." Ingeol news is published on either the main page or a section page, depending upon its perceived news value. For Green Wood articles, it is clearly stated that all responsibilities regarding the article be ascribed to the writer. (Only the titles of the articles can be viewed before they have been formally reviewed.) Recent statistics indicate that news guerrillas write about 150 of the 200 articles published every day at OhmyNews. The editorial department reviews the articles, and about 70% of them are published in the Ingeol section, with the remaining 30% in the Saengnamu (live tree) section. Ingeol articles are typically well received in terms of accuracy, importance, logic, and timeliness (Oh Yeon Ho, 2004).

In order to compete effectively against the entrenched press, OhmyNews has been cultivating the professionalism of its "guerilla" or citizen reporters. The routine reporter training, conducted by the specialist reporters, focuses on the basic skills of news gathering and article writing. A "citizen journalism school" was opened in November 2007 on the outskirts of Seoul to act as a "collaborative knowledge center" to develop new citizen reporters. Nevertheless, under intense (nonstop) daily pressure, limits in the production of news material suitable for a daily newspaper are inevitable. To solve this issue, OhmyNews is cooperating with communication companies to receive news articles. More often than not, the established media in South Korea report commercially interesting issues but then abandon them when readers' interest wanes. In contrast, OhmyNews takes a longer view, using an information database to keep track of issues as they slowly evolve over time.

In marked contrast with the authoritative nature of the mainstream media in the country, OhmyNews strives to be democratic and interactive. In other words, whereas the conventional press follows the interests of capitalist elites to lead public opinion in a single direction, OhmyNews has been encouraging readers to voluntarily express their interests and demands (Lee Hyo Seong, 2002). In this respect, the interaction with its readers is the biggest merit of OhmyNews. The site allows anyone, even those not registered as reporters, to share their personal opinions on a news article. This presentation of views takes place in two ways in the interests of cultivating dialogue. First, a reader contributes his or her opinions on a news article, and second, additional comments can be made on these opinions by other readers. A system is in place to recommend meritorious reader opinions (and their view-counts will be shown as well). This is intended to encourage discussions among readers and, naturally, articles on significant events accumulate a vast number of reader opinions and comments (Kim Eun Kyu, 2005). Moreover, OhmyNews allows readers to evaluate and rearrange articles posted on the Online Editorial.

Further strategies to develop interactivity abound. OhmyTV promotes interaction with readers in three ways. First, specialist or citizen reporters report significant events which require real-time coverage in a web-casting mode. Second, a citizen news announcer presents a web-casting news program based on key news articles gathered over the course of a week. This announcer is selected from citizen applicants irrespective of their class, age, gender, or educational background, and is constantly changing from one week to the next. Third, video clips shot by citizens are provided in a public access mode. As such, the operational mode of OhmyTV is receiving attention for providing multiple channels for participation in journalism from citizens in all walks of life.

Cyber forums and the activation of political mobilization have similarly made a critical contribution to the enhancement of OhmyNew's political influence. Discussion rooms are operated so as to encourage dynamic interactions among readers. Participants in discussion rooms observe self-regulatory rules of conduct—and all can freely express their opinions on any given article published in OhmyNews. Every day, hundreds of messages are posted in these discussion rooms. This forum has been widely recognized as an epicenter of political debate, one that is especially important for a country where democracy is such a recent phenomenon.

CONCLUSION

It is often taken for granted that the press exists to contribute to the development and enrichment of democracy. The reason why the virtues of the press—such as independence, freedom, and social responsibility—are given attention is because they are the fundamental values that should be present in order for a healthy democracy to flourish. If the press cannot perform its appropriate functions, democracy cannot survive. The primary importance of the success of OhmyNews, in my view, is that it has challenged the hegemony of the conservative press and successfully created a space for an alternative based on citizen reporting. The boundary between the producers and consumers of journalism has been transformed. Ordinary citizens serving as reporters take the lead in creating and proliferating discussions across the breadth of cyberspace. In opposition to the established press, these citizen journalists enable agenda setting and public opinion formation from the grassroots, thereby calling into question authoritative hierarchy. Their activities are motivated much less by monetary reward than by the appreciation and respect of the cyber community.

The factors giving rise to the success of OhmyNews are contributing to the development of participatory democracy across South Korea, namely by activating communication on multiple levels. This country, like many others, is currently experiencing serious challenges to its representative democracy. The alienation of politicians and electors, deterioration in political parties' capacity to intervene to advance civil interests, monopolized decision-making by policy-forming groups, and the continuous fall in voting rate at election time are perturbing signs of a looming crisis. The future of representative democracy, many agree, will require the active participation of citizens with energy, vitality, and desire for social change. In those countries where democratic traditions are relatively recent, these issues take on an even deeper significance. The threat of a possible regression to authoritarianism is ever present. Therefore, the citizen journalism of OhmyNews must continue to help build a bright future for South Korean democracy by promoting civil participation and communication through the internet.

REFERENCES

Allan, S. (2006) *Online news: journalism and the internet*. Maidenhead and New York: Open University Press.

Chang Woo Young (2005) "Online civic participation, and political empowerment: online media and public opinion formation in Korea." *Media, Culture & Society, 27*(6), 925–935.

Cho Hang Je (2002) *Democratization and media power in Korea*. Seoul: Hanul Academy.

Choi Jang Jip (2002) *Democracy after democratization: the conservative origins of Korean democracy and crisis*. Seoul: Humanitas.

Choi Yeong (2002) "A study on the possibilities of citizen journalism in online newspapers: with a focus on everyday practices." *Korean Journal of Communication & Information, 46*(6), 33–63.

Gurevitch, M., & Blumer, J. (1990) "Political communication systems and democratic values." In J. Lichtenberg (Ed.), *Democracy and mass media* (pp. 269–287). New York: Cambridge University Press.

Hong Seong Goo (2001) "The growth of the online press and the change in the press system." *Social Science Research, 42*, 237–253.

Im Young Ho (2002) "What is the media power?" *Opening Forum of Daehwa Film: Political Power and Media Power*, 13–23.

Kim Eun Kyu (2005) "Internet and citizen-participatory media: the experience of OhmyNews." *Eastern and Western Press, 9*, 325–350.

Korea Information Society Development Institute (2005) *Information society and informatization policy*, pp. 43–62. Seoul: Bakyeongsam.

Koreanclick (2005) *A report on internet*. koreanclick.com

Lee Hyo Seong (2002) "The possibility and restriction of independent online journalism." *Collection Papers, summer seminar, Communication and Information Research*, 1–12.

Mancini, P., & Swanson, D. (1996) "Politics, media and modern democracy: introduction." In D. Swanson & P. Mancini (Eds.), *Politics, media and modern democracy* (pp. 1–28). Westport, CT: Prager.

Mazzoleni, G., & Schultz, W. (1999) "'Mediarization' of politics: a challenge for democracy." *Political Communication, 16*(2), 247–261.

The Ministry of Information and Communication (2000) *Policy outputs and vision in the field of IT*. Seoul: The Ministry of Information and Communication.

National Information-Society Agency (2007) *2007 National Informatization whitepaper*. Seoul: National Information-Society Agency.

Oh Yeon Ho (2003) "2002 presidential election and changes in media power." *Sasang Quarterly, 107*, 116–137.

Oh Yeon Ho (2004) *Special product of the Republic of Korea: OhmyNews*. Seoul: Humanist.

Pfetsch, B. (1998) "Government and management." In D. Graber, D. McQuail, & P. Norris (Eds.), *The politics of news* (pp. 70–93). Washington, DC: Congressional Quarterly Inc.

Sisa Journal (2003) *Sisa Journal, 731* (30 October), 23–29.

Yun Tae Jin & Kang Nae Won (2001) "A study on the aspects of public journalism in online newspapers: with a focus on an analysis of special article in Joins.com, Internet Hangyoreh, and OhmyNews." *Korean Journal of Communication & Information 46*(1), 308–343.

CHAPTER TWELVE

Globalization, Citizen Journalism, AND THE Nation State: A Vietnamese Perspective

AN NGUYEN

While there is a prolific literature on the rise of citizen journalism in the developed world, little has been written about this phenomenon in developing countries. Where these countries are concerned, the Western media tend to celebrate citizen media as an autonomous counterweight to state censorship. The emergence of blogging in the little-known Vietnamese media environment, for example, has been depicted as having "taken [the country] by storm and spawned an alternative communications universe to dusty state media" (AFP, 2007).

This chapter looks at citizen journalism in Vietnam to show that this kind of celebratory coverage, often based on cursory anecdotal evidence from a technological determinist perspective, might be naive and unhelpful in providing a comprehensive understanding of the true power of citizen media in the developing world. To assess the extent to which citizen journalism is transforming sociopolitical processes in Vietnam, I will take a systematic look at how it operates both in global and local sociopolitical contexts. It is my contention that while globalized technological advances allow citizen journalism to develop beyond the control of the nation state in some aspects, it is also the case that its influence is largely kept within the boundaries of tolerance set down by the state's political elite.

THE RISE AND POWER OF VIETNAMESE CITIZEN JOURNALISM

By Western standards, Vietnam may seem to be an especially unlikely place to foster any kind of citizen journalism—understood here as the active efforts of citizens in collecting, analyzing, reporting, and disseminating news and information about current affairs (Bowman & Willis, 2003). Despite having liberalized the economy since 1986, the ruling Communist Party of Vietnam (CPV) still holds a strong grip on political processes. International media watchdogs continue to place the country near the bottom of the world's press freedom indices. And although Vietnam has been witnessing a rapid rate of internet penetration into daily life (with 18.5 million users, or 22% of the population, by December 2007), the country was listed among 13 "enemies of the internet" in 2006 by Reporters Without Borders. This makes the fact that Vietnamese citizen journalism has emerged and developed quite vigorously all the more interesting for our purposes here.

Breaking and Making the News

Citizen journalism started in Vietnam in the early 2000s, primarily in the form of chat room and forum discussions. In early 2004, an unidentified internet-savvy music fan conducted an online investigation for the benefit of an online forum, in which it was claimed that a top song of Bao Chan, an established pop composer, had been copied from a Japanese album. As the mainstream media brought the story to the attention of the wider public, offline investigations by relevant bodies eventually forced the initially stubborn plagiarist to issue a public apology and withdraw his by-line from the song. This stimulated a series of other, similar plagiarism exposures by online communities involving other famous pop composers. Not long afterward, online communities broke another serious plagiarism case, this time involving the apparent use of stolen foreign open-source codes in what was an award-winning content management system. As news of the scandal grew across the internet and in the mainstream media, the system's "authors" were suitably embarrassed into returning their award.

Vietnamese Citizen journalism's "tipping point" (Allan, 2006) was 2006, however, when blogs began to resonate throughout Vietnamese online communities. It was a year in which all of a sudden, one blog after another was born and, to quote a magazine article, "having no blog (was) now really a strange thing." With a minute-by-minute increase in the number of people joining the crowd, blogging became a buzzword, and citizen journalism began to be noticed as a social phenomenon. In November 2007, CNET reported that there were three million Vietnamese blogs, with most of them being hosted on Yahoo! 360°. A substantial number of blogs have attracted large and/or frequent audiences, with millions of page views, while some blog content has been bought and published into books. Here it is worth observing that Vietnamese blogs were emerging for a seemingly unlimited range of purposes: sharing personal observations, thoughts, and feelings with others; making new friends; forming new communities; collecting, storing, and sharing online materials; trading ideas for work/study purposes; inviting comments on literary/artistic works; promoting products/services; mobilizing others into certain tasks/actions; and many others. There are also the so-called black blogs—that is, blogs that promote or distribute pornographic content, pillory others for personal reasons, or perform other dirty deeds.

Citizen journalism, in relative terms, still makes up a small part of the Vietnamese blogosphere. This small portion, however, has shown its power in breaking important news stories that would have been held up, undiscovered, or ignored for some time (or even forever). By way of example, only two days before these words were written in Britain, it was thanks to blogs that I was more than a day ahead of most of the 88 million people at home to be aware that Vo Van Kiet—a respected former prime minister—had died quite unexpectedly in a Singapore hospital. Indeed, the news was immediately reported on some mainstream news sites but then, under some verbal order, was quickly taken off to wait for the CPV's Politburo to decide on the funeral arrangements and to issue an authorized obituary, which took 36 hours. The short life of the initial reports, however, was long enough for bloggers to snap, distribute, and redistribute them as webpage images. The news was further confirmed when a respected journalist close to Kiet posted a blog item detailing the arrival of Kiet's body from Singapore a few hours after his death. For those who understand Vietnam well, this was a remarkable event: for the first time since 1945, this type of news reached ordinary people before it was officially released by national leaders. By the time the mainstream media announced the death, the news was no longer news. Instead, it had entered a more substantive phase, when experts and laypeople alike had flocked to blogs, forums, and news sites operated by expatriate Vietnamese to pay tribute and present multifaceted analyses of Kiet's 86-year life and 70-year political career.

This is only one of many cases in which blogs have broken important news stories in Vietnam. In contrast to the example above, though, this is more typically done at the grassroots level by those close to or affected by events, either deliberately or by chance. As the media ceaselessly praised the success of the first Asia-Pacific Economic Cooperation (APEC) Summit hosted by the country in 2006, for instance, student volunteers reported on their blogs a range of behind-the-scenes problems, much to the annoyance of several distinguished international guests. The posts generated various blog and forum responses, which later surfaced on the national news agenda. A further example occurred in the summer of

2007, when the mainstream press was effectively ignoring a protest by hundreds of farmers from the southern provinces who had gathered in Ho Chi Minh City (HCMC) to challenge local authorities forcing them to leave their land without adequate compensation. Various witnesses to the protest brought news of it to the world by producing and distributing a wide range of eyewitness reports, photos, and video clips via blogs, forums, and social (file-sharing) networks such as Flickr and YouTube. In addition to these and related examples of serious news, citizen journalists have similarly been the first to report human-interest events that are quickly picked up by professional journalists, such as images of a police officer jumping onto the front of a moving taxi to stop its reckless driver, or those of a university student declaring his love to a fellow student in the middle of a colorful heart-shaped bed of roses in the courtyard of their dormitory.

Stimulating Debates and Civic Actions

Bearing these examples in mind, I would nonetheless suggest that the most pronounced contribution of citizen journalism in Vietnam so far is not grassroots reporting but rather its capacity to bolster critical discussions on public affairs among different groups of the public, especially the young. For many young Vietnamese, this has become an important part of their life. It is astonishing to find, when touring around citizen media, so many social, cultural, and political issues being discussed online without fear—issues that until recently were regarded as taboo topics in the offline world, such as press freedom, political pluralism, or even sex before marriage. "Like many other young Vietnamese, I belong to a very open generation," one blogger comments. "We are no longer afraid of and indeed aspire for sharing our feelings and thoughts with others." In a country where two-thirds of the population are under 35, and where social conformity is encouraged by the educational system, such a phenomenon is certain to have far-reaching implications for the future. This is not to deny that some blogs are highly objectionable—including hate-filled viewpoints expressed by some Vietnamese expatriates—but it is not hard to find high-quality, informed discussions oriented to consensus (i.e., to a general agreement based on critical reasoning). In my experience, the level of social capital in the Vietnamese blogosphere—the shared informal values or norms that permit trust and cooperation among its members—is fairly high. And the collective actions resulting from this type of social networking have the potential to inform offline civic actions on a large scale. So far, this has for the most part taken the form of joint charity efforts by netizens, which might seem normal but is in itself a break from the offline convention that charity efforts must be coordinated by party-controlled organizations such as the Fatherland Front.

In one recent political event, the power of citizen media went far beyond anyone's expectations. The story begins in December 2007, shortly after China set up an administrative unit named Shansha and included in it two strategic archipelagos in the South China Sea, the Spratlys and the Paracels. Both of these archipelagos have long been considered by Vietnam to be parts of its territory. The Paracels (Hoang Sa in Vietnamese) was attacked and taken by China from South Vietnamese forces in 1974, while the Spratlys (Truong Sa) is still partly controlled by Vietnam, China, and other countries. This act of "creeping assertiveness"—as Vietnam expert Carl Thayer calls it—was the latest in a chain of aggressive actions by China toward Vietnam, including firing and sinking a Vietnamese fishing boat near Truong Sa in July 2007 and shooting dead nine innocent Vietnamese fishermen off the Gulf of Tonkin in January 2005. As a close political ally of China, the Vietnamese government had been reacting to these events using gentle diplomacy. However, for many ordinary Vietnamese, who have never forgotten 1,000 years of Chinese invasion, Shansha was "the final drop into a full glass of boiling water," prompting an unprecedented array of angry criticisms in the media as well as a series of nationalist actions by Vietnamese netizens. At least one Chinese government website was defaced with obscenities, but the backlash was felt most strongly in blogs and forums, where historical documents regarding the archipelagos were collected, discussed, and distributed amid calls for offline protests. As a result, for the first time in more than three decades, hundreds of young Vietnamese—most of them university students—marched through the major streets of Hanoi and HCMC on December 9. Wearing t-shirts sporting the Vietnamese flag and a national map including Truong Sa and Hoang Sa, they stopped in front of Chinese diplomatic offices, shouting slogans such as "Down with China," "Hands off Vietnam," "Stop Chinese Expansion," "Chinese Hegemony Destroys Asia," "Defend Our Homeland," and "Vietnam: United We Stand."

Following this successful intervention, further demonstrations were organized via the internet. They took place in the two cities the next weekend, followed by worldwide anti-Chinese protests by overseas Vietnamese in Asia-Pacific, Europe, and North America. Since then, tensions have not shown any sign of easing, and China has made some implicit concessions. In April 2008, as the global media were keeping a close eye on demonstrations against China's human rights record along the global route of the Olympic Torch, they missed a similar, no less energetic effort by Vietnamese bloggers, who called for a widespread boycott of the torch relay in HCMC after discovering that China had included the archipelagos in its national map on the Olympics website. A young intellectual who was scheduled to be one of the torch bearers posted on his blog a letter to the president of the International Olympics Committee, arguing that China had politicized the

Olympics. Amid the mounting anger, Chinese officials removed the archipelagos from the map the day before the torch arrived in HCMC (they put them back afterward). In short the unfolding Vietnamese citizen media movement had shown—if only temporarily—the power of what Clay Shirky (2008) has aptly termed "organizing without organizations."

Implications for the Nation State

Such vigorous forms of citizen-led initiatives prompt the question of where the authority of the state is heading in Vietnam. Given its one-party political system, it is not surprising that blogging—as noted above—has been celebrated in some Western media accounts as resembling a revolutionary technological counterweight to state control. Meanwhile, inside Vietnam, it has become a serious concern of many people in power.

The rise of citizen journalism in Vietnam, in my view, is in part an outcome of larger processes of globalization. Globalization, for Scholte (2000), is a process of *deterritorialization*, in which the growth of supraterritorial (transworld or transborder) relations results in a less important role for traditional territories, weakening the ability of the nation state to control its own affairs. Often this involves the crucial aid of technologies that make transnational communication near-instantaneous (as opposed to simply fast).

In Vietnam, citizen media technologies bear a specific importance in this regard. Not only are they transnational in their reach, their interactive and anonymous nature helps to create authentic shared spaces between the domestic population and the more than three million homeland-dedicated Vietnamese around the world. Added to globalized technology, then, is the supraterritorial nature of citizen content hosting services such as YouTube, Blogger.com, or Yahoo! 360°. These preferred sites are created, owned, and run by transnational corporations that can operate beyond the control of national regimes. In Vietnam, blogs quickly rose to the central stage thanks largely to the introduction of the Vietnamese Yahoo! 360° service, which is hosted on a US-based server, run by a Singapore-based team, and owned by a global corporation that has not established a legal presence (i.e., not a registered business) in Vietnam. Together, as seen in the examples regarding the citizen reporting of the Chinese protests and Kiet's death, these globalized forces help Vietnam's fledgling online public sphere to be able to take shape beyond the wishes of the political elite. This online public sphere stretches beyond the country's S-shaped territory to vertically, horizontally, and diagonally connect different domestic and overseas groups, often with very different sociopolitical backgrounds, in near-instantaneous deliberation and debate over common affairs.

This is not to suggest, however, that Vietnamese citizen journalism has emerged in the frustrating witness of a powerless state. Globalization does not mean the end of the nation state because, as Bolton (2006) pointed out, the state operates not just on the level of giving permission to communicate (via licensing) but also by limiting and preventing certain actors from participating. While licensing Yahoo! or Google to run a blog-hosting or file-sharing service is hardly possible, for instance, Vietnamese authorities could stop them from participating in the local environment at any time by simply building a firewall to block Yahoo! 360°, YouTube, and the like. There might be other reasons for them not to have opted to do this (e.g., fierce responses by netizens), but as someone familiar with their "prohibition if uncontrollable" approach in other sociocultural areas, I see it at least as a sign of a laissez-faire tolerance. This can be seen in a comment by Duong Trung Quoc—a well-known historian and the only blogging congressman so far—when arguing for a self-regulatory blogosphere:

> Blogs form a virtual world but are a reflection of the real world.... We can employ technologies such as firewalls and we can extract and exploit evidence from the virtual world and treat it with the same laws applied in the real world. But it is essential to note that we are required to respect human rights.... We have to respect the right to privacy and the right to freedom of thoughts as recognized by the constitution.... For me, the most important thing is to mobilize and encourage people to build cultural and ethical behaviours online.... All bureaucratically imposed control approaches can only bring about negative impacts.... I think it is the real values of democracy that will be the soul of a healthy virtual world. (Duong, 2007)

This kind of openness, I believe, is a facilitator of citizen media. To agree with this, it is essential to go beneath surface evidence such as journalist arrests or repression of political dissidents (as media watchdogs such as Reporters without Borders do) in order to delve deeply into the many subtle but substantive day-by-day changes in Vietnam's conception of press freedom. In doing so, we need to be fair enough to recognize that the ruling party has been adopting an increasingly open, receptive, and relaxed approach to the media and civil society. As a former Vietnamese journalist and a current Western-educated academic observer of the Vietnamese media, I have often been struck by the way the CPV tolerates people who dare to open their mouths to speak against its policies or to expose corruption and other misdeeds of its senior members. Social feedback, social surveillance, and gatekeeping—things never associated with the Communist or authoritarian press theories in the Western literature—have become widely recognized functions of the local media. There are tacit limits or untouchable issues/people, but even so, the current level of freedom is something nobody would have imagined possible even 10 years ago. The need for a civil society is now openly discussed in the press, the coffee shop, the pub, and other places. The recent rise of blogs itself has been treated more as a healthy addition to national progress than as a potential source of sociopolitical evils. Even the minister for information and communication has recently called on the press to transform itself, in the wake of citizen journalism, from a mere propaganda lecture to a public conversation. In this sense, citizen journalism is being regarded as synonymous with the progressive democratization process underway in Vietnam.

I raise these issues to make several points about the potential of citizen journalism in Vietnam and probably other developing countries. The fact that citizen journalism is partly an outgrowth of an increasingly democratic environment that Vietnamese rulers accept and tolerate suggests that its fate is still within their control. Using coercion or technology to inhibit free speech can be little more than an emergency tactic. There are older but still effective tactics for the state to prevent blogs from disrupting its power. Generating public fear or stigma, via education and the media, is an example. The internet is global, but its participants are still subject to at least one local legislative and political system in the offline world, which can bring to bear the power of the state.

Indeed, at the same time as Vietnamese authorities are displaying a tolerance of blogs, they have been using media-related scare tactics to warn bloggers against providing or distributing "unhealthy content," that is, anything that titillates prurient desires, defames others, reveals state secrets, destroys the "great national unity," or incites anti-regime actions. Although it might become less effective for the younger and more politically demanding generations in the future, reinforcing this deeply rooted culture of fear—fear for oneself and for one's family—and its consequent self-censorship still works in Vietnam and other countries, especially Asian nations such as China, Burma, Indonesia, and Malaysia. For instance, although online technologies allow anonymity, many people are still so afraid of their IP addresses (computer identification) being tracked down by police that they do not dare to blog, email, or even read sensitive content on home computers.

Another, and probably more important, point related to the continuing power of the state is that the success of citizen journalism—either in developed or developing countries—depends much on the aid of the mainstream media (Nguyen, 2006). Despite all the hype, there are few cases in which citizen journalism can act alone to generate substantial changes in public life. A healthy public sphere requires its three key elements—journalism, social movements, and the discourses between citizens, experts, and policymakers—to constantly interact with each other. In most cases, the mainstream media initiate the issue, providing the material that is amplified via online citizen discussions/debates and then echoed back to the mainstream agenda. In other cases, citizens break and/or grab issues ignored or insufficiently covered by the mainstream media to create public pressure, after which mainstream journalism responds and works together with citizens to shed more light on the issues and/or to bring them to a broader context. Thus, the influence of most citizen journalism would remain relatively limited without the attention of professional journalism. When the state is still holding a tight grip on mainstream journalism, then, the influence of citizen journalism should not be overstated.

This is exactly what has been happening in Vietnam. The mainstream media have been responsive to the blogosphere, where issues are not deemed to be politically sensitive. But when it comes to events like the aforementioned farmers' protest, the rich amount of relevant citizen content distributed online is routinely ignored, and its effect inside the country is limited. In these cases, overseas Vietnamese's news sites, including those within global news organizations (e.g., BBC and Radio Free Asia), play an important role in amplifying the influence of citizen-generated content, but this should not be overvalued, because many of these sites are blocked and others could be blocked at any time. Even in the anti-Chinese movement, the media's role was pivotal. For students to distribute widespread online calls for offline demonstrations and to dare to march down the streets of Hanoi and HCMC, the strong passion displayed by respected journalists in quality news outlets such as Tuoi Tre or VietnamNet in the first days after the Shansha news—which appeared to exceed the "tolerance threshold" of the party (one ultimately led its editor-in-chief to be temporarily suspended)—acted as a strong stimulator and a "green light." In short, the blogosphere is still largely controlled, although indirectly, by the state. In the years ahead, unless Vietnam's authorities continue to be tolerant enough to allow for a certain level of press freedom, it will be difficult for citizen journalism to produce a major impact beyond a relatively small community of technically savvy and socio-politically active Vietnamese internet users.

CONCLUSION

In reviewing the rise and role of Vietnamese citizen journalism, this chapter has argued that with the aid of decentralized and globalized online technologies, citizen journalism is able to move out of the margins, inspiring people to debate and to act in a way that can threaten the authority of the state. At the same time, however, we need to go beyond technological determinism to recognize, as Brian McNair (2006, p. 168) has argued, that "the Internet does not create a climate for progressive democratic change where none exists, nor can it by itself force reform on an unwilling regime prepared to use violence and repression as tools." In Vietnam, repression and violence seem to have been the last resort, and the general climate surrounding the blogosphere has been shaped, at least until now, by the governing regime's confident tolerance. Although there remain many untouchable areas, there is sufficient evidence to indicate that a healthy democratization process is underway, one that will be both a facilitator, and a beneficiary of the rise of Vietnamese citizen journalism. And while there is a positive correlation between technological advances and the decline in authoritarianism, it is nevertheless important to bear in mind that the power of the nation state remains a crucial factor in the cultural chaos of our globalized news environment.

REFERENCES

AFP (2007) "Blogs sweep Vietnam as young push state-run media aside." *AFP*, 6 September.

Allan, S. (2006) *Online news: journalism and the internet.* London: Open University Press.

Bolton, T. (2006) "News on the net: a critical analysis of the potential of online alternative journalism to challenge the dominance of the mainstream media." *SCAN*, *3*(1).

Bowman, S., & Willis, C. (2003) *We media: how audiences are shaping the future of news & information.* Reston, VA: The Media Center at the American Press Institute.

Duong, Trung Quoc (2007) "Tra loi ve blog." *Quoc Xua Nay Blog*, 12 October.

McNair, B. (2006) *Cultural chaos: journalism, news and power in a globalised world.* London: Routledge.

Nguyen, A. (2006) "Journalism in the wake of participatory publishing." *Australian Journalism Review*, *28*(1), 143–155.

Scholte, J.A. (2000) *Globalisation: a critical introduction.* New York: Palgrave.

Shirky, C. (2008) *Here comes everybody: the power of organising without organisations.* New York: Penguin Press.

CHAPTER THIRTEEN

Citizen Journalism AND THE North Belgian Peace March

NICO CARPENTIER, LUDO DE BRABANDER,
AND BART CAMMAERTS

INTRODUCTION

In the long history of participatory (and potentially counterhegemonic) media practices, citizen journalism is one of the more novel concepts added to the vocabulary used to describe these practices. More than other concepts, that of citizen journalism focuses on the capacity of citizens to generate narrations with specific truth-claims, while at the same time avoiding the (traditional) professional link with mainstream media organizations. However, in the eagerness to sever the links with the mainstream media, the concept of citizen journalism brings with it certain risks, both theoretically and strategically.

Firstly, the concept of citizen media risks individuating processes of non-professional media production by detaching it from the embeddedness in media organizations, which is still a vital safeguard for these participatory processes. Other conceptual frameworks tend to emphasize how these processes are interwoven in the activities of community media (Howley, 2005), alternative media (Downing, Ford, Gil, and Stein, 2001; Atton, 2002), civil society media (Carpentier, Lie, and Servaes, 2003) or citizen media (Rodriguez, 2001). Secondly, "amateur" or non-professional media production risks becoming (too) detached from the broader social structure of civil society and (new) social movements (NSMs). Here it is important to understand the ways in which participatory media are situated within civil society, especially with regard to their (possible) affiliations with alternative or activist media organizations.

This chapter seeks to analyze these relationships between professionalism and amateurism, and between citizen journalists and activists within a civil society context, showing the interconnections between—and hybridity of—these discursive categories and the related mediated practices. More specifically, for purposes of illustration, we will focus on one specific example related to the political, legal, military, and humanitarian crisis of the Iraq War, and the (communicative) counterstrategies of the peace movement it provoked (and still provokes). The case study of a peace march organized on March 16, 2008, by the North Belgian peace movement and supported by a platform of 61 organizations, will allow us to unwrap many of the complexities that remain hidden behind the notion of citizen journalism, including its hybrid links to civil society and NSMs.

NEW SOCIAL MOVEMENTS' (NSMs) COMMUNICATIVE STRATEGIES

In the so-called digital age, the nature and structure of social movements has undergone a considerable degree of change, especially compared to classic social movements such as labor unions or even to NSMs such as the green movement. It could be argued that the majority of social movements nowadays are no longer purely membership-based, but are rather made up of networks of society-centered, advocacy-based organizations and fuelled by often-dispersed but highly prolific activists. Another major change is related to the transnational nature of many of the issues at stake, such as the environment, peace, global trade, migration, and so forth. As such issues need to be addressed beyond the sovereignty of the nation state, a drastic surge in transnational advocacy initiatives could be observed (Keck & Sikkink, 1998).

Starting from a framing perspective and drawing on the US civil rights movement, McAdam (2005) identifies six strategic challenges for movements that aim to become "a force for social change." The first two challenges are inward oriented: recruiting core activists and sustaining the organization. This has been covered extensively by the literature on social movements. (For an overview, see della Porta & Diani, 1999.) The four other challenges for activists can be characterized as more outward oriented. They relate to getting attention in the mainstream media, to mobilizing beyond those already convinced, to overcoming social control (and possible repression), and finally to "shape public policy and state action" (McAdam, 2005, p. 119).

McAdam's overview shows that we should avoid reducing all NSM activities to matters of communication exclusively, but at the same time we should also avoid underestimating the communicative dimensions of these activities. Media and communication strategies play an increasingly important role in the mediation and the convergence of different interests, spheres, and actors. This can be seen in terms of the emergence of alternative voices in mainstream public spaces—providing a platform for diverse discourses, in terms of representation—normalizing varied perspectives or lifestyles, but also in terms of being an agonistic battleground over meanings and conceptions of what constitutes the public interest and the common good (Mouffe, 1999).

Still, most recent studies on activism within media and communication studies focus almost exclusively on the opportunities and constraints that the internet provides to organize movements. Singled out for attention are efforts to facilitate the transnationalization of struggles, to increase networking and mobilizing capacities, as well as to strengthen the public sphere by facilitating discussion and the dissemination of counter-hegemonic discourses (see, e.g., Cammaerts, 2005; Gillan & Pickerill, 2008). Alternative information needs non-mainstream channels of distribution. The internet provides activists with a user-friendly and cost-efficient medium for the unbiased and unmediated distribution of alternative information across the boundaries of time and space. As Rucht (2004, p. 55) points out, the internet allows for movement-controlled media that "secure autonomy and operational flexibility."

However, while the internet increasingly constitutes an "opportunity structure" for activists and social movements, this clearly needs to be embedded in a larger communication strategy, including other channels to distribute their aims and goals, as pointed out earlier by McAdam. In this regard, face-to-face interaction, (positive) attention in the mainstream media, the use of pamphlets, or establishing a presence on alternative radio stations are as important as being active and present on the internet. While the relationships of NSMs with alternative media are often reasonably good (Bailey, Cammaerts, and Carpentier, 2008), making use of the mainstream media requires the development of what Rucht (2004, p. 37) calls adaptation strategies, or "the acceptance/exploitation of the mass media's rules and criteria to influence coverage positively." This is legitimized by the need of NSMs for mainstream media to "broaden the scope of conflict" and push their message to a mass audience, "because most of the people they wish to reach are part of the mass media gallery, while many are missed by movement-oriented outlets" (Gamson & Wolfsfeld, 1993, p. 116).

Arguably, NSMs are built on a combination of these different formal and informal communication strategies. But at the same time, their (communicative) networks are not limited to thematically or strategically affiliated organizations. The peace march case study that is discussed below will show the complexities of these alliances, and how the borders between participatory media, citizen journalists, and peace movement activists are being blurred.

CASE STUDY: THE BELGIAN ANTI-WAR PLATFORM
COMMEMORATING THE IRAQ INVASION

Months before the US-led coalition started a new war against Iraq (March 20, 2003), peace and other social movements, as well as many individual citizens from around the world, prepared for what would become one of the biggest protest events in history. The combination of the global indignation provoked by this crisis and the mobilizing and coordinating capacity of global social networks—in particular the Regional (European) and World Social Forums—resulted, on February 15, 2003, in more than 600 antiwar protests in over 60 countries with millions of participants. It became clear that "these were the largest and most momentous transnational antiwar protests in human history" (Epstein, 2003, p. 109). The Belgian protest march of February 15, 2003, was built on a similar structural basis and organized in a Platform of more than 200 organizations, including labor unions and third world, women's, environmental, youth, and political movements. An estimated 100,000 people joined the demonstration in Brussels.

However transnational this protest movement was, though, there were always specific national circumstances that resulted in important differences. In the Belgian case, most political parties were more or less opposed to a war, in contrast to countries like the United Kingdom, the United States, Spain, or Italy, where the governments had promoted a military approach to deal with Saddam Hussein's regime. This also had consequences for the media, as mainstream media coverage tends to stay in line with the national political consensus (Dimitrova & Strömbäck, 2005, pp. 13–14; Nohrstedt & Ottosen, 2000, p. 25). As in most other countries, the Belgian demonstrations continued to be organized even after President George W. Bush officially declared the end of the war. Between the antiwar movements worldwide, there was still some limited form of exchange of information through the internet or in meetings and conferences, but the international coordination of actions and demonstrations withered. Although the specific political demands that accompanied the demonstrations differed from country to country, in essence they mainly kept focusing on the "*Stop the war, stop the occupation*" slogan.

THE PEACE MARCH OF MARCH 16, 2008

As in previous years, the fifth anniversary of the invasion in Iraq was preceded by an international meeting of peace activists. On December 1, 2007, the World Against War Conference in London issued an appeal to launch global demonstrations between March 15 and 22, 2008.[1] Their final declaration demanded the retreat of troops from Iraq and Afghanistan and called for demonstrations as well against a possible attack on Iran.

The Belgian Anti-war Platform decided to hold a 27-kilometer peace walk from Leuven to the capital, Brussels, on March 16, 2008, under the banner of *"Five years of violence in Iraq = Enough! 1000 walkers for peace."* About 250 people started walking in Leuven, with several hundred activists joining the march along the way. Arriving at the endpoint, the Brussels Jubelpark, some 1,000 protesters formed a large peace sign. This event was supported by a coalition of 61 organizations from within the peace, north-south, women's, environmental, and youth movements, as well as labor unions and political parties. They signed a Platform text[2] asking for (among other things) the "withdrawal of the occupation forces" in Iraq and the termination of the agreement between Belgium and the United States that permits the use of the Belgian infrastructure for military transports to the Gulf. The Platform declaration also emphasized a "non-violent approach" to the tense relations with Iran and called for an ending of "the colonisation and annexation of Palestinian territories by Israel." While the political declaration clearly focused on Iraq, the Belgian NGOs of the Anti-war Platform—paralleling antiwar movements in other countries—linked the Iraq War to other conflicts in the Middle East.

Figure 1: The human peace sign at the end of the peace march

Photo: Olivier Van Acker (vzw Vrede—published on Indymedia) (http://www.indymedia.be/files/DSC04397.jpg & http://www.indymedia.be/nl/node/26625)

COMMUNICATION STRATEGIES IN A CHANGING CONTEXT

Over the years, the amount of media attention devoted to the Iraq War has gradually decreased. As in other countries, the yearly demonstrations in Belgium commemorating the invasion of Iraq have attracted ever-smaller numbers of protesters. As a result, groups such as the Belgian Anti-war Movement have had to develop a number of alternative strategies.

First, Platform activists decided to rely more on alternative communication channels, ranging from the distribution of posters and flyers, building a dedicated website (geenoorlog.be), publishing their arguments in the magazines and on the websites of the Platform members, using individual blogs, sending out (chains of) emails, organizing small conferences and antiwar meetings, and aligning themselves with alternative media. This strategy has resulted in the inclusion of two alternative media organizations (Indymedia.be and Radio Campus[3]), both based in Brussels, as Platform members.

Second, the Anti-war Platform developed a strategy to attract mainstream media attention. This was for them one of the most important reasons behind the decision to organize a long peace walk, followed by a mass meeting to form a large peace sign. Since a 27-kilometer march was not likely to attract massive mobilization, the organizers made the deliberate decision to make media interest the main objective in its own right. To avoid negative coverage on the expected small number of participants, the organizers took the precautionary measure of communicating the event as "1,000 march for peace." By focusing on the closing event—the meeting and the formation of a large peace sign—the Platform hoped to lower perceptions of the participation threshold for the protest. Moreover, it was hoped that having 1,000 people form a peace sign would provide journalists with compelling pictures and stories.

The latter strategy did prove reasonably successful, as most of the major newspapers, as well as Belgian television (VRT, RTBf, VTM) and radio (Radio1, Q-Music) stations covered the march. Two days before the march, the national news agency Belga had already used an Indymedia posting on the peace sign story, announcing the anti-war event. Not surprisingly, the meeting of the Platform organizations following the March 16 event gave the media coverage mixed reviews. The action had generated only short, factual articles focusing on the spectacular image and to some extent ignoring the political message the Platform organizations wanted to communicate.

In contrast, the more alternative channels generated more coverage. Print and online social movement magazines such as *Uitpers*, *Solidair*, *Visie*, and *Vrede* included articles on both the conflict and the actual peace march. In addition, the platform organizations produced a considerable number of (online) texts that dealt with the event. Excluding media websites, 24 different texts could be retraced on the websites of the socialist union ABVV, the (smaller) political parties Groen!, KP, and PvdA, and affiliated organizations such as Doctors for the People, peace movement organizations, ecological organizations, the third world organization Oxfam, and the feminist organization VOK. Even the municipal website of Leuven included a reference to the march.[4] Crucially, however, the Independent Media Centre (Indymedia.be) provided extensive coverage of the event. They published 18 postings on the march, which included 75 photos and one video.

Two weeks before the actual march, a number of articles had made reference to the march and sought to contextualize it. Two Indymedia articles (March 3 and 5), posted on behalf of Indymedia.be before the actual march, dealt with Indymedia's participation in the march. The March 3 posting explained that they were participating to "tell a story about the media and war" and will "put together some sort of an act on media and war."[5] The March 5 posting then showed the actual preparations of the Indymedia.be core staff members, planning to become "walking television screens."[6] From the day of the actual march onward, ten reports were posted detailing not only the march itself but also Indymedia.be's presence there.

Figure 2: The Indymedia delegation preparing for their peace march act
Photo: Han Soete (http://www.indymedia.be/nl/node/26307 & http://www.flickr.com/photos/hansoete/2312585064/)

CITIZEN JOURNALISTS CUM PEACE ACTIVISTS

The active presence of the Indymedia.be (volunteer) staff members at the march highlights the interwovenness of citizen journalism and peace activism. The Indymedia.be journalists not only reported on the march but at the same time were working to support its objectives. This blurring of otherwise distinct roles opens up a dialectical process of presence and representation.

In other words, this process of interwovenness moves in two directions. In analyzing the 18 postings on Indymedia.be, it becomes apparent that at least eight of these postings were made by authors clearly (and sometimes explicitly) affiliated with the peace movement. Five of these postings are authored by the spokesperson(s) of the Anti-war Platform, two of them by a journalism student doing his internship at one of the key organizations of the Anti-war Platform (Vrede vzw), and one other using a name (NatoGameOver) that refers to another peace movement organization (Bomspotting & Vredesactie). Yet two more postings were made by an author who is affiliated with Doctors for the People, an organization that is linked, in turn, to the PvdA, a left-wing political party, which is also one of the organizational members of the Anti-war Platform.

Through this process of interconnection, it becomes clear that participatory media like Indymedia are civil society media (or citizens' media—see Rodriguez, 2001) and need to be seen as an inseparable part of civil society, a societal segment considered crucial for the viability of democracy. These participatory media facilitate the access and participation of non-media professionals to the media, and through these participatory media citizens can be active in one of many (micro-) spheres relevant to daily life, organize different forms of deliberation, and exert their rights to communicate. At the same time, these media also contribute to democratization *through* media (Wasko & Mosco 1992, p. 13). Alternative media can overcome the absolutist interpretation of media neutrality and impartiality, and can offer different societal groups and communities the opportunity for extensive participation in public debate and for self-representation in a public space. In so doing, they enter the realm of enabling and facilitating macroparticipation.

These participatory media are also "rhizomatic" (Carpentier et al., 2003). That is, they are characterized by diversity, they cut across different boundaries (generated by market and state), they are part of large civil society networks, and they act as meeting points and catalysts for a variety of organizations and movements. The peace march case study illustrates how these different movements and organizations interact as part of a fluid civil society network, where different alliances are established, disintegrate, and then are reestablished again, according to specific needs. Moreover, the involvement of key staff members of the peace movement also shows the complexities of the non-professional status of participatory media producers. These authors perform professional tasks, including the promotion of the organization's rhetorical positions. From this rhizomatic/civil society perspective, all organizations can be seen as part of the NSMs network, with sometimes converging objectives to achieve specific aims through a combination of direct action, mobilization, and communicative strategies. This commitment to combining diverse forms of professionalism and amateurism recasts the traditional frontiers otherwise surrounding civil society.

Remaining crucial to this debate about citizen journalism, therefore, is its organizational embeddedness. The use of these technologies, especially with regard to their participatory potential, cannot be detached from bureaucratic imperatives. Participation needs to be organized. Even in the blogosphere, the existence of the individual writer-publisher is a romantic illusion because the blog infrastructure is provided by a variety of organizations and companies. Admittedly, in the web 2.0 era this organizational context is often—as Jenkins (2006) argues—a commercial and commodified context, which results in a combination of top-down business processes with bottom-up consumption and production processes. The web 2.0 platform YouTube, owned by Google, is a case in point here. But the interconnection of Indymedia and the peace movement discussed here shows that strong participatory media organizations independent from state and market can still play a crucial role as facilitators of mediation and participation.

Although citizen journalism can thrive in more commercial and commodified contexts, it is also faced by the threat of incorporation by a diversity of mainstream media organizations that reduce the intensity of the participatory process. Many mainstream media have been trying to develop business models to incorporate citizen journalists and to reduce their role as providers of information, keeping the media professionals' role as gatekeepers intact. Although far from perfect, strong participatory media organizations can provide a non-commercial and non-commodified context, where the top-down business processes play only a limited role, and where the risk of incorporation is less substantial. The peace march case study shows that the alliance of an online participatory platform with the peace movement can contribute to a viable civil society and to the democratization of our public spaces.

CONCLUSION

Citizen journalism offers a number of opportunities to better understand the contemporary conjuncture. The increase of mediated participations, at least partially through the popularity of web 2.0, has become a significant part of this contemporary conjuncture. It would be hard not to mention blogging, vlogging, webzines, internet radio (and television), podcasting, digital storytelling, and wikis here. The danger of focusing on online interactions and strategies is that the importance and capacities of "old" media are ignored. These media clearly still play an important role in the everyday lives of many people. Citizen journalism is a concept that facilitates the enriching of these participatory debates by emphasizing the potential of citizens to participate in the process of media production as non-professional journalists, thus disarticulating the need for professional employment in the media industry from the concept of journalism. The peace march case study illustrates that a diversity of non-media professionals from a variety of organizational origins can actually contribute to the in-depth coverage of a specific event that is considered relevant to all of them.

At the same time, each concept incorporates specific risks. For one, the concept of citizen journalism has become the object of a discursive struggle where mainstream media's practices have attempted to engulf and rearticulate it. This process of incorporation of citizen journalists into the mainstream media often reduces the journalistic role of citizen journalists, as professional journalists remain firmly in control in these kinds of settings. Moreover, it also reduces the participatory process to mere access and interaction, strongly reducing the power equilibrium that is constitutive for participation (Carpentier, 2007). Second, the concept of citizen journalism carries the risk of individuating participation, especially when the concept of citizenship is used in its reductive articulation generated through an exclusive citizen-state-market relationship. Citizen journalists are in danger of being detached from the structures of civil society, which are vital in constructing civility, being seen instead as individuals conforming to the (market) media or the entire polis.

For these reasons, the embeddedness in participatory organizations, which are in turn part of a rhizomatic civil society, is seen as necessary to protect citizen journalism. This does not imply that citizen journalism is impossible within a commercial or commodified context. It does mean, however, that civil society remains a nesting home and safe haven for citizen journalism, protecting it from incorporation and eventually annihilation. At the same time we should avoid a too-romantic position and recognize that power imbalances, authoritarian practices, and processes of exclusion can also arise within civil society. In the case of the peace march coverage, the lack of texts generated by non-networked citizens is a cause for concern. Furthermore, the complexity of different "professional" and "amateur" roles and positions should be recognized, leading to high levels of overlap and collaboration between different civil society (sub)networks. As we have sought to demonstrate, this fluidity should not be used to discredit citizen journalism; it should rather be seen as one of its many virtues.

NOTES

1. Declaration of World against War Conference, http://theworldagainstwar.org/
2. Peace in the Middle East: Now! On: http://www.motherearth.org/nowar/en/home_en.php
3. The case study will focus on the role of Indymedia.be because of spatial constraints. In doing so, it is not our intention to underestimate the role of Radio Campus.
4. This overview is based on a Google search with the combined Dutch keywords "peace march" and "Iraq" on be-websites only. Only texts with a clear focus on the peace march were selected. The search was performed on May 18, 2008.
5. http://www.indymedia.be/nl/node/26278
6. http://www.indymedia.be/nl/node/26307

REFERENCES

Atton, C. (2002) *Alternative media*. London: Sage.

Bailey, O., Cammaerts, B., & Carpentier, N. (2008) *Understanding alternative media*. Maidenhead: Open University Press/McGraw-Hill.

Cammaerts, B. (2005) "ICT-usage among transnational social movements in the networked society—to organise, to mobilise and to debate." In R. Silverstone (Ed.), *Media, technology and everyday life in Europe: from information to communication* (pp. 53–72). Aldershot: Ashgate.

Carpentier, N. (2007) "Participation and interactivity: changing perspectives. The construction of an integrated model on access, interaction and participation." In V. Nightingale, & T. Dwyer (Eds.), *New media worlds* (pp. 214–230). New York: Oxford University Press.

Carpentier, N., Lie, R., & Servaes, J. (2003) "Community media—muting the democratic media discourse?" *Continuum—Journal of Media and Cultural Studies, 17*(1), 51–68.

della Porta, D., & Diani, M. (1999) *Social movements: an introduction*. Oxford: Blackwell.

Dimitrova, D.V., & Strömbäck, J. (2005) "Mission accomplished? Framing of the Iraq War in the elite newspapers in Sweden and in the United States." *Gazette: The International Journal for Communication Studies, 67*(5), 399–417.

Downing, J., with Ford, T.V., Gil, G., & Stein, L. (2001) *Radical media: rebellious communication and social movements*. London: Sage.

Epstein, B. (2003) "Notes on the antiwar movement." *Monthly Review, 55*(3), 109–116.

Gamson, W.A., & Wolfsfeld, G. (1993) "Movements and media as interacting systems." *Annals of the American Academy of Political and Social Movements, 526*, 114–127.

Gillan, K., & Pickerill, J. (2008) "Transnational anti-war activism: solidarity, diversity and the internet in Australia, Britain and the United states after 9/11." *Australian Journal of Political Science, 43*(1), 59–78.

Howley, Kevin (2005) *Community media. People, places, and communication technologies*. Cambridge: Cambridge University Press.

Jenkins, H. (2006) *Convergence culture: where old and new media collide*. New York: New York University Press.

Keck, M., & Sikkink, K. (1998) *Activists beyond borders: advocacy networks in international politics*. Ithaca, NY: Cornell University Press.

McAdam, D. (2005) "Movement strategy and dramaturgical framing in democratic states: the case of the civil rights movement." In S. Chambers & A. Costain (Eds.), *Deliberation, democracy and the media* (pp. 117–35). Lanham, MD: Rowman & Littlefield.

Mouffe, C. (1999) "Deliberative democracy or agonistic pluralism?" *Social Research*, 66(3): 746–758.

Nohrstedt, S.A., & Ottosen, R. (2000) "Studying the media Gulf War." In S.A. Nohrstedt & R. Ottosen (Eds.), *Journalism and the new world order. Vol. 1: Gulf War, national news discourses and globalization* (pp. 11–34). Göteborg: Nordicom.

Rodriguez, C. (2001) *Fissures in the mediascape: an international study of citizens' media*. Creskill, NJ: Hampton Press.

Rucht, D. (2004) "The quadruple 'A': media strategies of protest movements since the 1960s." In W. van de Donk, B.D. Loader, P.G. Nixon, & D. Rucht (Eds.), *Cyberprotest: new media, citizens and social movements* (pp. 29–56). London: Routledge.

Wasko, J., & Mosco, V. (Eds.) (1992) *Democratic communications in the information age*. Toronto and Norwood, NJ: Garamond Press and Ablex.

CHAPTER FOURTEEN

Indymedia AND THE Law: Issues FOR Citizen Journalism

LEE SALTER

This chapter considers some of the legal issues facing citizen journalists, especially those engaged in "radical" or activist reporting, in an online context. It suggests that the conceptualization of the citizen journalist must consider the status of this type of journalism in relation to law, the application of which is especially challenging in an online environment that is said to transcend jurisdictions. The extent of legal provisions recognizing citizen journalists as being privy to special protection are in dispute, though there appears to be a growing recognition of their claim to substantive rights as citizens *and* as journalists. In this chapter, I shall argue that state authority and law is adapting—if rather slowly—to take account of changes in international relations (or globalization) with important implications for citizen journalism's forms and practices deserving of close attention.

To clarify this chapter's agenda, allow me to identify three critical questions for citizen journalists to consider:

1. What rights are assigned and responsibilities required of journalists compared to citizens?
2. How are journalists recognized as such and what implications does this have for citizen journalists working in an online environment?
3. What complications are there for the state in assigning rights and demanding duties of citizen journalists in an online environment?

I shall proceed to illustrate some of the corresponding issues, in the first instance, with an overview of legal concepts that apply to journalists. Next, I will discuss material derived from a case study of Independent Media Centers (IMCs) based on my participant observation with IMC UK and IMC Bristol.

IMCs are parts of a global federated network of media centers that aim to provide a space for politically active citizens, or activists, to report their news without the normal constraints of economic and administrative power. They are particularly interesting as projects that attempt to harness the potential of the internet to be used in a way that avoids the implicit and explicit power relations that are said to stymie traditional journalism. As such they are supposed to allow anyone to "be the media," not least by taking advantage of the perceived deterritorial, immaterial, and anonymous nature of the internet.

CITIZEN, JOURNALIST: RIGHTS, RESPONSIBILITIES, AND THE STATE

Online citizen journalism presents us with a conceptual conundrum: a citizen is the subject of a state, but the internet allows material to transcend the jurisdictional boundaries of the state. This conundrum, in my view, should not be seen as a discrete, novel problem, but rather placed in the broader context of change.

First, multiculturalism, migration, and competing obligations and loyalties create problems in the identification of legal subjects or citizens, on the one hand, and create legitimation problems for the state, on the other hand (see, for instance, Castles & Davidson, 2000). Second, the rise of multi-level governance has created a variety of sources of legal power and levels of citizenship (Held, McGrew, Goldblatt, and Perraton, 1999). Third, the supposed globalization (or perhaps, more accurately, internationalization) of politics and economics has outgrown the national basis of lawmaking, resulting in a profound shift in the constitution of people as political subjects and the state's claim to authority (Hardt & Negri, 2000; Falk, 2000; Jayasuriya, 1999). For many citizen-activist journalists, such as those working in IMCs, there is the further problem of the legitimacy of the state—many contest that they have a duty to obey what they conceive to be a manifestly and systemically unjust state.

These problems are compounded in the online environment where internationalization, virtuality, and deterritorialization are said to threaten the capacity of the state both to award rights and manage responsibilities as they relate to citizens and journalists. An online citizen journalist's copy may be written in Malaysia, about an event in Sudan, uploaded in Singapore to a server in Sweden by a German citizen. At what point is the citizen journalist recognized as such, and thereby awarded rights and/or held accountable for certain responsibilities? If rights are only made real by states, to which jurisdiction might the citizen appeal?

Can the journalist choose which state's right to claim or which responsibilities to adhere to? Should she be held to the Malaysian Press Institute's adherence to the principles of Rukunegara (the basis of the Malaysian state), which includes contributing to nation-building and upholding the standards of "social morality"? Perhaps most importantly, when can a state claim jurisdiction? Is it reasonable that citizen journalists should adhere to Germany's Töben ruling, which extends its Holocaust denial laws across all jurisdictions? Whose secrets, security, criminal code, and so on should such journalists obey?

Traditionally, journalists in liberal democracies have enjoyed basic rights, such as freedom of speech and freedom of the press, freedom from arbitrary arrest, and freedom of information provisions *as citizens*. That is, they have enjoyed *generally* applicable (to citizens) rights guaranteed by constitutional provisions (whether codified or not). At the same time, journalists have also enjoyed *specific* rights, awarded to them in recognition of their role in democratic states. As such, the ability to observe, scrutinize, and check power, and report to a public that governs itself, is made possible by journalistic rights and protections—specifically, with respect to questions of access, permissible speech, and legality of certain practices.

Citizen journalists may be concerned to secure rights of access (usually with a press card) and journalistic protection, for these are often not afforded to citizens as such. Access rights are those that allow journalists—usually gaining recognition through their attachment to institutions—to enter certain, sometimes restricted, institutions or areas *as journalists*. Speech rights for journalists sometimes go beyond those afforded to ordinary citizens, in the form of journalistic privilege—either absolute or qualified, usually offering protection against libel charges.[1] In the United Kingdom, absolute privilege only applies if the whole discourse is reported *contemporaneously*. Qualified privilege is reporting that may break a law, but which can claim a public interest qualification or a notion of duty to report.

The protection of journalistic material (or "shield laws") allows journalists to collect and store information of public importance. In the United Kingdom, section 10 of the 1981 Contempt of Court Act recognizes the journalist's right to protect a source but allows an exception if "disclosure is necessary in the interests of justice, national security or in the prevention of disorder or crime," unless outweighed by "public interest." Similarly, the 1984 Police and Criminal Evidence (PACE) Act protects "journalistic material," defined as "material acquired or created for the purposes of journalism," but in neither piece of legislation is "journalism" itself defined.

The rights available to journalists are usually awarded to institutions (rather than journalists as such), primarily because they offer some security for the state: institutions function to control workers and their products, especially through selection and socialization of personnel (Etzioni, 1967; Hatch, 1997). This approach makes the institution a legal subject with responsibility for legal compliance.

Many citizen journalists are *not members* of institutions or organizations, however. As we shall see, in the case of IMCs, for instance, the boundaries between who is and is not an Indymedia journalist are fluid, and there is no traditional hierarchy of editorial responsibility.

Citizen journalists may well find it difficult to gain recognition *as journalists*. Consequently, access rights and protections may not be forthcoming. This is especially pertinent when recognition is institutionalized. In the United Kingdom, for example, membership in the National Union of Journalists (whose press card is invaluable for access) is still in large part restricted to those who earn an income from journalism. IMC participants do not. However, a vast array of rights is available to them *as citizens*. In some countries, such as the United States since the 1972 *Branzburg v. Hayes* judgment, constitutional provisions for free speech prevent the federal government from making a distinction between citizens and journalists, though some states have opted to implement state-level shield laws. Citizen journalists who are concerned to be recognized as journalists in the United States may, then, have fewer concerns than expected elsewhere.

Nevertheless, recognition remains an important issue for activist citizen journalists online. Legal subjectivity is an essential mechanism for claiming rights, yet requires responsibility to obey laws. On one hand, a citizen journalist may seek rights as a journalist. On the other, he or she may seek protection in anonymity, virtuality, and the sense of freedom that stems from exploiting the supposed deterritorialization and jurisdictional complications provided by the internet, especially in states where liberal rights are not forthcoming. In this instance, the citizen journalist may reject the status as either a general (citizen) or specific (journalist) legal subject. These issues will now be illustrated in the case of IMCs.

INDEPENDENT MEDIA CENTERS

IMCs are key examples of radical forms of use of the internet. Born of the traditions of radical media projects that started with pamphleteering in the 17th and 18th centuries, through to radio and television in the 20th and 21st centuries, IMCs provide those excluded from mainstream media with the opportunity to "do it yourself." IMCs do not depend on any external institutional assistance and only continue to exist as long as ordinary citizens participate in decision making and related aspects of running an online media project. Consequently, issues, campaigns, and events that slip through the mainstream news net take center stage on IMCs and are reported and discussed in a manner far removed from mainstream discourses—reporting is frequently irreverent, controversial, judgmental, and active. IMC journalists do not consider themselves to be objective or neutral but stand on the side of the marginalized. As such, they are often "embedded" into the communities, movements, or campaigns they write about, embracing their subjectivities. They are not just advocacy journalists, but activist journalists.

IMCs are probably the closest thing we have to an autonomistic citizen journalism movement. Although individual IMCs make their own specific rules, they are held to global Principles of Unity (PoU). The PoU explain that IMCs must adhere to principles of equality, decentralization, and local autonomy. The emergence of new IMCs must derive from the "self-organization of autonomous collectives that recognize the importance in developing a union of networks." They must be organized on a not-for-profit basis, must "recognize the importance of process to social change and…[be] committed to the development of non-hierarchical and anti-authoritarian relationships," and thereby "organize themselves collectively and be committed to the principle of consensus decision making and the development of a direct, participatory democratic process that is transparent to its membership." IMCs must consider "open exchange of and open access to information a prerequisite to the building of a more free and just society." They must be "based upon the trust of their contributors and readers, [and] shall utilize open web based publishing, allowing individuals, groups and organizations to express their views, anonymously if desired." They must have a strong commitment to openness, by sharing resources, knowledge, skills, and equipment, while being committed to the use of free source code, thereby increasing the "independence of the network by not relying on proprietary software" (IMC, 2008).

As long as the PoU are adhered to, each IMC develops its own editorial policy and mode of operation. Though the degree of independence of each IMC means that generalizations are somewhat difficult, most IMCs can be roughly described as "anti-capitalist," attracting citizens who tend to be involved with "radical" groups, campaigning and taking actions against the bureaucratic-capitalist state. Taking a position of opposition to the state means that the normal mode of operation of news organizations is rejected. This means that there are no agreements, tacit or otherwise, between IMCs and the states in which they are situated. Indeed, relations are usually ones of opposition.

The fact that IMCs are based on a critique of what they see as a compliant corporate media system that operates in a grossly unfair social system means that compliance with the "rules of the journalistic game" is not forthcoming. This position of opposition to the state leads to conflicts that play out through the medium of law. Legal conflicts illustrate the frictional borders between activist citizen journalism and state power and demonstrate the persistence of the state in an international and virtual media environment, as will be illustrated in the following case studies. While Indymedia arose as an "alternative globalization" movement, it is arguable that its development from a global site to a network of sites that follow the contours of nation-states that the reality of the nation-state persists.

VIRTUALITY AND LEGAL SUBJECTS: LIBEL

Because of the commitment of IMCs to the right of free speech, copy on IMC sites (with the exception of some features) has no editorial input, faces no prior restraint, and should only be removed from an IMC site if it breaches editorial guidelines (such as no discrimination, no advertising, and no copy from mainstream bureaucratic organizations). Thus IMCs receive sporadic complaints from institutions and individuals who have been defamed, or from their lawyers. Unlike mainstream organizations, IMCs do not have legal teams but instead depend on volunteers—of which I am one—who might have some knowledge of law, to staff the legal list. Copy may be removed or edited if the charges are considered to be quite reasonable—for instance, the police sergeant accused of being a pedophile without any justification (January 2006), though more "political" cases will be fought.

On September 13 and 21, 2007, IMC UK received letters from Schillings law firm on behalf of the Uzbek billionaire Alisher Usmanov demanding the removal of an article written by the former British diplomat Craig Murray. Murray had accused Usmanov of being a heroin trafficker, a thug, and a criminal in his book and on his website. However, the latter's UK-based hosting company was served with a notice from Schillings. When Murray's website hosts took down his website, the article in question appeared on blogs around the world, many of which were also served with notices from Schillings, and some of which complied. The article was then posted to IMC UK, prompting the lawyer's letter.

The legal list was only notified of the letters some time after they were received, but soon initiated a discussion about how best to proceed. The volunteers were split between those who wanted to keep the original article and those who wanted to modify it.

IMC UK is a difficult "legal subject" insofar as most participants use pseudonyms, participation is fluid with people coming and going, and insofar as there is no formal hierarchy of office, participants may be regarded as virtual beings. This initially led some participants to consider themselves secure from such threats; however, it was suggested by some on the list that although most participants could not be identified (IMCs tend not to log IP addresses), an aggressive lawyer might realize that someone with a real identity must sign agreements with the web server company, domain name registrars, and so on. Such persons may be considered liable as legal subjects. However, the main thrust of the discussion was that IMC UK should claim journalistic rights under UK law.

As the discussions progressed over many weeks, participants contacted the original author to try to find out whether the publisher of the original book had had its legal department verify the claims made in it. Murray did not respond. Although no one was able to decide conclusively the veracity of the article, some participants declared themselves prepared to go to court to defend it. However, without verification of the claims, no truth-defense could be made, so some participants argued against the idea. The "Reynolds Judgment" might have offered a public-interest defense had the claims been proven untrue, but the fact that there was no attempt to include the (potential) claimant's position would have invalidated this defense.

While this was going on, a participant noted that a Member of the European Parliament had repeated Murray's claims in parliamentary debate. Some proposed that IMC UK could keep the article up and claim statutory qualified privilege. However, the claim was based on a misunderstanding. In the sense intended by some of the participants, privilege was understood as the right to report comments made in Parliament (in this case the European Parliament). However, privilege tends to be considered to extend only to the words directly reported *in context* and does not then extend to the rest of an article.

Although there was some consideration that it would be unlikely that a court would award significant damages to Usmanov, on the basis that he was a billionaire and IMC UK is a not-for-profit and has no significant assets, most participants (besides some of the more "radical" participants who stood aside) agreed to a proposal to rewrite the article as a front-page story (the original was buried deep within the site) about an attack on IMC UK by Usmanov, repeating the original claims *as allegations*.

Shillings did not contact IMC UK again with regard to Usmanov, but libel notices from others have continued. In this instance, the institutional virtuality of IMC UK may have prevented effective legal action from taking place. However, libel law has adapted to the "deterritorialized" internet, with countries such as the United Kingdom allowing people to "libel shop" when something is published internationally, that is, to choose the jurisdiction in which libel cases will be heard.

THE STATE, DETERRITORIALIZATION, AND JURISDICTION: SECURITY

Just as libel law is adapting to internationalization, so too are "security" laws. So-called anti-terrorism laws have multiplied and intensified since 2001. Such laws have had significant effects on the ability of journalists and ordinary individuals to seek information about the state, yet increase the capacity of state authorities to survey and investigate citizens. Indeed they provide some evidence to challenge the "end of the state" (Ohamae, 1996) thesis that developed states retain an ultimate monopoly over coercive resources.

One of the promises of the online environment was that it would transcend political boundaries, that states would be unable to control it. However, citizen journalists as material beings are legal subjects whether they like it or not, and their tools are similarly subject to laws as material items. Thus, the internet does not entirely transcend jurisdictional control. It may not be as easy to control as licensed media or institutionalized media, but control *can* be exerted over all material items, especially when issues of security are in play.

On Thursday, October 7, 2004, the Indymedia UK website went offline. Few of the participants were aware of how and why this happened—the site just disappeared. It was not, however, just IMC UK that went down. Another 21 IMC sites were also brought down. The problem for IMC UK was that its site was hosted on the servers of a US hosting company, which had been requested to comply with a subpoena from the Federal Bureau of Investigation.

In 2003–2004 an Italian magistrate was investigating a number of "terrorist" acts committed in Italy and elsewhere in Europe, in particular the attempted bombing of Romano Prodi, responsibility for which was admitted by a contributor to an Indymedia web site. However, the magistrate found that the site was not hosted in Italy, but in the United States—exploiting deterritorialization to receive greater constitutional protection. Therefore, in April 2004, she requested that the US Judicial Authority obtain log files from Indymedia's web-hosting company, Rackspace. The magistrate had requested that the US authorities subpoena Indymedia Global for IP logs. However, although Rackspace is a US company, the servers in question were physically located in the United Kingdom. This meant that the FBI could not directly comply with the request. Instead it had to make the request to the UK authorities. The important point about these requests is that they were made under the Mutual Legal Assistance Treaty, an agreement among countries to cooperate on legal investigations across borders without necessarily having formal laws in common.

We see here, then, mechanisms in place that affirm jurisdictional control over citizen journalists: they are still subject to law as countries adapt to a changing legal environment. Indeed, the international scope of the internet does not mean that it escapes countries and their laws, but instead that it may be subject to the laws of many countries.

THE STATE, RECOGNITION, AND THE ACTIVIST JOURNALIST: INCITEMENT

A notable feature of mainstream journalism is that it tends, usually in the name of neutrality, to take a passive relation to the world around it. Neutrality is not, however, motivated only by principle or professional values. For example, incitement laws effectively prevent mainstream journalists from taking an advocacy role, at least on certain topics.

The promise of activist citizen journalism has always been to report actively from within movements. However, the issue of incitement to commit crime presents reporters with problems. If facts are not neutral, how can a proposed mass trespass of a military base be reported? How can the disabling of nuclear submarines be reported actively without incitement?

Under the United Kingdom's 2006 Terrorism Act, the issue of incitement has become especially problematic, wherein the *encouragement* and *glorification* of "terrorist acts" domestically and *overseas* constitutes a crime. Indeed, encouragement applies to "a statement that is likely to be understood by *some* or all of the members of the public to whom it is published as a direct or *indirect* encouragement or other inducement to them to the commission, preparation or instigation of acts of terrorism." Again, the limit of the supposed virtuality and borderlessness of the internet becomes apparent.

Of course incitement is not restricted to terrorist acts; it is more often applied in relation to crime. In June 2005 the police raided Bristol IMC and seized its web server under the Police and Criminal Evidence (PACE) Act and arrested a participant for incitement to criminal damage. The server was seized as the police sought access to the IP log (as did the FBI in the IMC UK case above) to identify the person who had written a story about a "direct action" they had initiated. (In this case materials were thrown at a train carrying cars from the port through the city of Bristol in a protest about climate change.)

In keeping with other IMCs, Bristol IMC preserves the anonymity of participants by deleting IP logs. The police had originally requested the IP logs, but when they were not forthcoming, they confiscated the server. Naturally, even this course of action was unfruitful. As Bristol IMC was merely a conduit, it claimed no responsibility for the posting, the author being entirely anonymous. One of the key arguments that the IMC put to the police was that the server should have been treated as "journalistic material" using the same PACE Act under which it was seized. In the first instance it was immediately clear that because Bristol IMC is not recognized as a journalistic institution in the same way as, say, the *Bristol Evening Post*, it was not treated equivalently. Its irreverence worked against it.

Further to this, although the argument that its servers be treated as journalistic material was well supported by other organizations that sympathized with Bristol IMC, such as the National Union of Journalists, it was somewhat misplaced. In the first instance, journalistic privilege is not protected in the same way as, say, lawyer's privilege. Journalistic privilege (in this instance to protect a source and journalistic material) is significantly qualified. Although journalistic material is protected under the PACE Act, that protection can be easily overturned by a judge or even by the invocation of special procedures. Furthermore, as outlined above, the protection of journalistic material is subject to other issues, especially the "public interest." It is clear that a judge would see the action as criminal damage, and its reporting as the glorification of vandalism, and therefore there is no public-interest defense.

Bristol IMC has since instituted a system of editing so that when the collective is informed that copy might be considered to incite criminal activity, the particular passages are edited and replaced with a disclaimer.

CONCLUSION

Activist citizen journalism will always be at a disadvantage compared to mainstream journalism—politically, economically, culturally, and legally. IMCs advocate causes and actions and may report in ways that do not correspond with the rules of the journalistic game, norms, or laws. Because of this, neither IMC journalists nor other citizen journalists can simply and straightforwardly claim the rights afforded to journalists. It is not enough to claim privilege, for privilege is dependent upon adherence to the rules.

Though adherence to a legal system that is considered to reflect and sustain gross inequalities may not be desirable for IMCs, better knowledge of the law would help IMCs and citizen journalists more generally. Such knowledge would prevent participants from assuming journalistic protections are greater, and jurisdictions lesser, than they actually are. It might also enable them to consider claiming more general laws and rights as citizens rather than as journalists as such.

Some of the characteristics of citizen journalism mean that legal problems are not as great as they might initially appear to be. Though there are figures who are more easily identifiable, it would prove difficult to link them personally to legal transgression. Also, in libel cases, the visibility of the publication counts for a great deal—citizen journalists might claim that the number of people who read a specific story is very small, and perhaps of politically marginal importance, so large libel awards against them are unlikely.

The political decision of IMCs (and many bloggers) to protect participants through the use of pseudonyms and deletion of IP logs has proven effective. However, the question must be asked whether this will be allowed to continue and whether repressive aspects of law withdraw or advance in the face of new media practices. If it does not continue, citizen journalism will lose one of its most potent protections but may, perhaps, gain recognition as a journalistic enterprise proper.

NOTE

1. While the United Kingdom has some of the strictest libel laws in the Western world, they have been loosened somewhat with the 2001 "Reynolds Judgement."

REFERENCES

Bentham, J. (1843) *Anarchical fallacies.*

Castles, S., & Davidson, A. (2000) *Citizenship and migration: globalization and the politics of belonging.* London: Routledge.

Etzioni, A. (1967) "Social control: organizational aspects." In *International Encyclopaedia of Social Science* 14, pp. 369–402.

Falk, R. (2000) "The decline of citizenship in an era of globalization." *Citizenship Studies* 4(1), 5–17.

Hardt, M., & Negri, A. (2000) *Empire.* Cambridge, MA: Harvard University Press.

Hart, H.L.A. (1994) *The concept of law.* Oxford: Oxford University Press.

Hatch, M.J. (1997) *Organization theory.* Oxford: Oxford University Press.

Held, D., McGrew, A., Goldblatt, D., & Perraton, J. (1999) *Global transformations: politics, economics and culture.* London: Polity.

IMC (2008) "Principles of unity." *Independent Media Center.*

Jayasuriya, K. (1999) "Globalization, law, and the transformation of sovereignty: the emergence of global regulatory governance." *Global Legal Studies Journal* 6, 425–455.

Locke, J. (1924) *Two treatises of government.* London: Everyman.

Ohamae, K. (1996) *The end of the nation state: the rise of regional economies.* New York: Free Press.

Salter, L. (2005) "Globalizzazione, tecnologia e il mito dell'indebolimento dello Stato: una critica alle dinamiche della postmodernità" [Globalization, technology and the weakening state: a critique of the dynamics of postmodernity]. In O. Guaraldo & T. Tedoldi (Eds.), *Lo stato dello Stato: riflessione sul potere politico nell'era globale* (pp. 64–84). Verona: Ombre Corte.

CHAPTER FIFTEEN

Citizen Media AND THE Kenyan Electoral Crisis

ETHAN ZUCKERMAN

The crisis surrounding the disputed 2007 presidential elections in Kenya served as a stark reminder of how fragile young democracies can be. It also put into sharp focus the power new media technologies give citizens of developing nations to report news and organize responses to crisis situations. A number of Kenyans demonstrated how technically sophisticated and globally connected their country is at precisely the moment when their leaders demonstrated a willingness to sacrifice the nation's reputation for stability in exchange for continued governing power.

While Kenyan citizen journalists and community organizers have a great deal to be proud of in their response to an electoral crisis and the concomitant ethnic violence, information technology was also used both by the government and civilians to amplify tensions and coordinate violent attacks. The technologies used by citizen reporters and community organizers were the same ones used by forces in the government who sought to rig the election, and agitators who attempted to expand ethnic violence. One lesson from the use of information technology in the Kenyan crisis, this chapter will argue, is that the technology itself is neutral. It can be used powerfully either to give citizens a voice in crisis situations or to aggravate those same crises.

A BRIEF HISTORY OF THE 2007 ELECTIONS

Mwai Kibaki became the third president of Kenya in 2002 after winning a landslide election against Daniel arap Moi, who was widely accused of corruption.

Kibaki promised to address problems of government corruption and experienced some early victories, leading the International Monetary Fund (IMF) to resume lending. The resignation and flight of anti-corruption advisor John Githongo in early 2005 was a major blow to this new program and suggested that corruption problems were endemic to the Kibaki government.

Kibaki, who had promised a new constitution when elected, put a draft constitution up for vote on November 21, 2005. The constitution consolidated presidential power, making it easier for the president to dismiss uncooperative ministers. Raila Odinga led the opposition to the referendum, choosing an orange as his campaign's symbol, in contrast to the banana chosen by Kibaki. The defeat of the referendum was viewed as a major embarrassment for Kibaki as well as a precursor to a challenge by Odinga in the next presidential elections.

On December 27, 2007, presidential and parliamentary elections pitted President Mwai Kibaki and his Party of National Unity (PNU) against Raila Odinga and the Orange Democratic Movement (ODM). Odinga led in polls before the election. Early results showed substantial losses in parliament for the PNU and suggested that Odinga led Kibaki. At the same time, delays in announcing election results raised concerns about possible election rigging.

Three days after the elections, the Electoral Commission of Kenya (ECK) declared Kibaki the winner of a closely contested election, with a margin of 230,000 votes. Kibaki was quickly sworn in as president, as members of the ECK held a press conference to express concerns about voting irregularities. Riots erupted in the Kibera neighborhood of Nairobi, an opposition stronghold. The new government banned live television coverage of the protests and deployed troops to keep the peace and block demonstrations. Odinga attempted to hold an alternate inauguration on December 31, but the event was banned, and Uhuru Park, where it was to be held, was sealed off by riot police.

The situation took a brutal turn on January 1, 2008, when more than 100 ethnic Kikuyu (the tribe Kibaki belongs to) were burned to death by a gang of Kalenjin, Luhya, and Luo men (tribes associated with Odinga) in a church outside Eldoret, in the Rift Valley. Over the next weeks, as African and international leaders flew into the country to mediate, clashes between ODM and PNU supporters, and between Kikuyu and minority ethnic groups, were responsible for more than 1,000 deaths and up to 600,000 internally displaced persons.

In early February, as party leaders began negotiations in earnest, violence slowed, possibly reflecting the political nature of the clashes, or perhaps as a result of the separation brought about by internal migration of threatened ethnic groups. On February 28, a power-sharing agreement mediated by Kofi Annan was signed by Odinga and Kibaki, establishing a new position of prime minister, to be held by Odinga. Lengthy negotiations led to agreements on composition of a new cabinet, creating seats for 40 ministers, an unprecedented and expensive number.

DIGITAL MEDIA IN KENYA

Understanding the role of citizen media in the elections crisis also requires a brief history of Kenyan digital media. With an estimated 3 million internet users (Miniwatts, 2008), Kenya has one of the highest levels of internet penetration in sub-Saharan Africa, at 7.9%. (Of major sub-Saharan African countries, i.e., discounting those with populations under a million, only Zimbabwe and South Africa have higher net penetration.) Eleven and one-half million Kenyans—roughly 30% of the population—have mobile phones, a penetration rate that again outpaces many sub-Saharan African nations (Afrol News, 2008). Kenyan companies have been early adopters of mobile money transfer systems like M-PESA and complex SMS-based systems like Kazi560, which matches jobseekers and employers via their phones.

Against this backdrop, it makes sense that Kenyans would emerge as early adopters in citizen media. Prominent Kenyan blogs, including Daudi Were's Mental Acrobatics, have been online since early 2003. Starting in 2004, Kenya Unlimited has aggregated posts from individual blogs on a central site and provided a "webring," a navigation mechanism that links related weblogs together. In 2006, a nationwide blogging contest—the Kenya Blog Awards or "Kaybees"—helped bring together individual Kenyan bloggers into a community (Kenya Unlimited, 2006). Afrigator, an African blog aggregator based in South Africa, cites two Kenyan blogs in its list of 25 top-ranked blogs, giving the country the second-best representation on that list (after South Africa, which dominates) (Afrigator, 2008).

Kenyan bloggers have an influence beyond their online readership. They have emerged as sources for ideas and stories for mainstream papers. Indeed, this influence has included cases where newspapers have taken stories, word for word, from blogs and have been forced to apologize for their plagiarism (Zuckerman, 2008). Kenyan bloggers have not been shy about using their online platforms to agitate for political change. Ory Okolloh, author of the popular Kenyan Pundit weblog, launched Mzalendo in early 2006, a site designed to provide increased transparency and insight into the Kenyan parliament.

BLOGGING THE 2007 ELECTIONS

Several Kenyan bloggers took pains to document the 2007 election, but there is little indication from their posts that any anticipated the unusual events that would follow the election. In the midst of a thorough post describing his voting experience, and the precautions taken by the ECK to prevent election fraud, Daudi Were observed:

> One thing I noticed was that no one was wearing any political party merchandise and the conversations in the queue were distinctly non political. Rather than being divided, by queuing together to exercise our civic duty and responsibility we were bound together in a sort of patriotic camaraderie. We all felt it was worthwhile to take part in the vote and that ultimately was what mattered. (Were, 2007a)

The joy in a smooth-functioning democratic process extended through December 28, 2007, as it became clear that the elections had ousted a large number of incumbents. Ory Okolloh observed:

> Folks this is a historic election by Kenyan standards, regional standards and international standards—I don't think there is a precedent for the number of incumbents that are going down despite having massive resources behind them and attempts to bribe voters. And I challenge you to find an election in the Western world in recent times where people have come out with such determination, conviction, and a strong sense of civic duty. I'm very very proud of Kenyan voters and you all should be no matter who you are supporting. (Okolloh, 2007a)

The tone—and focus—of coverage changed sharply on December 30, as it became clear that the disputed election would be declared in Kibaki's favor. The ban on live media reports particularly incensed Okolloh, who had been monitoring television, radio, the internet, SMS, and local gossip to produce several election updates per day. When the live coverage ban was announced, she declared:

> All live broadcasts have been suspended by the government. The order was released as ODM was addressing their press conference. This is now officially a police state. So we have no idea what ODM is saying, and what the security situation is around the country. (Okolloh, 2007b)

In the wake of a ban on live media, some Kenyan bloggers responded by redoubling their efforts as citizen reporters. Reeling from the violence in her native Eldoret, Juliana Rotich began posting brief bulletins on refugee movements, fuel shortages, and road and airport closures. Some were posted via SMS using Twitter to disseminate messages to a wider audience; others featured photos and were uploaded to Flickr using a GPRS modem. Daudi Were took to the streets on January 3, following ODM activists as they attempted to march to Uhuru Park to attend a banned rally. His photos documented the empty streets of the usually-bustling capital and the tense standoffs between activists and security forces and provided insights on the confrontation that were hard to find in international media covering the confrontations (Were, 2008a).

As it became clear that Kenya would be in crisis for more than a few days, bloggers began to search for ways to share their workload. Okolloh, who resides in Johannesburg, returned home on January 3, 2008, after a difficult debate over whether she should stay to document the crisis or prioritize the safety of her young child. Three days after arriving in South Africa, she added a new feature to her blog: "diary entries" written by guest bloggers and submitted to her via email. In the month the diary was active, it featured 26 posts from a variety of Kenyans, including regular bloggers who sought an opportunity to reach a larger audience, and from people who had not previously published online. The tone was sharply different from Okolloh's opinionated but news-focused reports—the diaries were personal reflections on the crisis, providing context for readers interested in how the crisis was affecting individual Kenyans.

In her first post on returning to Johannesburg, Okolloh proposed another form of distributed reporting, a Google Maps mashup that showed incidents of violence reported throughout Kenya:

> Google Earth supposedly shows in great detail where the damage is being done on the ground. It occurs to me that it will be useful to keep a record of this, if one is thinking long-term. For the reconciliation process to occur at the local level the truth of what happened will first have to come out. Guys looking to do something—any techies out there willing to do a mashup of where the violence and destruction is occurring using Google Maps? (Okolloh, 2008a)

The reaction to this idea, one of nine points in a long roundup, helps demonstrate Okolloh's influence and reach in the blogger community. (Technorati lists Kenyan Pundit as the #15,282nd-most-popular blog in its index, a very high rank for an Africa-focused blog). Within three days of her January 3 blog post, a prototype version of the system she proposed had been built. By January 9, it was live at Ushahidi.com (the term Ushahidi means "witness" in Swahili). A day later, a partnership with Kenyan mobile phone operators allowed Kenyans to post reports using an SMS shortcode.

The authors of the Ushahidi system were, without exception, people deeply involved in Kenya's citizen media community. David Kobia, the lead author of the system, administers Mashada.com, the leading bulletin board site for Kenyans and the Kenyan diaspora. The chief architect of the system was Erik Hersman, author of the Afrigadget and White African blogs. Bloggers Daudi Were and Juliana Rotich built partnerships with NGOs in Kenya to promote the service and generate reports from outside the web community. Hersman reports that 75% of Kenyan blogs linked to Ushahidi by January 10, helping launch the site to local and global audiences (Hersman, 2008a).

Ushahidi is best understood as a form of collaborative citizen journalism. Individuals submit reports of violent incidents—as well as of peacemaking efforts—via a web form or SMS message, including details of the incident, its geographic location, and supporting information, including photos or video. Ushahidi's administrators attempt to verify reports (by cross-checking against mainstream and citizen media reports), to resolve multiple reports into a single record, and to make the reports visible on an interactive map. The result is a powerful visualization of the complexities of violence and peacemaking in post-conflict Kenya.

The Ushahidi project is now focused on creating a sustainable, open-source platform to allow citizen crisis reporting anywhere in the world. The platform was adopted in late May 2008 by United for Africa, a South African project that documents xenophobic violence. On May 28, Ushahidi won the NetSquared N2Y3 mashup challenge, a prominent software competition that awarded the project a $25,000 first prize. Humanity United, a new foundation focused on "building a world where modern-day slavery and mass atrocities are no longer possible," has committed funding to the Ushahidi team, allowing expansion and maintenance of the platform.

WHO IS THE AUDIENCE FOR CRISIS MEDIA?

Since Ushahidi is built by SMS and web submissions, but chiefly visible via the web, it is worth asking whether the main audience for the site is inside or outside the country. This question is complicated by the fact that the possible audience for these projects includes Kenyans living domestically and Kenyans in the diaspora, as well as non-Kenyans. Kenya's diaspora is a powerful political and economic force—some estimates put remittances from the diaspora at more than US $1 billion per year, more than 2% of GDP. Diaspora Kenyans have political debates in Washington, DC, and stay deeply involved with national politics through groups like the Kenyan Community Abroad (Nyanchama, 2007).

Some of the most innovative efforts in response to the Kenyan crisis were aimed, wholly or in part, at motivating the Kenyan diaspora to support reconstruction efforts. Mama Mikes, for instance, is an online business that accepts payments via the web and delivers goods to addresses within Kenya (a system some have termed "alternative remittance"). During the crisis, they began offering diaspora Kenyans the opportunity to give online, purchasing relief materials that the company staff delivered to displaced persons camps in the Rift Valley. Mama Mikes documented the materials purchased on their staff blog, thanking donors by name and documenting their trip to the camps. To encourage donations and support, either through Mama Mikes or directly to the Red Cross, Juliana Rotich began photographing conditions in displaced persons camps and food distribution efforts. One effect of this coverage was to add transparency to the relief efforts and reassure donors in the diaspora that goods were reaching people in need (Rotich, 2008a).

It's difficult to determine the extent to which citizen media efforts affected news coverage and perceptions of Kenya outside the diaspora population. But it is apparent that many Kenyans were concerned with the international perception of their country in the wake of the crisis. A group called Concerned Kenyan Writers, led by celebrated Kenyan author Binyavanga Wainaina, sought to organize Kenyans to write op-eds in international newspapers in order "to present a human face to the Kenyan post-election crisis; to counter the static images and impressions of escalating violence and anarchy in the foreign press and to document this turning point in our nation's history for posterity" (Wainaina, 2008). In editorials like Wainaina's "No Country for Old Hatreds" in *The New York Times*, authors challenged portrayals of the crisis as an eruption of ethnic hatred, suggesting instead that the events reflected systematic manipulation of ethnic stereotypes by political parties seeking political gains (Wainaina, 2008). Bankelele, a popular blog focused on banking and investment in Kenya, challenged the narrative that Kenya would become another Rwanda with sober, thoughtful analyses of the implications of the crisis for Kenyan economics.

It is also clear that many Kenyans were interested in raising their voices, either through projects like Ushahidi, Concerned Kenyan Writers, Kenyan Pundit's diaries, or through their own blogs. On December 30, 2007—early in the crisis—Daudi Were posted instructions on starting one's own blog in response to the avalanche of comments he had received on his own posts. Many of these comments criticized existing bloggers or demanded that certain posts or comments be removed from the Kenya Unlimited blog aggregator. Daudi responded, "If someone writes something you disagree with by all means let your voice be heard as you present your counter view, and the best place to do this is on your own blog" (Were, 2007b). This raises some open research questions: Did the Kenyan elections crisis cause more Kenyans to start blogging? Will they continue beyond the crisis? Should efforts to introduce citizen media to new populations focus on crisis-response efforts?

THE DARK SIDE OF CITIZEN MEDIA

It's an oversimplification to view online reactions to the Kenyan crisis purely as a proud moment for citizen media. One of the most dramatic lessons of the crisis is that technologies useful for reporting and peacemaking are also useful for rumor mongering and incitement to violence.

As the Kenyan crisis unfolded, many cellphone owners received SMS messages that urged them to drive neighbors from their houses: "If your neighbor is a Kikuyu, just kick him or her out of that house. No one is going to ask you anything" (AFP, 2008). Messages included expressions of ethnic hatred, warnings that one ethnic group would attack another, and rumors that implicated Kenyan companies and institutions in promoting violence. The Nation Media Group, a major Kenyan media company, was forced to issue a press release specifically to counter rumors that its vehicles were being used to transport arms throughout the country to increase violence.

Kenyan mobile phone operators cooperated with the Kibaki government to send messages to subscribers, urging them not to send or forward inflammatory messages. Juliana Rotich reported receiving the following message on her mobile phone in Eldoret: "The ministry of Internal security urges you to please desist from sending or forwarding any SMS that may cause public unrest. This may lead to your prosecution" (Rotich, 2008b). On January 1, 2008, Ory Okolloh reported "Bulk sms has been blocked by the government to prevent guys from sending inciteful messages" (Okolloh, 2008b).

Firoze Manji, a Kenyan human rights activist and editor of *Pambazuka News*, pointed out that these messages from the government had the effect of challenging legitimate political organizing via mobile phone. Blocking bulk SMS may have been intended to stop spreading ethnic hatred, but it also created obstacles for the ODM as they attempted to organize rallies and protests. Manji was particularly offended by a message from Kibaki shortly after he was inaugurated, urging all Kenyans to remain calm: "How did Kibaki get my phone number? This is a major breach of privacy" (Manji, 2008).

The ministry of information may have been premature in threatening prosecution for forwarding messages that incited violence. *The Nation* reported on March 1, 2008, that the government had compiled a list of 1,700 people who had forwarded messages that incited ethnic violence. However, "there is no law governing hate speech over mobile phones, radio and television" (Querengesser, 2008). Groups like the Kenya National Commission on Human Rights have been advocating such a law, unsuccessfully. It is possible that concerns about the role of SMS in the crisis situation may reopen debate on electronic hate speech.

Ethnic incitement was not limited to SMS messages. Bloggers discovered that their comment threads were becoming increasingly hostile and featured many hateful sentiments, sometimes expressed in tribal languages so as to be understandable only to members of that group. Daudi Were's post on January 4, 2008, outlining the guidelines for commenting on his site, left little doubt about the content he was being forced to moderate:

> I am not here to spoon feed you or even debate with you what does or does not make valid commentary. My younger cousins who are just out of their teens and about to join high school know the difference between intellectual and valid commentary and hate speech. So do you. I will not enter into a lengthy debate on whether your comment, that we should "finish" this or that tribe is valid because of some socio-economic-political-historical injustice you quote. For crying out loud our country is burning. You fuel the flames here and I will burn your comment, i.e. I will delete it. (Were, 2008b)

Moderation problems became so intense on Mashada, Kenya's leading bulletin board site, that David Kobia had to take extraordinary steps. He shut down the site for a cooling-off period and briefly explored paying moderators to continue their work, as they were quickly resigning after trying to cope with floods of hateful messages. On January 29, he shut the forum down entirely, noting "Facilitating civil discussions and debates has become virtually impossible" (Kobia; cited in Hersman, 2008b).

A few days later, Kobia launched a new site, I Have No Tribe. Like Ushahidi, it was centered on a Google Maps mashup. However, this mashup showed posts from Kenyans around the country and around the world wrestling with the statement, "I have no tribe.... I am Kenyan." Kobia redirected the Mashada site to the new site, and it rapidly filled with comments—both combative and supportive—as well poems and prayers. Kobia reopened the forums on February 14, 2008, having elegantly demonstrated that one possible response to destructive speech online is to encourage constructive speech.

CONCLUSIONS

In the wake of the political crisis, bloggers found themselves playing unusual roles in Kenyan media environment. Bloggers took on the role of reporters, first documenting the election process, then the violence, protests, and police response. Blogs became spaces for discussion of the future of the nation and for practical discussions of ways to document the crisis. Techniques and software developed by the Kenyan citizen media community, including the Ushahidi platform, are likely to be useful in future crises, inside and outside Kenya.

While the reaction to the election crisis was a proud moment for Kenyan bloggers, it also served as a stark reminder that communications tools can be used to spread strife as well as to promote harmony. Mobile phones allowed reporting from rural locations, but also permitted messages spreading ethnic hatred. Website operators found themselves moderating hateful messages and struggling to maintain online civility. The intense pressure of the post-election political environment showed the potential power of citizen media in crisis areas but offers no definitive answer as to whether this power is more likely to be used to promote peace or to disseminate strife.

REFERENCES

AFP (2008) "Text messages used as a tool of hate in Kenya." *AFP*, 19 February.

Afrigator (2008) *Top ranked blogs in Africa.*

Afrol News (2008) *Telkom Kenya joins stiff mobile phone market.*

Hersman, E. (2008a) "Activist mapping" [PowerPoint presentation]. *White African.*

Hersman, E. (2008b) "Mashada forums: Kenyas first digital casualty." 29 January. *White African.*

Kenya Unlimited (2006) *Kaybees winners 2006.*

Manji, F. (2008) "Remarks" made at the *Fill the Gap conference*, Amsterdam, Netherlands, 12 January.

Miniwatts Marketing Group (2008) *Internet world stats: Usage and population statistics.*

Nyanchama, M. (2007) "Diaspora has deep pockets to build country." *East African Standard*, 17 April.

Okolloh, O. (2007a) "Election results update 12:30 pm Dec 28." *Kenyan Pundit*, 28 December.

Okolloh, O. (2007b) "Media blackout announced." *Kenyan Pundit*, 30 December.

Okolloh, O. (2008a) "Update Jan 3 11pm." *Kenyan Pundit*, 3 January.

Okolloh, O. (2008b) "Post-media blackout update Jan 1 4:30pm." *Kenyan Pundit*, 1 January.

Querengesser, T. (2008) "Hate speech SMS offenders already tracked." *The Nation* (Nairobi), 1 March.

Rotich, J. (2008a) "Bloggers for Kenya, and hope in Jamhuri Park." *Afromusing*, 14 January.

Rotich, J. (2008b) "Quick update from Eldoret, Rift Valley." *Afromusing*, 1 January.

Wainaina, B. (2008) "No country for old hatreds." *The New York Times*, 6 January.

Were, D. (2007a) "Voting experience—Kenyan election 2007." *Mental Acrobatics*, 27 December.

Were, D. (2007b) "Citizen media—Kenyan Election 2007." *Mental Acrobatics*, 30 December.

Were, D. (2008a) "ODM rally 3rd Jan—Kenyan election 2007." *Mental Acrobatics*, 3 January.

Were, D. (2008b) "Site administration—ground rules on comments." *Mental Acrobatics*, 4 January.

Zuckerman, E. (2008) "Meet the bridgebloggers." *Public Choice, 134*(1), 47–65.

CHAPTER SIXTEEN

Citizen Journalism as Social Networking: Reporting the 2007 Australian Federal Election

AXEL BRUNS, JASON WILSON, AND BARRY SAUNDERS

The 2007 Australian federal election campaign will be remembered for a number of reasons. It was only the second time that a sitting prime minister lost his seat. It was the first time those voters born after 1988 had experienced a change in government, after the Howard Government had been in charge since 1996. It also brought about the Australian Labor Party's domination of all territory, state, and federal parliaments. Beyond this, it also marked the beginning of a transformation of the Australian mediasphere, signaling a substantially greater role for online and citizen media. This trend was previously observed during the 2004 US presidential campaign, but the 2007 election saw the trend arrive here with its own uniquely Australian inflection.

Such dramatic changes, of course, do not come out of the blue. Long-established news and commentary blogs, such as Road to Surfdom, JohnQuiggin.com, or TimBlair.net, had gained some prominence in Australia already. Public intellectual and citizen journalism sites from On Line Opinion to Crikey were instrumental in developing an alternative public sphere, and many interested citizens were prepared to seek them out in the years preceding 2007. The potential of online developments had also been well recognized by some key players in the media and journalism industries. Crikey was sold to corporate media interests in 2005, Road to Surfdom's Tim Dunlop accepted a position in News.com.au's line-up of opinion blogs, and Tim Blair combined his blogging with prominent mainstream media work. Over at the national broadcaster, ABC Online gradually developed a range of experiments in citizen media, including expanded discussion and commentary functions for its readers and a number of blog-style opinion sections involving staff and guest writers.

2007 saw a further broadening of citizen journalism approaches to the coverage of Australian federal politics, however, and it is possible to point to signs of a marked impact on the Australian mediasphere of such extended citizen involvement in political coverage, debate, discussion, and deliberation. This was discernible in a number of ways. Overall, there was an increase in audience and attention (not always laudatory) for political bloggers. In particular, specialist bloggers—economists, psephologists (or poll specialists), and "insider" political gossip sites—came to the attention of media professionals and political junkies. Their credibility was enhanced during the election, arguably at the expense of paid commentators in the mainstream media (see Bruns, 2008b). Australia's first successful crowdsourced citizen journalism projects were also run during the campaign, including our industry linkage project Youdecide2007, run at Queensland University of Technology in collaboration with public broadcaster SBS, On Line Opinion, and Cisco Systems. Perhaps most tellingly, the winning party, the ALP, and its successful prime ministerial candidate, Kevin Rudd, were themselves seen to embrace social media, online forums, and feedback, while the outgoing Liberal Party refused to engage with online campaigning beyond a very limited use of YouTube. This chapter will examine these manifestations of change in Australia's mediasphere through the prism of the 2007 campaign and will offer a close account of our citizen journalism project, Youdecide2007.

THE "OZ" VERSUS THE BLOGS

The clearest indication that political bloggers were having an impact on political reporting by 2007 was a negative one: the new readiness of mainstream media commentators to go after bloggers who had criticized them in the editorial pages of newspapers. There was some provocation: internationally, citizen journalism's first target is often the established mainstream media, and Australian political bloggers and citizen journalists made great sport in the election lead-in of analyzing and critiquing mainstream commentary. The prominence of some of these political news and commentary blogs in Australian election coverage can be explained in the context of Australia's broader mediascape. For an affluent industrial nation with a vigorous democratic culture, Australia has a comparatively underdeveloped mediasphere. This is due in part to the unusual distribution of the majority of the Australian population into a handful of geographically remote major centers, separated by sparsely populated countryside. Australia constitutes not one, but perhaps four or five more or less separate media markets. Addressing all of these markets sustainably at a national level is possible only for a very few major commercial media operators. For this reason, then, ownership of Australia's commercial print media is largely concentrated in the hands of only two major corporations: Rupert Murdoch's News Ltd., and John Fairfax Holdings. Most Australian state capitals have access to only one major local newspaper, and Reporters sans Frontières regularly ranks Australia relatively low in its annual Press Freedom Index—the country ranked 28th in the 2007 edition, up from 41st in 2005 (Reporters sans Frontières, 2007).

The breadth and depth of political reporting in Australia is limited by these structural factors. Anecdotally, there is also evidence that the relatively small band of serious political journalists at national and state levels—aware of their precarious situation—tend to form relatively close working arrangements with long-lived state and federal governments. Such arrangements sometimes give the appearance of "source capture"—they ensure a steady flow of political information but can inhibit more critical political reporting. Additionally, media proprietors and editors themselves may also pursue specific political agendas, which affect the framing of their staff's work. In a small market, unbalanced reporting by significant players can significantly affect the democratic process. Inadequacies of political coverage are highlighted especially at times of heightened political awareness—most of all, during state and federal elections.

The emergence of blogs and similar citizen journalism and citizen commentary sites as alternative sources of political information and commentary during the 2007 federal election campaign was motivated to some degree by such deficits. While (as is evident from opinion polls and the eventual election results) a significant majority of the Australian population had already committed to a change of government several months prior to the election date, some news outlets and journalists seemed less enthused. In some newspapers, political allegiances and the depth of personal connections between government sources and many leading commentators combined to generate coverage that actively supported the Howard government. In particular, reporting of opinion polls in *The Australian* was consistently optimistic about the government's chances of staying in office—much more so than the polling data seemed to warrant; consequently, the paper served as the lightning rod for blogosphere criticism of media bias.

The persistence and vigor of this grassroots criticism appears to have had a surprisingly strong impact on the news media in general, and on *The Australian* in particular: on July 12, 2007, the paper published an extraordinary article that openly attacked bloggers and other "sheltered academics and failed journalists who would not get a job on a real newspaper" (*The Australian*, July 12, 2007).

This was ostensibly for daring to voice their disagreement with *The Australian*'s own journalists' and pundits' interpretation of the political mood of the electorate. The piece, understood to have been authored by the paper's editor-in-chief, Chris Mitchell, denounced grassroots online commentators as "out of touch with ordinary views" and culminated in the remarkable statement that "unlike [daily political email newsletter] Crikey, we understand Newspoll because we own it."

Such reactions by journalists and commentators may only serve to illustrate veteran blogger-journalist Dan Gillmor's well-known claim that "my readers know more than I do" (2003, p. vi). On a range of topics—opinion polling and election speculation included—it is now possible to find specialist bloggers and citizen journalists providing deeper insights than is possible for a journalist operating under the pressures of the modern newsroom. While citizen journalists are often depicted as amateurs attempting to do the work of professionals, in this case there was the spectacle of professional journalists (but manifestly amateur psephologists) criticizing expert election analysts who happened to share their insights through the medium of blogging. In the end it was the bloggers under attack, rather than *The Australian*'s scribes, who called the election result correctly, from a long way out.

HYPERLOCAL CITIZEN REPORTING—YOUDECIDE2007

Incidents such as this one reproduce international experience that suggests that bloggers have no trouble producing political commentary that is at least the equal of their industrial counterparts. From the 2007 campaign forward, it is safe to say that a group of bloggers has been recognized by a politically literate audience (and their mainstream "competition") as providing a legitimate source of alternative political commentary. Nonetheless, what is often perceived as the Achilles heel of citizen journalism is an inability to conduct investigative or first-hand reporting. A number of projects have recently addressed this problem, with varying success: the U.S.-based Assignment Zero was described as "a highly satisfying failure" (Howe, 2007), while the German MyHeimat.de appears to have been thoroughly successful in attracting strong communities of contributors in many of the geographic areas that it covers, even to the point of being able to generate print versions of its content that are distributed free of charge to households in selected German cities.

Building on MyHeimat's principles, Youdecide2007.org (YD07)—a collaboration between researchers at Queensland University of Technology and media practitioners at the public service broadcaster SBS, the public opinion site On Line Opinion, and technology company Cisco Systems—was developed as a dedicated space for a specifically hyperlocal coverage of the 2007 election campaign in each of Australia's 150 electorates, from the urban sprawls of Sydney, Melbourne, and Brisbane to the sparsely populated remote regions of outback Australia.

While Australian news and politics blogs such as Larvatus Prodeo and Possums Pollytics are constructed around specific intellectual interests and pursuits, Youdecide2007 (not to be confused with News Ltd.'s election site You Decide 2007 or similarly named sites in the United States covering the presidential primaries) took a very different approach to its attempt to foster Australian citizen journalism. Youdecide2007 employed a hyperlocal methodology to its election coverage: it provided contributors with the tools and platform to cover their local electoral races for a wider audience. This is particularly appropriate to the Westminster-style Australian electoral system, which (for the lower house) ultimately breaks down into 150 individual contests for local electorates.

YD07 provided training materials for would-be citizen journalists and encouraged them to contribute electorate profiles, interview candidates, and conduct vox-pops with citizens in their local area. The site developed a strong following, especially in its home state of Queensland, and its interviewers influenced national public debate by uncovering the sometimes controversial personal views of mainstream and fringe candidates. At the same time, the success of YD07 was limited by external constraints determined by campaign timing and institutional frameworks. As part of a continuing action research cycle, lessons learned from Youdecide2007 were also translated into a further iteration of the project, QldDecides.com, which covered local government elections in the Australian state of Queensland in March 2008, and developments subsequent to these elections.

Youdecide2007 contributors were encouraged to interview their local candidates (including but not limited to those of the major parties), conduct vox-pops with local voters, and report on the issues central to their own electorate; these reports were posted on the site in text, audio, and video format. Additional material, some of which transcended individual electorates, was also prepared by YD07 staffers, who also appeared on a number of state and national radio broadcasts and in a weekly election talk show on Brisbane's community channel Briz31. In essence, Youdecide2007 was therefore a hybrid or professional-amateur ("pro-am") citizen journalism project, designed to stimulate grassroots, citizen-generated coverage of the political contest by using institutional backing to put in place a sophisticated framework for citizen-journalistic activity.[1]

While YD07 had a relatively short run-up to the election, it nonetheless managed to attract citizen journalists in roughly one third of all Australian electorates, including many that had been largely overlooked by election coverage in the national press. In fact, the site's most active contributor, Kevin Rennie, reported from the remote Western Australian electorate of Kalgoorlie. This placed it well as a hyperlocal complement to the national coverage of both industrial journalism and topical citizen journalism, and enabled it to cover stories and feature candidates otherwise excluded from journalistic coverage.

In a number of cases such reporting became newsworthy on a wider level: Youdecide2007's perhaps best-known story was an interview with the Liberal member for the Queensland seat of Herbert, Peter Lindsay, who blamed young people's "financial illiteracy" for the unaffordability of housing being experienced by many younger voters. "I remember my own case," he claimed. "We sat on milk crates in the lounge room until we could afford chairs. We had makeshift shelves to put ornaments on and so on, but you did that in those days. You waited until you could—you didn't live beyond your means and you didn't try to keep up with the Joneses. Things were more responsible" (Wilson, 2007a). These comments also became the basis for a question in parliament to PM John Howard by Opposition Leader Kevin Rudd, who asked, "apart from the milk crate solution, what is your plan to deal with Australia's housing affordability crisis or is it simply to blame the states?" (Wilson, 2007b).

Though extraordinary, this incident highlights the potential inherent in hyperlocal and other forms of citizen-journalistic news reporting, especially where citizen journalists are able to build on a solid set of resources and tools for their work. In a political context, it makes elected representatives and rival candidates more directly accountable to reporters who act in a double role as both citizens and journalists—and this similarly applies for fields other than politics as well—and, by relying on a broader community of citizen journalists, it is able to uncover a wider range of stories than is accessible to the limited workforce of the journalism industry. Some of these stories, in turn, may prove to be of significance beyond the local environment, but even where they are of interest to locals only, such citizen journalism offers an important addition to the material available from the mainstream press.

Throughout its active life, the site attracted around 2,000 registered users, who submitted some 230 stories. We received stories from over one third of Australia's 150 electorates, and citizen journalists submitted print, video, audio, and photographic materials. At its peak, the site attracted over 12,000 readers a week and received more traffic than all but one of the major political parties' sites. It broke stories that were picked up by the national press and was able to send a correspondent to the National Tally Room on election night. Although ambitions for such services tend to be high, Youdecide2007 was considered a successful effort as a citizen journalism service, especially in the Australian context, where little has been attempted in this area.

JOURNALISM AS SOCIAL NETWORKING

One of the important outcomes of the project was in discovering what the work of facilitating citizen journalism consists of. Given the "limitations of the crowd" (Simons, 2008) and the need for "go-to" people (Howe, 2007) to keep such services on an even keel, it was important to learn more about the role of "professionals" in citizen journalism's "pro-am" equation. Despite the conflict between professional journalists and bloggers noted earlier, by thinking through the work of facilitating a community of news and content makers, it is possible to transcend the stale "pro-am" dichotomy by pointing out ways in which professional practice is changing in order to accommodate citizen-generated content.

We discovered that this new model of journalism—which we might call "journalism as social networking"—takes place in four dimensions. Although these dimensions of practice are distinct from one another, they share one aim: promoting, maintaining, and extending an active community of citizen journalists. Firstly, *content work* includes editing citizen content (for quality and legal issues) and producing pro "seed" content to draw in "produsers" (users able to and interested in taking on content creation roles; see Bruns, 2008a) to a news service. While publishing amateur, citizen content will be a major part of the rationale for any citizen journalism service, "pro" content can draw in readers, ensure a steady flow of content for the service, and provide "models of practice" for citizen reporters. Though ideals of free speech are often also part of the inspiration for citizen journalism experiments, they do not take place in a legal vacuum. Local publishing laws, which are often complex and uneven, still often apply to online publishing, and not all jurisdictions guarantee free speech in the same way that, say, the United States does. Australia's defamation laws provide an example of legislation that restricts what can be published—amateur journalists are often not fully apprised of the application of such laws, and require guidance for their own protection, and the long-term viability of the service. Users also often welcome editorial input on issues of quality.

Secondly, *networking* involves both making and maintaining contacts in the mainstream and independent media, and procuring and republishing content across the networked news environment. Although false dichotomies between mainstream and citizen journalism are often posed, the best way to attract a community to citizen journalism services is to promote the services in the mainstream media, since any media appearances attract more users and contributions. Being able to syndicate material in other online forums also helps to draw people to services and means that contributors get more readers or viewers and more value from their participation. Appropriate licensing models are important here, and Creative

Commons licensing allows extensive republication. Most important of all, though, is a willingness to go beyond the idea that citizen and mainstream journalism are opposed to one another, and instead to consider them as elements of an ecology of "networked journalism," where a range of professional and amateur contributors and industrial and independent outlets together form the diverse totality of contemporary news production.

Thirdly, *tech work* involves both running the online services and using appropriate technologies to syndicate content, communicate with users, and assess the performance of the service. Obviously, citizen journalism itself is often internet-driven and necessarily requires the ability to design, use, and maintain an online platform for journalism. But those operating citizen journalism services may also be involved in republishing content to services like Flickr or YouTube, communicating with users via Skype or Instant Messaging, and obtaining and processing reliable site metrics. In a small team, a wide range of basic technological skills will be required, and this is even more true where the generation of multimedia "pro" content is necessary.

Fourthly, and most important of all, *community work* involves gathering and serving an online newsmaking community. This means not only bringing users to a community, but serving their needs and rewarding their investment of time and skills in a particular service. Users may require guidance in using technology or writing stories, and communities may require staff to lead or moderate discussions. Successful services will be those that take special care to establish good relations with the relatively small number of users who are regular or prolific contributors—in a very real sense, these "super-contributors" are even more vital to the health of citizen journalism communities than staff are. Given the international trend toward mainstream news organizations harnessing user-generated content, this more community-oriented form of journalism, which we mapped during the Australian election, is likely to become more important in the future. It is our belief that journalism education needs to start taking some of the lessons of citizen journalism projects on board.

In spite of its achievements, Youdecide2007 cannot be described as an unqualified success; it serves in the first place as a proof of concept for further hyperlocal citizen journalism experiments. This is hardly surprising, as most produsage sites and projects in citizen journalism and elsewhere take years to generate a sustainable, committed community with shared values and protocols, while YD07 operated for just under three months between its launch and the election date. This brief pre-election lifespan left little time for the site to establish a reputation that would have allowed its contributors' work to be picked up more regularly by mainstream news outlets (including project partner SBS), so that most of the mainstream media coverage of the site occurred through third-party mentions (as in the case of Kevin Rudd's "crate-gate" question in federal parliament) or through reports which focused on the Youdecide2007 project itself, rather than on individual political stories published on the site by its citizen journalists.

However, by engaging in original reporting that fills a gap left open by the national news media, hyperlocal citizen journalism sites are able to position themselves outside of conventional "citizens vs. journalists" frameworks altogether: they operate from a third place that is neither necessarily in opposition to nor supportive of the mainstream journalism industry, and neither limits itself to analysis and commentary only nor avoids extended discussions of topics of relevance to its contributors. A well-established network of committed citizen journalists operating across the nation would appear to be able to make a significant contribution to Australian journalism, and it is likely that further phases in the research project that produced Youdecide2007 will pursue such possibilities.

PARTICIPATORY TRANSFORMATIONS IN POLITICAL COMMUNICATION

In the long run, perhaps the most significant shift to occur during the 2007 election was a move to new, online, socially inflected models of political communication. It is notable in this context that the victorious Australian Labor Party (ALP) dipped more than a toe into the waters of more consultative, two-way models of political communication. By various means—starting Facebook pages, offering the facility for comments and questions on a central "Kevin07" website, and direct methods such as targeted emails, the ALP dominated an area of campaigning that Liberal/National Coalition strategists either ignored or handled poorly. Whether or not this new direction in campaigning translates into a more consultative and deliberative approach to governance and policy formation remains to be seen.

Although the ALP's embrace of online and social campaigning methods may not have been decisive in the election, it did help to underscore the ALP's central campaign message of "new leadership." Significantly, the internet and ICTs themselves became campaign issues during the election, with the ALP promising laptop computers for every high school student, and more importantly offering to fix the country's antiquated broadband infrastructure. This raft of 21st-century issues, along with the promise of generational change, were accented positively by the employment of new modes of political communication.

It is unlikely that the ALP will similarly dominate the online area in future campaigns, however, and already the Liberals are moving to improve their online performance. Along with the ALP's own campaign, progressive online campaigning organizations such as GetUp[2] worked to organize online and shift the issues agenda through progressive campaigning.

While political allegiances on both sides may change by 2010–2011, we would expect that both sides of the pro-am divide will once again battle to establish their leadership in interpreting opinion polls and taking the overall political pulse of the nation. Indeed, continuing financial strain for commercial news organizations and growing public recognition of citizen journalism outlets may combine to shift the advantage in this conflict further toward the bloggers. At the same time, projects such as Youdecide2007 also indicate that compromise is possible, especially, as we have noted, for projects that operate at a larger, nationwide scale and aim to advance beyond commentary to do first-hand reporting. For us, the presence of quasi-journalistic staff, addressing the four dimensions of pro-am work that we have identified, appears to be necessary to the success of citizen journalism. Enterprising news organizations in Australia are now taking their first steps toward experimenting with such pro-am models, and we would expect them to have reached a level of substantial maturity by the time of the next regular federal election.

Ultimately, such developments stand a chance of overcoming some of the structural deficits that have been a long-time feature of the Australian media landscape. By incorporating a greater level of citizen-sourced content, they may be able to increase the diversity of coverage and commentary in Australian political journalism. By providing the tools and infrastructure for journalistic activity, they may be able to generate better reporting, especially from the chronically underserved regional and rural areas outside of the major Australian capitals. Perhaps most critically, by injecting citizen participation into political news, they might be able to break up the "echo chamber" effect that limits the variety of perspectives covered by the Canberra press gallery. Journalists and news organizations that seek to delay or insulate themselves from such changes may prove to be increasingly left out of mainstream political debate, while those who actively pursue such new opportunities may well turn out to be the opinion (and market) leaders of tomorrow.

NOTES

1. It should also be noted in this context that there was no overt commercial impetus for any of the industry partners to be involved in this project. SBS's and On Line Opinion's participation was driven largely by their respective missions to stimulate diversity and generate quality in Australian political debate, while Cisco Systems participated in the project presumably on the understanding that an increased use of online media for political debate would have beneficial, indirect flow-on effects for its sales of networking technology.
2. As of July 2008, and during the writing of this paper, one of the authors, Jason Wilson, became E Democracy Director at GetUp.

REFERENCES

The Australian (2007) "History a better guide than bias." *The Australian*, 12 July.

Bahnisch, Mark (2007) "Government Gazette fights back." *Larvatus Prodeo*, 11 July.

Bruns, Axel (2008a) *Blogs, Wikipedia, Second Life, and beyond: from production to produsage.* New York: Peter Lang.

Bruns, Axel (2008b) "Citizen journalism in the 2007 Australian federal election." Paper presented at the AMIC 2008 conference: *Convergence, Citizen Journalism, and Social Change*, Brisbane, 26–28 March.

Gillmor, Dan (2003) "Foreword." In S. Bowman & C. Willis, *We media: how audiences are shaping the future of news and information.* Reston, VA: The Media Center at the American Press Institute.

Howe, Jeff (2007) "Crowdsourcing: the importance of community." *Crowdsourcing*, 17 June.

Milne, Glenn (2008) "ALP's secret web weapon." *The Australian*, 7 July.

Ramsey, Alan (2007) "Polls apart at the sausage sizzle." *Australian Politics*, 14 July.

Reporters sans Frontières (2007) "Worldwide press freedom index 2007." 16 October.

Shanahan, Dennis (2007) "Rudd 'relaxed' about Howard's poll comeback." *The Australian*, 10 July.

Simons, Margaret (2008) "Journalism: the limitations of the crowd." *Creative Economy*, 15 February.

Thurman, Neil (2008) "Forums for citizen journalists? Adoption of user generated content initiatives by online news media." *New Media and Society*, *10*, 139–157.

Wilson, Jason (2007a) "Interview with Peter Lindsay MP (LP, Herbert)." *Youdecide2007*, 10 September.

Wilson, Jason (2007b) "Youdecide2007 influences national debate!" *Youdecide2007*, 19 September.

Wilson, Jason (2007c) *Interview: Camilla Cooke.* 18 December.

CHAPTER SEVENTEEN

Crisis Alert: Barack Obama Meets A Citizen Journalist

TOM FIEDLER

Although the battle for the Democratic presidential nomination raged furiously on that April 2008 night, Barack Obama felt he was in safe harbor at a campaign fundraiser near San Francisco, off limits to the press and attended only by admiring contributors. The critical Pennsylvania primary loomed just ahead, yet the Illinois senator responded casually and bluntly when asked to describe that working-class state's small-town voters.

They have been neglected and beaten down by their leaders, Obama began. "So it's not surprising that they get bitter; they cling to guns or religion or antipathy to people who aren't like them" (Fowler, 2008).

And so began "bittergate," a campaign dustup that gave Obama's rival, New York Senator Hillary Clinton, a potent weapon in her effort to portray Obama as an elitist. A chastened Obama later pled guilty to clumsy speaking—uncharacteristic of this painstakingly careful wordsmith—but a clumsiness induced by the assumption that no campaign reporters lurked among that privileged crowd.

But Obama overlooked a different conduit to the outside world—a conduit in the person of Mayhill Fowler, who attended the fundraiser as a contributor and avowed Obama partisan. Fowler also happened to be a neophyte blogger for OffTheBus.net, a website birthed by *Huffington Post* founder Arianna Huffington and New York University journalism professor Jay Rosen as an experiment in on-line "citizen journalism." Fowler, despite her partisanship, had been enlisted by the site to cover (without pay) the senator's campaign.

After four days of wrestling with her dual roles as citizen journalist and Obama partisan, Fowler reported the candidate's ill-chosen words in one of her folksy blogs, albeit wrapped gently amid other campaign musings. Then she watched in a mixture of horror and pride as the words leapt from the web and ignited a political firestorm that engulfed his campaign, labeled him an elitist, and nearly knocked the sheen of inevitability from his campaign.

"I'm 61," Fowler told *The New York Times*'s reporter Katharine Q. Seelye later. "I can't believe I would be one of the people who's changing the world of media" (Seelye, 2008).

Indeed she is, for better or worse. Obama, despite this episode, survived his collision with the blogosphere and made history as the United States's first African American president. But even as an historical footnote, the "bittergate" episode, as it came to be called, illustrated just one of the myriad ways in which the so-called new media—the catch-all words for internet communication—upended the 2008 presidential campaign and raised questions about journalism's place in it.

Matt Bai, *The New York Times Sunday Magazine*'s political writer, had it right when he said of the internet's role in politics: "This changes everything."[1]

Indeed it did; historians may point to 2008 and declare it the first campaign of the internet age. For candidate Obama, the internet's impact on the process was far more positive than not. His campaign modeled how the web could be used to find supporters—especially the young with no ties to organized political parties—and raise vast sums (more than $640 million by Election Day, an astonishing total). Text messaging and social-networking tools like Facebook, MySpace, and YouTube enabled the candidate to bypass the news media's filters and communicate directly to supporters, and they to communicate with each other. It became clear that the old ways of campaigning—the need for endorsements from party bosses, to pay fealty to deep-pocketed (and favor-seeking) donors, to pander to special-interest groups, and to flatter the oligarchs of the press—became in 2008 as anachronistic as the smoke-filled room.

Of all these changes, however, none is more important than what the internet is doing to journalism as we have known it for generations. Up for grabs, in fact, is the very definition of the term "journalist."

BLOGGING ENTERS THE MAINSTREAM

In campaigns as recent as four years before, Mayhill Fowler—as an unpaid and admittedly partisan participant—couldn't find herself in the same sentence with the word journalist, even with the adjective "citizen" in front of it. But as "bittergate" showed in 2008, you don't need a printing press or a broadcast license to join an army of people determined to report what they see. The foot soldiers in this army don't need journalistic experience, ethical training, or even expense accounts. To become a blogger requires little more than access to a computer, an internet connection, and a web address.

There's something to be said for this. Howard Dean, former governor of Vermont, presidential candidate and chairman of the Democratic Party in the months leading up to the 2008 election, described the internet as "the most democratic invention since Gutenberg and the printing press; the Internet is Gutenberg on steroids."

That's *democrat* as in egalitarian. Dean is right that the web creates a game in which everybody can play and all players appear equal. It enabled Mayhill Fowler's blog to have the kind of impact that was previously the province of the press's big guns, which was precisely the vision when celebrity-activist Arianna Huffington, founder of the on-line opinion site *Huffington Post*, teamed with Professor Jay Rosen to create OffTheBus.net. The name was a twist on the label given decades ago to campaign reporters as the boys on the bus. Their idea was to cobble together a bunch of political junkies—all self-supporting—who would cover the campaign from the vantage point of those who didn't have seats on those buses.

But Huffington recognized that if the volunteer bloggers posting to her site were to compete with the sites staffed by mainstream journalists, she would need to strive for similar standards of professionalism. She hired such veteran journalists as Thomas Edsall, recently retired after a distinguished career at *The Washington Post*, and Betsy Morgan, former general manager of CBSNews.com, to put such standards in place. Morgan's former boss told *The New York Times* that moves of this type are significant in what they bode for the future.

"New media companies weren't doing this before," said Larry Kramer, a former CBS executive. "I think it shows that traditional media companies are further down the road than people think" in terms of "being very helpful for how new media plans to expand" (Carter, 2007).

In addition, a rapidly increasing number of sites are launching on the web, staffed by journalists trained in and adhering to traditional practices. Among the longest running are Salon and Slate (now owned by *The Washington Post*'s parent company). And one of the newest practicing this form of crossover journalism is Politico.com, backed by Washington, DC, businessman Robert Allbritton.

Politico debuted in January 2007, edited by two of *The Washington Post*'s most prominent political writers, John F. Harris and Jim VandeHei, who had been lured away by Allbritton with a promise of long-term financial backing. Its start-up staff also included veterans of such mainstream publications as *The New York Times*,

Time magazine, *The Philadelphia Inquirer,* Cox newspapers, *The Baltimore Sun,* and *USA Today,* to list a few.

Although in its mission statement the on-line publication said it would push against the constraints of newspapers that "tend to muffle personality, humor [and] accumulated insight," it also promised to practice journalism that "insists on the primacy of facts over ideology." Perhaps auguring things to come, Politico also publishes a real newspaper of the same name aimed at a Capitol Hill and K Street audience in Washington, DC.

TOO MUCH DEMOCRACY?

But Politico and the handful like it that adhere to journalism's traditional ethos are more the exception than the rule. Far more common are the newer entries into the process with varying credentials—if any—to expound upon the political process or the issues that arise within it. Quite suddenly a dizzying array of contributors with oddly named blogs vie with the traditional press to get the attention of voters. They are the free agents of the media taking every advantage of their egalitarian access.

But this carries with it profound implications, many of them troubling. Do Americans actually want their political information to be truly democratic, where every participant's voice is to be treated as the equal of all others? Where something gleaned from the "old" media of major newspapers, wire services, and networks is treated no differently from something gleaned from a citizen journalist's blog on the Web?

A British journalist took aim at the notion of an egalitarian Web in an article published in a trade-union magazine. The writer, Donnacha DeLong, ridiculed the notion that a blogger with no particular credentials should be accorded the same credibility as a professional journalist's reporting and commentary. "It's like saying anyone can play for Manchester United," DeLong wrote, referring to England's powerhouse soccer franchise. "In one of the main examples given to explain Web 2.0, Wikipedia replaces Britannica Online. Is that the kind of democracy we want—where anyone can determine the information that the public can access, regardless of their level of knowledge, expertise or agenda?" (cited in Weinberger, 2007a).

DeLong's reference to Wikipedia bears exploring. Wikipedia is the wildly popular internet encyclopedia that proudly operates on the idea that there is more wisdom to be found in its crowds of anonymous readers than in the brains of editors and academics. More than 700 new entries are made daily to Wikipedia, with few restrictions as to who can create them. Every entry is subject to review by every other reader, however, and if one or more of those readers spots a factual error—or at least perceives an error—that reader can jump in and change or challenge it.

As Wikipedia's co-founder Jimmy Wales envisioned it, an entry could start with a simple skeleton of information—for example, the name of a notable person with birth date, hometown, education, and profession. Then as others came to the page with even more information about that person, they could add other pieces until a fully fleshed-out person emerged. In short, the crowd can contribute more than any single individual.

The concept is certainly brilliant—except for this weakness: the accuracy of any entry depends on the quality of the information that those crowd members bring and their collective good will. In other words, it assumes a crowd of "reasonable people" who will create and edit the entries.

Sadly, that isn't always the case. Wikipedia's emergence as a credible source of information was badly damaged shortly after its launch when someone hiding behind an opaque username rewrote the entry about John Seigenthaler, Sr., a prominent journalist at *USA Today*, *The Nashville Tennessean*, and a former aide to late Attorney General and US Senator Robert F. Kennedy. The bogus entry stated that Seigenthaler may have played a role in the assassinations of Robert in 1968 and President John F. Kennedy in 1963. It also said that Seigenthaler had lived in the Soviet Union for 13 years until 1984 and upon his return started one of the nation's largest public relations companies.

None of this was true. Yet it remained posted on Wikipedia for four months and was picked up and reproduced without change on two other websites. Finally Seigenthaler's son, a reporter for a network news organization, found it and warned his father, who had the false information removed and a correction posted in its place. But there is no liability: Wikipedia and similar sites have been insulated by law against libel suits arising out of information they carry.

The distinguished journalist recounted his experience with Wikipedia in a column for *USA Today*, where he concluded with a story: "When I was a child, my mother lectured me on the evils of 'gossip.' She held a feather pillow and said, "If I tear this open, the feathers will fly to the four winds, and I could never get them back in the pillow. That's how it is when you spread mean things about people."

"For me," Seigenthaler continued, "that pillow is a metaphor for Wikipedia" (Seigenthaler, 2005).

Getting things wrong—and escaping responsibility for it—is just one of the problems of this democratized internet. Author Cass R. Sunstein, in his book *Infotopia*, also faults the internet for making it too easy for people to seek out and support those websites and bloggers who already share their views. Liberals gather with liberals and conservatives gather with conservatives in "echo chambers" and "information cocoons" where objective information is the first casualty, he says (Sunstein, 2006).

Fortunately, this is not an either/or paradigm where the consumer's choice of information is relegated to the "old" media with its limitations or the "new" media with its many flaws. The web (with examples such as Politico.com) and the blogosphere are increasingly populated by writers and readers who not only represent more mainstream—as opposed to extreme—opinions, but who also subscribe to the values of traditional journalism.

Matt Bai, the *Times's* political writer who has specialized in the new media's impact on campaigns, likens the blogosphere to a teenager who is fast maturing as he or she approaches adulthood. Bai told me in an interview that as recently as 2003 the online conversations were shaped by "early adapters and they tended to come from the outer edges of society." Little wonder that the opinions batted about back then reflected youthful exuberance.

By the end of 2005, a survey by the Pew Internet & American Life Project found that 60-something Americans went online to get their news in roughly the same percentages as those Americans in so-called Generation Y, or between 21 and 40 years of age. And at the dawn of the recent campaign, Pew found that 71 percent of American adults used the web to get their news (American Society of Newspaper Editors, 2007).

"In 2008 you have everybody on the Web," Bai said in the interview. "They've changed the nature of the internet community. It has become more diverse, more representative of more constituencies. And the more mainstream the technology becomes, the more mainstream will be the sensibilities of those who use it."

Another factor is at work driving internet news toward the centerline: "old media" is rapidly occupying this new media's space and soaking up much of the audience. The news reports of newspapers, television networks, National Public Radio, local television and local radio stations, and other traditional producers are expanding on the web, even as their historic operations have cut back. Between 2007 and 2008, the online audience for newspaper sites rocketed upward by 16% and now reaches 41% of all internet users. And in a hopeful sign for these traditional media, 29% of the so-called Generation Y visit newspaper sites "regularly" (American Society of Newspaper Editors, 2007, p. 15).

Most of these "old media" sites also host blogs written by their staffers, which provide counterweight—and maybe role models—to the more extreme bloggers. In a typical week during the run-up to the 2008 presidential primary season, the number of visitors to *The New York Times's* political coverage and its blog, The Caucus, far outnumbered the hits on ultra-liberal Daily Kos or the conservative Red State.com. Even the pioneering blog Drudge Report, which has evolved into an aggregator of story links from being a source of sensational scoops, devotes the vast majority of its space to mainstream newspaper and broadcast coverage barely distinguishable from Google News.

Some see this convergence of "old" and "new" media as a win for both sides. Journalism professor Jay Rosen, co-founder of OffTheBus.net and one of the early advocates of web-based journalism, contends that "The rise of blogs does not equal the death of professional journalism. The media world is not a zero-sum game. Increasingly, in fact, the Internet is turning it into a symbiotic ecosystem—in which the different parts feed off one another and the whole thing grows" (Rosen, 2005a).

That optimistic view of the future is gathering force. Rosen has enlisted a half-dozen small newspapers in an experiment where beat reporters are linked to on-line social networks that have grown up around that beat. For example, a local government reporter for a small newspaper (the professional) would enter an alliance of sorts with bloggers who write about that government (the amateurs). The idea, according to Rosen (2005b), is to create a "pro-am" relationship. Although the "old" media can no longer act as gatekeepers of information—it is no longer "sovereign" in Rosen's phrase—he is quick to add that "not sovereign" doesn't mean the traditional press disappears from the process.

But the change in the way news and information is delivered and received will be profound. The old-media model entails a vertical flow of news, produced at the top by mainstream journalists, then passed downward to passive consumers. The new-media model is horizontal, with the consumer in the middle of a flow of information coming from a variety of sources, each bit of information seemingly the equal of every other bit, some of it credible, some of it not. At first glance, this would seem to leave the consumer vulnerable to the vagaries of the mob, unable to distinguish good information from garbage.

But David Weinberger, in his book *Everything Is Miscellaneous*, contends that this horizontal world will become self-regulating and that there will be little need for mediators to screen information for credibility. In Weinberger's example, a consumer sits at the hub while information flows toward him in "packets." If two packets come together and are in agreement, Weinberger, a fellow at Harvard's Berkman Center for the Internet & Society, says they become the sum of the parts, twice as powerful and thus more credible. If the two packets come together but disagree, they cancel each other out. "That's how validation would work," Weinberger says. This model would appear to have a critical vulnerability in that it assumes there to be more "packets" of truth than falsehood (Weinberger, 2007b, pp. 131–140).

But there is reason for Weinberger's confidence that truth will win out, based on what James Surowiecki called the "the wisdom of crowds," which is the central premise of prediction markets. These work on the idea that if only one person places a bet on a certain outcome, the reliability of that forecast is weak at best. An opposite bet by someone else cancels it out entirely. But if vast numbers of people—a crowd—place bets on the same outcome, and each has a monetary stake in being right, the odds are good that the predictions will be accurate.

Scholars would have us believe that the way to snuff out misinformation on the web is to overpower it with correct information. It's a reverse Gresham's Law where the good eventually will drive out the bad.

Still, there remains an obvious problem with this free-market solution: a calumny can survive a long time before it "collides" with correcting information and is driven out. Even then, a percentage of people who read the initial bogus information may never catch the correction. Mark Twain famously observed that "a lie can get half-way round the world while the truth is still tying its shoelaces." On the internet some lies will never be run down by the truth.

But the forces for good appear to be growing on the web at a pace far faster than the other side. Many self-motivated bloggers, for example, are embracing restraint by joining such groups as the Media Bloggers Association, which is attempting to bring more professionalism to the new field. In return for getting access to major events—presidential campaigns, press conferences, and conventions, for example—the MBA asks members to adhere to a statement of principles that could have been lifted from the Society of Professional Journalists' code of ethics. The MBA statement says in part: "We accept the Wikipedia definition of journalism as "a discipline of collecting, verifying, reporting and analyzing information gathered regarding current events, including trends, issues and people." It further encourages bloggers to meet such standards as "honesty, fairness and accuracy, [to] distinguish fact from rumor and speculation [and to] act responsibly and with personal integrity" (Media Bloggers Association, 2008).

But imposing ethical constraints on bloggers addressed just a part of the new-media environment. Consider the impact of YouTube: before it arrived in 2005, a candidate's gaffe—or, more rarely, a brilliant sound bite—might be captured by a news camera and, if deemed worthy by an editor, have a brief, ephemeral life on television before the news would move on and the moment would pass into history.

But today, such moments can be captured by anyone on the typical cell phone, uploaded to YouTube, possibly altered in programs like Photoshop, and passed in ever-widening ripples through Facebook and MySpace pages—all without passing through a single journalistic filter where assessments can be made about credibility, context, relevance, and even fair play. The potential for YouTube to impact politics became clear in a 2006 US Senate campaign in Virginia in which the incumbent seeking re-election, Republican George Allen, became annoyed at finding his campaign appearances videotaped by a young worker for the rival campaign of Democrat Jim Webb. That worker, though born in the United States, was the son of immigrants from India and was dark-skinned. With the young man's camera rolling at an appearance in rural Virginia, Allen's temper got the best of him. He called the crowd's attention to the young man and referred to him as a "macaca," a word considered a racial slur in some parts of the world. (Allen claimed he had made up the word and wasn't aware of its meaning) (Segal, 2006). When the video was uploaded to YouTube it became an instant internet and media sensation, replayed countless times. The rattled Allen campaign never regained its footing and went down to defeat.

Despite the optimistic claims of those who foresee self-correcting mechanisms, what seems certain is that without those journalistic filters, rumors, half-truths, and lies will travel farther and penetrate further into credulous corners of the electorate than ever before. No doubt, too, that as people deputize themselves as news gatherers without understanding—or perhaps while ignoring—the conventions that journalists embrace, ethical corners will be cut. Inevitably, it seems that the definition of "journalist" will be rewritten in the public's mind—much to the dismay of journalism's true practitioners.

But thicker skin and a citizen's code of caveat emptor might be the price to pay for a process that gets much closer to being open to all people than the one that came before. And, in truth, it does no good to protest. During the 2008 presidential campaign, YouTube—which hadn't existed in the previous cycle—had become entrenched enough to co-sponsor a presidential primary debate. Candidates created their own channels where friends and foes alike could see the latest television ad, campaign speech, or blunder by the opponent. In the 10 weeks between the Obama-Biden ticket's nomination and the election on Nov. 4, more than 20 million visitors viewed video on the YouTube channel. Millions of amateurs weighed in with their own "ads," parodies of ads, commentary, or reporting.

A new era is born and, like it or not, the era when influence was reserved for the high clergy of the press—the era when Mayhill Fowler's musings wouldn't have traveled beyond her holiday card list—is no more.

ACKNOWLEDGMENT

An earlier version of this article appeared in the Summer 2008 edition of *Nieman Reports* published by the Nieman Foundation for Journalism at Harvard University. It is adapted here with permission.

NOTE

1. Remarks by Matt Bai, political reporter, *The New York Times Sunday Magazine*, author of *The Argument: Billionaires, bloggers and the battle to remake Democratic Politics* (New York: Penguin, 2007) at a political forum, Graham Center, University of Florida, April 17, 2008.

REFERENCES

American Society of Newspaper Editors (2007) *Growing audience.* American Society of Newspaper Editors. January.

Carter, B. (2007) "CBSNews.com chief to lead a news and blogs site." *The New York Times*, 2 October.

Fowler, M. (2008) "Obama: no surprise that hard-pressed Pennsylvanians turn bitter." *The Huffington Post*, 11 April.

Media Bloggers Association (2008) "About." *Media Bloggers Association.*

Rosen, J. (2005a) "Bloggers vs. journalists is over." *PressThink*, 21 January.

Rosen, J. (2005b) "Bloggers vs. journalists is over." *Blogging, Journalism and Credibility Conference*, 21–22 January, Berkman Center for the Internet & Society, Harvard University.

Seelye, K.Q. (2008) "Blogger is surprised by uproar over Obama story, but not bitter." *The New York Times*, 14 April.

Segal, D. (2006) "True blue, or too blue." *The Washington Post*, 2 April.

Seigenthaler, J. (2005) "A false Wikipedia biography." *USA Today*, 29 November.

Sunstein, C.R. (2006) *Infotopia.* Oxford: Oxford University Press.

Weinberger, D. (2007a) "Is the Web as weak as its weakest link?" *Everything is miscellaneous*, 28 October.

Weinberger, D. (2007b) *Everything is miscellaneous: the power of the new digital disorder* (pp. 131–140). New York: Times Books, Henry Holt and Company.

SECTION THREE: FUTURE CHALLENGES

CHAPTER EIGHTEEN

Citizen Journalism IN THE Global News Arena: China's New Media Critics

STEPHEN D. REESE AND JIA DAI

Optimists about globalization often argue that its processes inexorably yield greater transparency. Powerful pressure is being exerted on journalism itself, they observe, which must now serve multiple global audiences, many of whom are equipped with sufficient information from alternative media to challenge mainstream news reports. Professionals have been placed in dialogue with citizens, the latter with their own forms of expression distributed easily through online platforms. Traditional forms of news reporting, when subjected to such scrutiny and critique, risk appearing problematic.

A particularly compelling example of this practice of journalistic critique is found in China, where in spite of remarkable strides in economic and social development, the likelihood of greater transparency has been brought into question. A highly developed communication structure provides ever-growing capacity for citizen journalism and public deliberation but provokes government attempts at control. The number of Chinese internet users now surpasses that of the United States, but centrally guided human monitoring and computerized filtering continue, leading to direct and self-censorship. Official management of the online environment does not mean, however, that significant openings within the society have not taken place, but they must be understood in the right framework. Here we want to consider this deliberative space with particular interest in the forum it provides for media criticism by citizen journalists. Indeed, we may go so far as to expect that the emerging engagement with journalism by citizens in China will help produce higher standards for press performance. The nationalistic impulse behind citizens' criticism of Western media should—if directed inward—raise expectations for their own news organizations. To see how, we need first to understand the broader context of public communication.

Restrictions on press freedom ebb and flow, but they now take place against this backdrop of globalized connectivity. China has plugged into this communication network in several ways, most visibly when a window on the society was provided by the 2008 Beijing Olympics. According to Victor Cha, director of Asian Studies at Georgetown University, the Olympics created unprecedented social change in one of the world's most rigid systems, change that cannot easily be undone (Cha, 2008). Moves toward greater openness were met by increasing expectations of further liberalization. A similar ratcheting up of expectations has been occurring for some time with citizen expression online, where the vast Chinese social networks, online chat forums, and blogosphere have shown how space can be opened up for public deliberation. Western journalistic reports have often minimized Chinese blogs as a politically insignificant place to "blow off some steam," incapable of yielding any actual social change, but that is giving them too little credit.

"Social responsibility" bloggers, for example, recognized for their contributions in nationwide contests, feature a number of posts and comments that would qualify in any Western definition of public deliberation. They include problem-solving and analytical discussion, with comments that dissent from the original posts. The blogs of celebrities far outnumber them in popularity and traffic, but even a significant percentage of those blogs contain comments and information that could be considered serious discussion about solving public problems (Dai & Reese, 2007). As the Chinese media have transformed and grown into vast competitive commercial enterprises, and as international media have become more available within China, journalistic performance itself has become one of these key problems for deliberation.

THE WATCHDOG IN THE GLOBAL NEWS ARENA

As "doing" journalism has become more universally possible, "being" a journalist has become a more difficult boundary to define. Nevertheless, it is still useful to retain some distinctions between citizen and professional, if only to see how they interact with each other in a larger structure of public accountability. Professional media signal a claim to institutional authority and economic resources rooted in their organizations, while citizen journalists are not typically commercially viable and do not require adherence to a professional code in order to participate, just the desire to express an idea or support a cause. This distinction is meaningful because in this chapter we focus specifically on how citizen journalism operates to critique professional journalism, and how doing so may steer the discursive space toward more clearly articulated values and greater transparency. In what Reese (2008) characterizes as the "global news arena," a synchronized discursive space is made possible by communication networks, which conceptually encompass both citizen and professional efforts. Certainly, the blogosphere is constituted by both forms, each feeding on and complementing the other (Reese, Rutigliano, Hyun, and Jeong, 2007).

Media watchdogs across the political spectrum have been a fixture in the United States for many years and in other countries with advanced press systems, but less so where press bias and political alignments are taken more for granted. They have brought much greater skepticism and awareness of journalistic techniques to the public, but the difference now in the online environment lies in the ability of citizens to respond on a much larger scale across and within societies. People know how they are portrayed, and others know that they know (or soon will). As a constructed product, news has been deconstructed with great enthusiasm as online citizen critics have joined organized media watchdog groups in monitoring how their interests are portrayed. Not surprisingly, this style of media criticism has become globalized along with everything else, and other parts of the world are taking up the task from their own perspectives as part of this larger discourse. Media criticism becomes less an organizational activity and more of a practice embedded in the citizen journalism network.

Chinese media criticism operates with a different ideological dynamic depending on whether directed inward or outward. Western observers are more aware of the latter, of course, given that they are directly implicated, but the amount of inward-looking critique may be underestimated. Language differences restrict circulation outside the country, and national pride, particularly among the young and well-educated, makes many Chinese reluctant to criticize their own media to foreigners (Osnos, 2008). But that does not mean a lively conversation on press performance is not taking place within the borders.

EXTERNAL PRESS CRITICISM

Traditional criticism of international news has dwelled on the weaknesses and blindspots of Anglo-American media with respect to other parts of the world. The hegemonic system of global "news flow" meant that the dominant Western media covered the world from the perspective of the West and to the disadvantage of the rest, which were led to understand their own societies through the lens of the dominant powers. This unbalanced news flow model has been rendered less useful in a networked system of media and communication, which gives traditional global news organizations less gatekeeping authority. In the long-standing debate over the quality of international news, the Chinese now have invoked the principles of media analysis to forcibly critique the performance of the world press, particularly as the Olympics became a flashpoint of heightened awareness as to how the nation is portrayed (with what the Chinese have regarded as unfair emphasis on, for example, Tibetan protest and government restrictions on the Falun Gong). To the extent that expressions of nationalism suit its interests, the government has given free reign to criticism of Western media, with Chinese online critics attacking CNN with the kind of vigor typical in the past from viewers of its American rival, Fox News Network (e.g., Anti-CNN.com). Chinese media monitors are observing problems of skewed news coverage that echo long-standing criticisms elsewhere in the world of sensationalism, negative conflict-based stories, unbalanced news flow, and a "coups and earthquakes" mentality. These concerns, although familiar press tendencies in the academic research, are amplified when they intersect with a defensive nationalism.

The Tibet Riots and Anti-CNN.com

In March 2008, Tibetans engaged in a series of activities to protest the Chinese central government's rule. The initial political demonstration eventually turned violent, with Tibetans attacking and looting non-Tibetans and burning their property. The reporting by the Western media was conducted without much historical context regarding the long-standing political conflict between the Chinese central government and Tibet over the issue of autonomy. Coverage, therefore, was perceived as depicting the Chinese government trampling human rights, overriding the desire of Tibetans to be independent of China—using deadly force if necessary. CNN, for example, published a photo on its website of a Chinese army garrison arriving in a Tibet town to crack down on the protests, and the accompanying news article emphasized the death toll among protestors. In fact, a group of Tibetan rioters attacking the army's vehicle with stones had been cropped out from the original AFP/Getty Images photo. The misleading discrepancy was quickly located on the internet and highlighted by Chinese netizens, who objected to the way CNN depicted the Chinese authorities and not the rioters as the instigators of the disturbance. Thus, local media critics used one Western news organization's work to compare to another's in searching for examples of visual framing unfavorable to China.

In response to this distortion, 23-year-old student Jin Rao established Anti-CNN.com, calling up netizens to "collect, classify, and exhibit the evidence of misbehaviors of Western media, and to voice our own opinion" (Anti-CNN, 2008). The website soon received an enthusiastic response from Chinese, both at home and abroad, who have been participating in evidence collecting, sorting, translating, and technical support ever since.[1] The collective action eventually led to requests for formal responses from CNN and other Western media such as RTL news in Germany. Following the Tibet riot, Anti-CNN's effort to protest the portrayals by Western media kept growing. The site now claims about 500,000 visits per day, 60% of which are from China. Regarding it as "a war resisting the Western dominance of news discourse," Anti-CNN's criticism now extends to other international media. Characterizing itself as a cyberwar headquarters, the site works to challenge media credibility whenever China becomes the subject. In this initiative, the criticism began with a presumption of anti-China media "misbehaviors" and left it to citizens to find examples that fit.

The Olympic Torch Relay

Critiques of Western media from Chinese netizens surged again one month later, in April 2008, when the world press reports of the global Olympic Torch processions in London, Paris, and San Francisco were deemed to be unduly supporting the Tibetan demonstrators while belittling the Chinese government. Chinese netizens blamed the Western media's prejudice against China for turning the Olympic Torch processions into controversial publicity stunts around the globe and tarnishing their pride in the long-awaited games. This outrage over perceived media bias became evident across countless websites, blogs, and bulletin boards. The BBC, a well-known and respected brand in China, provoked anger because of its emphasis on the "peaceful" pro-Tibet protests while ignoring the presence of thousands of pro-Chinese supporters in the London torch relay. CNN incurred similar criticism when covering the relay in San Francisco.

The Chinese objected to what they regarded as the demonizing of their nation and their fellow citizens. For example, in an article "unmasking" Chinese guardians of the Olympic Torch, *The Times* in Britain focused on their "paramilitary training," "aggressive methods of safeguarding," and identified their paramilitary colleagues back in China as the force responsible for restoring order following the Tibet riots—thus linking the two incidents. Interviewees in one article all presented negative viewpoints about the guardians, labeling them as "thugs" and "robotic" (McCartney & Ford, 2008). *The Guardian* described the guardians as "flame retardants," while the *Daily Mail* labeled them as "horrible Chinese thugs." Particularly objectionable to the Chinese, given the high-profile media role of the speaker, was the remark by CNN commentator Jack Cafferty, who appeared on the program *Situation Room* about the same time to accuse the Chinese government of being "the same bunch of goons and thugs they have been for the past fifty years."

The most remarkable action taken was the online petition against the Western media (especially CNN—inevitably, perhaps, given its claim as the "global news leader"), which reportedly accumulated tens of thousands of signatures and comments. Netizens demanded that Western media respond to their petition, stop publishing irresponsible comments, and apologize for biased news coverage of China. To support the petition, citizens trans-posted Jack Cafferty's photos and uploaded the video and text of his objectionable comments. The video, titled "Jack Cafferty CNN insulted Chinese people by racism words,"[2] became a popular YouTube posting. Although Cafferty denied that he was prejudiced against China, the vigorous petition and crusade successfully invited public examination into and suspicion toward the Western media in general, beyond the objections raised by these specific incidents.

Also widely shared in blogs and chat rooms were videos made by average citizens that satirized CNN and other Western media. For example, a music video made by a web singer, "Don't be too CNN," achieved strong online popularity in webspace, causing the title to be adopted by netizens to mean "don't ignore the truth." The "human search engine," a search system that encourages human participation in filtering information provided by online search engines, exhibited its enormous power when online communities mobilized to track down specific individuals and facts missing in media coverage. In the Paris relay, for example, a pro-Tibet protester attempted to grab the torch from Paralympics torchbearer Jing Jin, but this incident was not seen in most Western media. Angry netizens initiated an internet manhunt to locate the protester, in order to examine his background and to launch an attack on him. The "human search engine" took four days to find the person with detailed information, including name, home address, and association with the Tibet independent movement. Netizens arguably went too far in disclosing such personal information, but their collective efforts clearly provided information ignored by most Western media.

INTERNAL PRESS CRITICISM

The Olympics provided the most compelling vehicle for citizen critics of the international media, but other kinds of critiques have been growing within China. Setting aside the dimension of national pride, which helps guide outward-directed criticism, the inward-looking discourse points more directly to professional journalistic principles, both individual and institutional. Three recent examples exemplify this tendency.

Wenchuan Earthquake

The Wenchuan earthquake, on May 12, 2008, in the Sichuan province of China, received wide international attention and sympathy, but particularly so within China where the government's response was carefully watched. Given the extent of victims and witnesses, the earthquake was not only newsworthy but also accessible for citizen coverage, using cameras, cell phones, and video cameras (see also Chapter 7, this volume). Personal experience with the event gave citizen journalists a special vantage point and perspective for their online press criticism. Most of the critiques focused on the sensitivity of professional media, especially journalists' sensitivity to their subjects. For example, when Luyu Chen, a well-known anchorperson at Phoenix TV, wore Chanel sunglasses and carried a parasol during a live report from the disaster scene, she incurred the anger of netizens who disdained her for being frivolous and insensitive to the victims.[3] The same anger emerged online toward journalists when they forced busy rescuers and seriously injured or dying victims to be interviewed, when they took up seats in rescue helicopters, when they presented the tragedy of the earthquake with bloody and graphic pictures and descriptions, or when they shot flash photos of victims' faces without regard for the trauma the bright lights would inflict on those who had spent so much time trapped under the ruins in darkness.

Beyond this simple insensitivity, the professional integrity of journalists also came in for attack. For example, CCTV (Chinese Central Television) correspondent Na Xu was referred to as a "runaway" and became the target of raging criticism when she admitted live on camera that she was not at the front line of a destroyed middle school at Dujingyan but in a hotel in Chengdu, a hundred miles away from the quake zone. Worse was her inaccurate comment while far from the scene that "the rescue at the school is almost over." At that time, to the contrary, the rescue had just started, with hundreds of students still in the ruins and their parents nearby, anxiously waiting for rescue news. The text and video of this live connection were posted on major news websites and forums, and Xu's performance was furiously condemned as neglect of journalistic duty.

This criticism of personal integrity eventually broadened to target the media organization itself when Feike Shi, Xu's former colleague at CCTV and now a well-known netizen and blogger, defended Xu against public criticism. In his blog post, trans-posted to many major online forums by netizens, Shi urged audiences to question CCTV's internal operation as well. He wrote that since the CCTV news channel rarely does live reporting on large-scale events like the earthquake, journalists have insufficient experience dealing with live news coverage. CCTV's strict control on reporting scope also was deemed responsible for inadequacies in coverage. With constant warnings from their supervisors of what could be reported and what could not, Shi argued, journalists engaged in self-censorship, causing them to flinch from their professional duty (Feike, 2008).

Shi's blog post and the enthusiastic trans-posting created a space for the public to examine and discuss journalistic operation, not only at the individual level but also at the organizational and ownership level. Since CCTV is regarded as a propaganda machine for the Communist Party, any critiques toward its operation are ideologically and politically sensitive. Although not the first time, the challenge to CCTV by netizens who were able to link it to such a highly publicized national event signaled to the public the possibility of defying a media authority, particularly one that is regarded as both politically correct and professionally paradigmatic.

The South China Tiger

In October 2007, the Provincial Forestry Department of Shaanxi published photographs of a South China tiger as proof that the rare creature still existed in the wild. Although covered by various professional media including CCTV, the authenticity of these photos was soon questioned on Xitek.com, the biggest photographic website in China and an online platform for photographers to exchange ideas and opinions about equipment and techniques. In its picture forum, some photographers questioned the photo's lack of depth, making it appear like a flat "paper tiger." Before long, the photos aroused widespread suspicion among all major web forums organized and participated in by ordinary citizens, leading to demands that media professionals review the issue. Some newspapers even sent reporters to Shaanxi to investigate the authenticity of the photos. Meanwhile, major gateway websites such as Sina.com (the leading news website), QQ.com (the leading internet community in China, based on its instant messenger services), and 163.com (the leading website based on online community building and online games), set up special sections to incorporate information and opinions from professional media, officials, experts, and citizens.

To locate the origin of the image in the photo, the "human search engine" again was employed. With numerous netizens involved, the original was found and posted in Xitek.com a month later, proving the South China tiger photos were fakes.[4] Without the assembled expertise and intelligence of average citizens, scholars, and experts, major media reports would never have been challenged. In spite of pressure from tourism-minded local authorities, who sought to uphold the tiger's authenticity, citizen reporting was successful in urging professional media to give their performance greater scrutiny and pursue the truth of questionable facts. Citizen journalism, as this example illustrates, can be an effective check on journalistic practice, with professional media sites even seeking to integrate these efforts into their own platforms.

San Lu Contaminated Formula Issue

In September 2008, lethal bacteria were found in San Lu baby formula manufactured in China. A baby died, and many were diagnosed with kidney stones, a health scare that traveled worldwide given the product's broad export. The problem was revealed when some company insiders disclosed that tainted product had existed for years but that media coverage was kept quiet as a result of San Lu's powerful public-relations manipulation. The social responsibility of the entire Chinese media was brought into question when the extent of their cooperation in promoting a corporate image was revealed. David Bandurski, a researcher in the China Media Project in the Chinese University of Hong Kong, noticed that two reporters, Wanfu Miao and Jingxue Jia, frequently appeared in the mainstream media with consistently positive news about San Lu (including *China Food Quality News*, the newspaper designated by China's State Council as the primary vehicle for disseminating food quality and supervision policies and regulations). These two "reporters," as Bandurski revealed, were San Lu's public-relations mangers:

> The complicity of China's media is doubly disturbing because it underlines a dangerous trend resulting directly from the party's policy on media—an amplification of falsehood driven by the narrowest commercial ends attended by state news censorship that suppresses information that is critical to the well-being of ordinary Chinese.... [U]nless the media are given greater freedom to monitor officials and corporations on behalf of the people, the cruel and cynical contrast between public relations ploys and hidden realities will persist. (Bandurski, 2008)

Bandurski's article was originally published in English at the "China Media Project" webpage but soon was translated into Chinese and trans-posted onto websites with heavier traffic. Because many feared it might be screened by the Chinese internet "Great Firewall" because of the politically sensitive words (i.e., criticism of the Communist party's policy on media), they quickly trans-posted it to their blogs and to chat forums so as to save copies of the article, or at least prolong the existence of it (even if blog posts would be deleted). In this case, the threat of censorship ironically caused an even quicker online viral distribution.

The impact of such criticism on the Chinese media is still unclear, but certainly closer attention is now being paid to professional practices, including those of the online portals themselves. After the San Lu issue was disclosed, an "internal document" appeared online disclosing that the company was trying to invest 3 million RMB (Chinese yuan) in Baidu, the biggest search engine in China, to help screen negative news. This document aroused immense surprise and indignation among citizens, who demanded that Baidu respond. Eventually, Baidu claimed that it had denied the invitation of cooperation and promised to provide objective, timely, and comprehensive information about the issue to the public.

CONCLUSION

Taken globally, these developments in China point to new ways of understanding social change. Previously, theories of political economy and cross-national news flow emphasized the effect of one power bloc on another, or the imposition of one system on another, in a process of "McDonaldization." In the "world culture" perspective on globalization, however, beliefs emerge, not as the result of imposition and force, but out of spaces of mutual awareness in which standards evolve in a reflexive process (Robertson, 1995). That dynamic lies not always in the obvious government controls on citizen and journalistic expression but in the implicit spaces that emerge with their own pressures toward social change. Rather than declaring one country authoritarian and another free, as Westerners are prone to do, it is more helpful to examine—as we have done—these spaces for public deliberation created by fluid networks of expression that do not always track national boundaries or traditional distinctions between the political and non-political.

One of the most important consequences of citizen journalism is the structure of accountability it provides for traditional, "professional" media. Nothing stimulates the deliberative space like a perceived failing of the press, particularly in this case when it is a failing of the foreign press regarding China. We continue to be intrigued with the prospects of this deliberative criticism for democracy. Although operating within an authoritarian framework, Chinese netizens are expressing their opinions, disagreeing with others, making their choices among options—all behaviors that constitute the world of democracy. In a *New York Times* report, "Google's China Problem," Clive Thompson (2006) argued that internet communication is bringing a revolution to China, not with dramatic changes in ruling party or governance, but with a revolution experienced "mostly as one of self-actualization: empowerment in a thousand tiny, everyday ways."

In examining public deliberation in China, we find this idea provocative, suggesting the deliberative features of the blogosphere help to promote a "democratic rehearsal" process (see also Dai & Reese, 2007). If the kind of citizen media criticism we have reviewed here has a similar effect in the Chinese context as it has elsewhere, we should ask what that will mean for the quality of press performance.

As perhaps China's post-Olympics concern for its world media image wanes, we can imagine that enthusiasm for media critique and concerns for press bias being refocused internally, raising the same expectations for home-grown press performance with a continuing nudge toward transparency.

NOTES

1. Examples of distorted photos available at: http://www.anti-cnn.com/index2.html
2. http://www.youtube.com/watch?v=2j2bvOq3fLA
3. Tianya chat forum about the performance of Chen, available at http://laiba.tianya.cn/laiba/CommMsgs?cmm=281&tid=2600915412149663923
4. Xiaoyu Bobobo, November 16, 2007. "The result of human research engine: The antetype of the tiger photos were found," available at: http://forum.xitek.com/printthread.php?threadid=484393&pagenumber=1

REFERENCES

Anti-CNN (2008) "About us." Anti-CNN.com.

Bandurski, D. (2008) "Sanlu's public relations pawns: a relay of lies in China's media." *China Media Project*, 28 September.

Cha, V.D. (2008) "Beijing's Catch-22." *International Herald Tribune*, 4 August.

Dai, J., & Reese, S.D. (2007) *Practicing public deliberation: the role of celebrity blogs and citizen-based blogs in China*. Paper presented at the Harmonious Society, Civil Society and the Media Conference, Beijing.

McCartney, J., & Ford, R. (2008) "Unmasked: Chinese guardians of Olympic Torch." *The Times*, 9 April.

Osnos, E. (2008) "Angry youth: the new generation's neocon nationalists." *The New Yorker*, 28 July.

Reese, S.D. (2008) "Theorizing a globalized journalism." In M. Loeffelholz & D. Weaver (Eds.), *Global journalism research: theories, methods, findings, future* (pp. 240–252). London: Blackwell.

Reese, S.D., Rutigliano, L., Hyun, K., & Jeong, J. (2007) "Mapping the blogosphere: citizen-based media in the global news arena." *Journalism: Theory, Practice, Criticism*, 8(3), 235–262.

Robertson, R. (1995) "Glocalization: time-space and homogeneity-heterogeneity." In M. Featherstone, S. Lash, & R. Robertson (Eds.), *Global modernities* (pp. 25–44). London: Sage.

Thompson, C. (2006) "Google's China problem (and China's Google problem)." *The New York Times*, 23 April.

Shi, F. (2008) "To defend for Xu Na." *My1510*, 24 May.

CHAPTER NINETEEN

User-Generated Content
AND Journalistic Values

JANE B. SINGER AND IAN ASHMAN

The various forms of user-generated content (UGC) described in this book not only raise practical issues for journalists but also challenge long-standing occupational values. Who decides what is credible, true, or even newsworthy? What happens to the prized journalistic norm of autonomy in this interconnected environment? When the content space is shared, who is responsible for what it contains? What might an optimal relationship between journalists and user/contributors—the people Bruns (2007) calls "produsers"—look like, and what are the obstacles to achieving it?

The rapid advent of UGC in the digital media environment has given a new twist to long-standing journalistic ambivalence—at best—about citizen journalism. A perception that any move toward civic journalism (the term for prototypical efforts to explicitly incorporate public input into deciding what to cover and how to cover it) would undermine journalists' ability to make autonomous news judgments was at the heart of professional resistance to the idea in the 1990s (McDevitt, 2003). More recent objections have included protests that citizen journalism is not really journalism at all, notably because much of what users create seems to have little to do with the broader public interest (Stabe, 2006).

At issue, essentially, is journalistic control not merely over definitions but also, as this chapter explores, over the norms that journalists see as framing their own products and processes, but not necessarily those of users. We examine the topic by looking at how journalists at Britain's *Guardian* newspaper and its internationally popular website—part of a media organization in which clearly articulated values are culturally embedded—are assessing and incorporating UGC.

GUARDIAN MEDIA AND THE SCOTT TRUST

The *Guardian* and Sunday *Observer* are flagship newspapers of the Guardian Media Group, a company wholly owned by a trust whose core purpose is to safeguard the financial and editorial independence of its holdings. The Scott Trust states that profit must be used "to sustain journalism that is free from commercial or political interference"—journalism that in turn must uphold a set of values articulated by *Manchester Guardian* editor C.P. Scott on the paper's 100th anniversary in 1921. "Comment is free, but facts are sacred," he declared. Newspapers have "a moral as well as a material existence," and "the voice of opponents no less than that of friends has a right to be heard" (Guardian Media Group, 2007). Applying those values to a digital age, current *Guardian* editor Alan Rusbridger wrote:

> The character of Scott Trust journalism depends on its independence of ownership, behaviour and belief. Our journalists should be fierce in their protection of that independence. In the absence of a proprietor, our journalists' main relationships are with other colleagues and with readers, viewers or listeners. There should be a high premium on transparency, collaboration and open discussion. (Forgan, n.d., pp. 7–8)

The *Guardian*, *Observer*, and guardian.co.uk together employ nearly 800 journalists. About 10% work on the award-winning website, which includes hundreds of blogs from staffers and commissioned writers. The "Comment Is Free" section, launched in 2006, is Britain's leading commentary blog, attracting 350,000 comments or more a month. Its stated aim is to provide "an open-ended space for debate, dispute, argument and agreement" (guardian.co.uk, n.d.). Aside from topics deemed especially sensitive, such as "Blogging the Qur'an," comments are not pre-moderated. As of this writing, the *Guardian* allows relatively little free-form "citizen journalism"—that is, material not directly tied to content it has provided.

Although most readers of the printed newspapers live in the United Kingdom, two-thirds of the website users are outside the country. *Guardian* journalists accustomed to writing for, and getting feedback from, a British audience must therefore now accommodate an international readership.

JOURNALISTIC VALUES IN A NETWORKED ENVIRONMENT

Building on work that traced the encroachment of blogs on journalists' occupational turf (Lowrey, 2006), researchers have turned to the ways in which journalistic culture encompasses, or not, material from users that increasingly occupies the same digital space. Deuze and his colleagues suggest that participatory ideals do not mesh well with notions that journalists should keep their professional distance, "notions which tend to exclude rather than to include" (Deuze, Bruns, & Neuberger, 2007, p. 335). Journalists interviewed by Thurman (2008) in his study of UGC in nine British news outlets highlighted content concerns including newsworthiness, quality, balance, and decency.

In their multinational study of UGC on media websites, Domingo et al. (2008) found that news organizations in Europe and the United States are interpreting online user participation mainly as an opportunity for readers to debate current events; the core journalistic culture remains largely unchanged, as professionals retain the decision-making power at each stage of the news production process. Similarly, Hermida and Thurman (2008) found that UK journalists are retaining traditional gatekeeping roles in adopting user content on their websites.

Deuze (2005) places normative values including autonomy within what he calls the ideology of journalism, a system of beliefs that enables a group to produce meanings and ideas. In considering the challenges to journalists posed by citizen journalists and other external content providers, Singer also highlights autonomy, along with accountability. She suggests that in a networked environment, where all communicators and all communication are connected, "the notion of autonomy becomes unavoidably contested" (Singer, 2007, p. 90).

Autonomy and accountability, as well as authenticity, are normative values related to journalistic credibility that Hayes and his colleagues suggest need to be both strengthened and reinterpreted in a digital environment, where "old assumptions about journalistic roles and values can no longer be accepted uncritically nor old approaches to them continued indefinitely" (Hayes, Singer, & Ceppos, 2007, p. 275).

This chapter offers empirical evidence about journalists' views of these values in an environment that includes citizen journalism and other forms of user input. It is based on interviews with 33 print and digital *Guardian* journalists between November 2007 and February 2008. Brief questionnaires also enabled journalists to provide up to three words or short phrases associated with credibility (related to authenticity), responsibility (accountability), autonomy, and competence; in addition, they were invited to highlight a key ethical issue related to audience input into the news product or production process. All but five completed at least some parts of the questionnaire.

The questionnaire data provide a benchmark for understanding how these journalists define their occupational values. A relatively small set of traits are seen as essential. Accuracy stands out as central; the two dozen journalists who answered this question mentioned it most often in connection with credibility, responsibility, and overall competence.

Other associations also spanned more than one construct. Honesty and balance/fairness were associated with both credibility and responsibility; thoroughness and expertise, including notions about authority, were highlighted in connection with credibility and competence. Independence was seen as an important aspect of credibility, as well as comprising the core of journalistic autonomy.

UGC AND JOURNALISTIC VALUES AT THE *GUARDIAN*

The 15 journalists who identified key issues related to UGC focused mainly on credibility and civility—and the potential for "debasing journalism" by their absence, as a print editor wrote. "The platform gives credibility to people whose comments may be completely inaccurate, offensive or without foundation in fact. It arguably undermines the work of professional journalists by placing the words of people who have no training or professional responsibility alongside, or even on a par with, those who do," wrote an online journalist.

At the same time, respondents linked UGC to values of free speech—"letting people have their voice heard without intimidation," as an online editor wrote— and strengthened relationships. "We're no longer writing for people, but having a conversation with them," a print editor wrote. "The relationship is more balanced than ever before." Some tied UGC to what they felt the paper stood for. "It is a challenge to extend the *Guardian*'s values and ethics," an online editor wrote, "which on many counts we are achieving successfully and others not."

The 33 interviews expand on these ideas and suggest others. We will take the three concepts of authenticity, autonomy, and accountability in turn, then examine how *Guardian* journalists see relationships with users evolving in this increasingly shared, global media space.

Authenticity

For *Guardian* staff, being a "true" or authentic journalist encompasses occupational norms of credibility, authority, and accuracy. The extent to which UGC jeopardizes or undermines personal and institutional authenticity was a major concern.

Most agreed that users pose a challenge to journalistic authority—but opinions differed on whether this was a good or bad thing. Some saw democratization of discourse as healthy. "The old model of top-down, from-the-pulpit editorializing just doesn't do anymore. The vitality of the whole [Comment Is Free] enterprise is in the debate," an online editor said. "You're not there to give people definitive answers." Others felt UGC was not credible or authoritative enough to be inherently beneficial. They saw a crucial ongoing role for "the expert journalist who can interrogate and understand and all of those sorts of things in a way that the citizen reporter just can't," as a print editor said.

Notions of authority and credibility were closely related. Journalists believed they took adequate steps to ensure that what they wrote was credible but had little or no way either to assess or improve the credibility of what users provided. One editor said she had no expectation that users would be credible, citing issues of "what they know, what they don't know, what motivation they have, and what views they bring with them."

Institutional authenticity is also at stake. Respondents were universally supportive of "*Guardian* values"—and proprietary about protecting them. They saw their employer as providing a quality product and standing for things they approved, including enabling diverse voices to be heard. But they worried that those voices would harm the paper's own place in the world of credible opinion, potentially undermining the brand by sheer nastiness.

Another threat to authority was more direct: Users do not hesitate to challenge, often stridently, what journalists write. The challenge takes three forms: personal attacks, disagreement over opinion, and disputes about factual information. All three require time and energy to deal with, resources not always in adequate supply. Journalists who feel they already have too much to do wonder "why would I want to respond to BigDick119?" an online editor said.

Otherwise, journalists favored a different response to each challenge. Personal attacks were easiest, in theory: Grit your teeth and try to ignore them—if you can. "Sometimes I snipe back," one online writer confessed. "I try to take a deep breath, be positive and say, 'Well, the reason we said this was because...' But to be honest, I don't feel it's part of my job to go and disabuse people of notions they shouldn't be holding in the first place." A print editor said his reaction to abusive users was "YOU set the tone for the discourse—you can't expect us not to respond in kind. If you call us ignorant imbeciles, you've got to expect that we'll take it to heart a little bit."

Differences of opinion drew mixed reaction, though particularly among online staffers, honest (and civilly expressed) disagreement was seen as providing healthy opportunities for meaningful engagement and even self-reflection. Having one's opinions challenged "removes complacency," a print editor said, and responding constructively to users involves explaining why you disagree with their point of view: "You have to question yourself as well as them."

Challenges of factual statements were also valued, though for a different reason: knowing their work would be open to comment made journalists pay extra attention to getting it right in the first place. One blogger said she asks herself if what she has written is "bullet-proof": "I'm going to go and triple-check it because I know someone will shoot me down if I don't, and obviously that will destroy the credibility of anything else you say." However, responding to challenges can be time-consuming. "It's good that people can raise things. The internet gives them more standing to do that. The difficulty is it can then involve the media in long and tedious work to justify themselves," an online editor said. "They often question very basic assumptions."

Autonomy

In challenging "basic assumptions" and otherwise questioning what journalists write, UGC has the potential to erode professional autonomy as well as authority. Indeed, journalists see the concepts as closely related. An online editor said user feedback did not threaten his autonomy because "ultimately, I'm still in charge of it, and they're not," adding "you want to please them, but that's different from eroding your sense of autonomy."

Most interviewees treasured the large amount of individual autonomy they felt they had. Online staffers in particular commented on their freedom to write—and post—what they liked, in comparison to more protracted print-editing processes. A former newspaper writer who had moved online said the editor who "scrutinizes everything" before publication has been replaced to some extent by users who "can act as whistle blowers if there's dodgy content."

Input into decisions about what and how to write is not necessarily desired, however. The main area where UGC was seen as potentially impinging on journalistic autonomy related to the ready availability—indeed, the seductiveness—of hit logs and comment counts. Journalists accustomed to their work being part of a package for which only aggregated readership figures are available (and those only a few times a year) can see exactly how many people read their stories—and how many feel compelled to respond. Some saw such information as useful. "I have an enormous amount of independence. I can write about anything," an online journalist said. "But there's got to be a reason for it and a demand for it and an audience for it. Online, you do have this kind of instant knowledge of whether something you've written is of interest to people or not.... We may feel 'well, that obviously was really popular, what else can we do along those lines?'"

However, most were reluctant to say that usage information either did or should dictate what they wrote or how they wrote it, a practice a print writer described as "traffic whoring." They stressed the importance of journalistic autonomy in content decisions. "I wouldn't ever throw the more in-depth stuff out the window just to get comments," said an online writer. "If you're going to start chasing hits, you're just going to end up writing about gratuitous remarks," said another. "It appalls me, the idea of what you'd have to do for popularity."

Some journalists phrased their objections in terms of safeguarding the *Guardian* brand as distinct from the British "red-tops" or down-market tabloids. "You have to balance the desire for hits with what we think the paper should represent," an online editor said. Several said that while "dumbing down" their content, for instance with celebrity gossip, would attract more hits, such appeals to "the lowest common denominator" ultimately would alienate "real" *Guardian* readers.

Accountability

The interviewees felt a clear responsibility to those readers, one related both to the quality of the content—"my responsibility to the community is to put up good quality stuff that is interesting and accurate," an online journalist said—and to the quality of the resulting discourse. Indeed, they felt that sense of responsibility distinguished them from users. "With citizen journalists, it's all rights and no responsibilities," a print writer said. "They can opt out at any moment, and I can't," a print editor said.

For journalists, overlapping considerations of honesty, transparency, and trust all related to accountability in an interactive environment. "It works by being honest," a print editor said. "What makes people cross is if they think you're being unfair or dishonest or disingenuous." An online editor said users now expect journalists to "step out from behind articles, defend, and discuss them." Another journalist cited the need to "be seen putting our hands up" when they got something wrong.

One simple aspect of being accountable is having a byline. "Commenters behind a shroud of anonymity don't have that responsibility" not to be cruel, an online writer said. "They don't care. But I can't do that." Indeed, almost all the respondents who mentioned anonymity suggested it was a factor in the too-often abusive tone of online discourse. "People feel licensed to say things in content and style that they wouldn't own if publishing as themselves," said an online editor.

Several respondents also touched on a perceived responsibility to be fair and balanced. An online journalist cited a need to "consciously signal" efforts to look at a topic from different perspectives. Once an item is published, she said, "You're going to get loads of perspectives! So if you haven't even thought about one of them, I think it undermines your initial attempt."

Negotiating New Relationships

All these views highlight the many complexities journalists face in negotiating new forms of interaction with other citizens. Some interviewees valued the more open and dialogic relationships. "It's made it a much more balanced site," an online editor said. Despite a few disruptive contributors, "most are eloquent, intelligent, and able to add to the debate." Interviewees embedded in online communities outside their *Guardian* role were notably more comfortable. Veteran journalists asked to engage with users want to know 'why am I being thrown to the lions?' Whereas I don't see them as lions," a blogger-turned-journalist said. "They're part of the tribe that I am still part of, but in a different way."

Others were taken aback by what they saw as disturbingly confrontational discourse. Several characterized it as blatantly sexist. "Female journalists tend to be subject to abuse," one woman interviewee said. "It tends to be like a big boy's playground." Some saw it as rude to the point of being abusive. An editor said one of his writers told him, "If I want to be called a cunt all day, I'd become a traffic warden and do it in the open air." Some confessed to feeling hurt or upset. "You get really, really depreciative comments," an online writer said. "Whatever kind of maxims you repeat to yourself about how anything good always has haters, it subconsciously works away."

At the time of the study, the *Guardian* had no explicit policies for journalist-user interaction, though informal guidelines were emerging. They suggested thanking users who correct errors, engaging with those who raise valuable (in the journalists' eyes) points, and trying to ignore the irredeemably obnoxious. Several interviewees indicated they were coming to see encouragement of cogent contributions as having more long-term value than discouragement of the less cogent. "You can ignore the very hostile ones and respond to the more constructive ones," an online editor said.

Some said that though interaction was great, a bit of professional distance was also needed. Reading through comment threads, an online editor said, can lead to "getting very depressed: 'They all hate us, what's the point, why don't we just pack it all in?' And that's where the sense of autonomy comes in, and you have to say, 'Actually, this is still our website, and this is what we're trying to do here.' You have to remember what you're there to do in the first place." She cited the Scott Trust mandate to enable debate of issues of the day: "If we didn't have our autonomy, we wouldn't be producing that range of voices that we do produce."

In general, *Guardian* journalists conveyed a feeling that the interactive terrain was one they were only just learning to navigate and had considerable ambivalence about. One online journalist said her colleagues were not trained or prepared for the "slip from professional discourse into a more personal discourse." Their role is no longer simply to inform or entertain; it is to engage and interact with a hugely diverse range of unseen, but definitely not unheard, people all over the world.

SUMMARY

The *Guardian* journalists studied here expressed concerns about the credibility of UGC itself and about the effects of anonymous and/or uncivil comments on personal and institutional credibility. The perception that UGC potentially challenged their authority was widespread; though they said they appreciated the fact that more voices could now be heard, many clearly felt that too many of those voices were not worth listening to. One perceived value of UGC, however, was that it encouraged increased attention to accuracy, a paramount professional virtue.

Autonomy was highly valued, and most journalists were adamant that usage data—direct and immediate feedback from users about what they were interested in reading—should not be allowed to encroach on their professional news judgment. However, they also felt accountable to those users and indeed saw having explicit responsibilities as something that set them apart. The simple fact that users can be anonymous while journalists cannot was highlighted as an important component of online accountability.

All these issues—from autonomy to accountability, credibility to civility—are connected to the challenges inherent in negotiating new relationships. *Guardian* journalists, particularly the ones more deeply embedded in the traditional media culture, expressed considerable ambivalence about those relationships. Long-standing cultural norms position autonomy as a safeguard of credibility, and accepting explicit interdependency can be a lot to ask. Moreover, many were taken aback by the tone of some user contributions. Although most saw a theoretical value in broadened discourse, the reality presented a more profound challenge to their professional sensibilities than they had perhaps anticipated.

More broadly, this work suggests that journalists are thinking about the issues raised by citizen contributions in terms of an existing cultural framework defined by occupational norms—with varying degrees of accommodation and resistance. They face challenges in an open, global, and networked media environment that they did not confront when the product they alone produced was one they alone controlled.

When journalists control the product and the discourse surrounding it, relations with users are destined to be held at a distance. Yet in a seamless network, with its flattened or even obliterated hierarchies, all are in close proximity, a click of a mouse away. Journalists are increasingly comfortable seeing themselves as citizens of this networked world, but they have doubts about whether the reverse—that citizens are journalists—is also true.

*Portions of this chapter were previously published in "Comment Is Free, But Facts Are Sacred": User-generated content and ethical constructs at the *Guardian*,' *Journal of Mass Media Ethics 24* (1): 3–21.

REFERENCES

Bruns, A. (2007) "Produsage: towards a broader framework for user-led content creation." Proceedings of the 6th ACM SIGCHI Conference on Creativity & Cognition.

Deuze, Mark (2005) "What is journalism? Professional identity and ideology of journalists reconsidered." *Journalism*, 6(4), 442–464.

Deuze, Mark, Bruns, Axel, & Neuberger, Christoph (2007) "Preparing for an age of participatory news." *Journalism Practice*, 1(3), 322–338

Domingo, David, Quandt, Thorsten, Heinonen, Ari, Paulussen, Steve, Singer, Jane B., & Vujnovic, Marina (2008) "Participatory journalism practices in the media and beyond: an international comparative study of initiatives in online newspapers." *Journalism Practice*, 2(3), 326–342.

Forgan, Liz (n.d.) "Foreword" (pp. 7–8). In *A Hundred Years* (CP Scott, original work published 1921).

guardian.co.uk (n.d.) "Comment is free: about this site."

Guardian Media Group (2007) "The Scott Trust: the Scott Trust values." *Guardian Media Group*.

Hayes, Arthur S., Singer, Jane B., & Ceppos, Jerry (2007) "Shifting roles, enduring values: the credible journalist in a digital age." *Journal of Mass Media Ethics*, 22(4), 262–279.

Hermida, Alfred, & Thurman, Neil (2008) "A clash of cultures: the integration of user-generated content within professional journalistic frameworks at British newspaper websites." *Journalism Practice*, 2(3), 343–356.

Lowrey, Wilson (2006) "Mapping the journalism-blogging relationship." *Journalism*, 7(4), 477–500.

McDevitt, Michael (2003) "In defense of autonomy: a critique of the public journalism critique." *Journal of Communication*, 53(1), 155–164.

Singer, Jane B. (2007) "Contested autonomy: professional and popular claims on journalistic norms." *Journalism Studies*, 8(1), 79–95.

Stabe, Martin (2006) "The four critiques of 'citizen journalism.'" Pressgazette.co.uk, 9 June.

Thurman, Neil (2008) "Forums for citizen journalists? Adoption of user generated content initiatives by online news media." *New Media & Society*, 10(1), 139–157.

CHAPTER TWENTY

Wiki Journalism

PAUL BRADSHAW

The past few years have seen the news industry begin its first experiments with web-based applications that allow multiple authors to add, remove, and edit content in a process of collaborative authoring. These experiments are better known as wikis.

From the open nature of the Wikinews website ("The free news source you can write!") to the aborted reader-editable *Los Angeles Times* editorial (which collapsed within 24 hours as internet users scrambled to overwrite one another's edits), these experiments have demonstrated the potential of wiki technology, for better and for worse, that is, both to reach out to and engage a readership—and to fall foul of vandalism and abuse.

This chapter explores the forms and practices of "wiki journalism." We begin by briefly tracing the development of the technology that underpins it, before turning to assess current thinking about its potential as a medium for citizen reporting. The economic role of wikis receives particular attention, not least because of news organization interest in them as a basis for a new business model on the internet. Against this backdrop, I propose a number of criteria for assessing wiki journalism that, taken together, constitute a taxonomy of different types. Bearing this range of types in mind, I argue that we are entering a new stage in the evolution of wiki journalism and outline the strategies on which its future rests.

WIKIS AND WIKI JOURNALISM: A HISTORY

First employed in 1995 on WikiWikiWeb, wikis—like blogs—are platforms that can contain almost anything the user wants to use them for. Alongside project plans, encyclopedia entries, and scientific research, various forms of citizen journalism have been hosted on wikis for almost as long as the technology has existed—from the product reviews of ShopWiki and travel guides of WikiTravel (Gillmor, 2004, p. 150), through to wiki-based reports on the treatment of detainees at Guantánamo Bay Naval Base (Dorroh, 2005), and comprehensive coverage of global stories at Wikipedia's "current events" section (Kolodzy, 2006).

In addition to the popularization of wikis since 2001 by the online encyclopedia Wikipedia, their growth has been facilitated by a range of free wiki services. Setting up a wiki is now as easy as setting up a blog. It can contain one or more pages, and users can add further pages if they feel it is necessary to do justice to a topic. In addition to the most up-to-date version of a wiki page, wikis normally include a number of other important features, including:

- a system whereby authors are notified of changes to pages and can revert to older versions if necessary;
- permissions, whereby users may have different levels of editorial control. Some wikis also include password protection;
- records of previous versions of the page, so users can see how the subject has changed over time;
- discussion pages, where authors can discuss the subject and reach consensus on page content.

The most significant attempt to use wiki technology for news-based journalism has been that of Wikinews, launched by the Wikimedia Foundation in 2004. The site relies on users to monitor the site and requires that all sources "must be cited, and they must be verifiable, at least in principle, by someone else. In the case of original reporting, field notes must be presented on the article's discussion (Talk) page" (Allan, 2006, pp. 136–137)—a transparency of process rarely seen on commercial news websites.

Wikinews has been most successful in covering news events involving large numbers of people, such as Hurricane Katrina (see Chapter 4, this volume) and the Virginia Tech shootings, where the availability of first-hand accounts forms a substantial part of the entry. The sheer breadth and range of such forms of reportage—especially when informed by eyewitness accounts—makes this type of central "clearing house" (Thelwall & Stuart, 2007) or community "gathering spot" (Yamamoto, 2005) invaluable.

Kolodzy (2006) describes Wikinews coverage of such major events as follows:

> The first stories have the feel of initial wire service reports on the events. [Wikinews] operates under the premise of publishing first and then editing, albeit the editors are Wikinews users who become contributors. Some edits can involve punctuation, adding a subhead, or correcting spelling. Others add new information, such as the death toll updated by authorities during the London bombing or Prime Minister Tony Blair's statement. (p. 238)

In marked contrast, the *Los Angeles Times* example cited at the outset of this chapter was widely seen to have failed in its experiment with wiki technology. Its "wikitorial" on the Iraq War, in which an editorial was published inviting readers to "rewrite" it using wiki technology, may have sounded like a good idea, but it simply did not work in practice. The experiment was quickly terminated following vandalism by users—a result foreseen by Ross Mayfield (2005) of SocialText, who put it down in part to the departure from the "Neutral Point of View" (NPOV) policy of Wikipedia and Wikinews. The NPOV policy is similar in principle to the ideals of impartiality and objectivity, though, in keeping with the collaborative nature of wikis, it dictates that "contributors should seek *collectively* to produce a fair representation of all available points of view" (Thorsen, 2008, p. 939; emphasis added).

There has been a steady increase in experiments since, including *Esquire* magazine using Wikipedia itself to publish a draft version of an article about Wikipedia; *Wired* using its own wiki to post a draft article about the technology; and the subsequent launch the *Wired* How-To Wiki, a blog-style collection of editable how-tos. CNET has launched wikis about interactive television and the Indian technology industry (Dorroh, 2005; Kolodzy, 2006). The *San Diego Tribune*'s "AmpliPedia" (wiki.amplifysd.com) invites readers to contribute information on the local music scene, and the *Online Journalism Review* (now defunct) launched a collection of wikis in January 2007 that succeeded in helping to raise their profile among journalists.

Mainstream news organizations have introduced internal wikis, such as The N&Opedia at Raleigh's *News & Observer*, which provides a central repository of useful documents for breaking or ongoing stories, as well as information about expertise within the newsroom and general information about competitions and training (Ebbs, 2006). The *Columbus Dispatch*'s newsroom wiki "Dewey Answers" was started in December 2005, emerging from a local stylebook to provide wiki-tipsheets. It eventually evolved into a source of background information on news events and newsmakers, timelines and buildings. The wiki is controlled by librarians and senior editors, and the newspaper has a monthly "Dewey Answers meeting"

(Hunter, 2006). Similarly, the *St. Louis Post-Dispatch* also has a wiki for the research department, containing research and standard procedures (Meiners, 2006). Even the BBC has on occasion made use of wiki technology for writing formal documents, policies, guidelines, and manuals—their guidelines on employee weblogs and websites, perhaps the most publicly advertised example (Reynolds, 2008).

STRENGTHS OF WIKI JOURNALISM

Wikis allow news operations to effectively cover issues on which there is a range of information so broad that it would be difficult, if not impossible, for one journalist or one article alone to summarize effectively. Jay Rosen (2006) explains it as follows:

> A professional newsroom can't easily do this kind of reporting; it's a closed system.... The weakness is the organization knows only what its own people know. Which wasn't much of a weakness until the Internet made it possible for the people formerly known as the audience to realize their informational strengths.

Organizations willing to open up wikis for their audience to define the news agenda may also find a way of identifying their communities' concerns: Wikipedia, for instance, notes Eva Dominguez (2006), "reflects which knowledge is most shared, given that both the content and the proposals for entries are made by the users themselves."

Internally, wikis also allow news operations to coordinate and manage a complex story that involves a number of contributors: journalists are able to collaborate by editing a single webpage that they all have access to at once. News organizations interested in transparency can also publish the wiki "live," so readers can watch as it develops and look at previous versions—as is already the case with Wikipedia and Wikinews, whose instantaneous editing process make them examples of citizen journalism in process.

For traditional news organizations, the discussion space that accompanies each entry has the potential to create a productive dialogue with users. There is also the potential for users to translate articles into other languages, as takes place with Wikipedia entries, so as to help transcend linguistic—and national—barriers.

There are obvious economic and competitive advantages to allowing users to create articles. News organizations face increased competition from all sides, what with the growth of low-cost micro-publishing facilitated by the internet, and entry into the online news market by broadcasters, publishers, and online-only startups. At the same time, print and broadcast advertising revenue is falling, while competition for online advertising revenue is fierce and concentrated on a few major players (Rayport, 2007). Wikis offer a way for news websites to increase their reach, while also increasing the time that users spend on their website (Francisco, 2006), a key factor in attracting advertisers.

When successful, a wiki can also engender a sense of community (Gillmor, 2004; Bowman & Willis, 2003). Lih (2004) notes, for example, how wikis function primarily as social software, fostering communication and collaboration with other users: "Users become stakeholders in the content and in the outcome of their articles" (2004, pp. 15–16).

Economically, wikis appear to offer the attractions of free citizen journalism—or "user-generated content" as some prefer to describe it—and, in the case of published articles, free subediting. But these attractions are sometimes overstated: the disadvantages of the form mean costs elsewhere, in community management (Howe, 2007), maintenance, and monitoring (Levine, 2006).

WEAKNESSES OF WIKI JOURNALISM

In addition to their susceptibility to vandalism, questions have been raised about the relative authority and accuracy of wikis as obstacles slowing down the adoption of wikis as a form of citizen journalism (Allan, 2006; Richmond, 2007; Lih, 2004). Wikis such as Wikipedia have generally taken a "soft security" approach to such issues, making damage easy to undo rather than attempting to prevent its occurrence in the first place:

> When vandals learn that someone will repair their damage within minutes, and therefore prevent the damage from being visible to the world, the bad guys tend to give up and move along to more vulnerable places. (Gillmor, 2004, p. 149)

"Edit wars" are a related problem, where contributors continually overwrite each other's contributions because of a difference of opinion. The worst cases may require intervention by other community members to help mediate and arbitrate (Lih, 2004).

Attempts to address the security issue vary, depending on how the publisher balances the need to attract users with the need to maintain standards. Wikipedia's own entry on wikis explains:

> Basically, "closed up" wikis are more secure and reliable but grow slowly, whilst more open wikis grow at a steady rate but result in being an easy target for vandalism.

A further complication for news organizations used to the deadlines and production cycles of print and broadcast are the long timescales involved in building a successful wiki and the communities needed to maintain it. Wikinews contributor Erik Möller notes the reduced incentive for readers to contribute to articles with a short shelf life: "Wikinews articles are short-lived, so there is a reduced feeling of contributing to a knowledge base that will last a lifetime" (Weiss, 2005).

Further issues around authorship and remuneration also need addressing: Bruns (2005) notes that while there is no well-defined system as yet, models do exist, including the Creative Commons initiative and the system used by OhmyNews (see Chapter 11, this volume). The latter shares copyright and insists contributors disclose bank account details for payment.

A TAXONOMY OF WIKI JOURNALISM

As the nature of journalism moves from the document-based "final versions" of print and scheduled broadcast toward a more iterative journalism, wikis represent a particularly effective way to facilitate and manage that "unfinished" quality (Lih, 2004; Bruns, 2005). The format also has the potential to fit Hume's "resource journalism" (2005), which

> works to combine news about problems with news about a range of potential solutions to those problems.... [It] tries to offer a relevant selection of deeper information resources, a range of clearly labeled, diverse opinions, and interactive access points for citizens who may want to get involved.

Similarly, wiki journalism "uniquely addresses an historic 'knowledge gap'—the general lack of content sources for the period between when the news is published and the history books are written" (Lih, 2004, p. 4).

A number of frameworks for looking at citizen journalism (Bruns, 2005; Lasica, 2003; Bowman & Willis, 2003, p. 10) suggest that wiki journalism is far from homogenous. A review of examples of wiki journalism, in particular, suggests that there are key qualities that must be identified when examining the use of wikis in journalism:

- whether the topic is defined by an editor, or a user;
- whether the first draft is produced by a journalist paid to do so, or by a user;
- whether the material could have been produced without using wiki technology;
- whether the timescale is finite ("frozen" for print publication), or infinite (ongoing);

- whether the wiki draft is professionally edited further for "final" publication (in contrast to those that are edited solely by users).

Based on variations in the above, we can identify five broad types of wiki journalism:

- **Second-draft wikis**: a "second stage" piece of journalism, during which readers can edit an article produced in-house (*Wired* article, *Esquire*, *Los Angeles Times* wikitorial);
- **Crowdsourcing wiki**: a means of covering material that could not have been produced in-house (probably for logistical reasons), but that becomes possible through wiki technology (*San Diego Tribune*'s AmpliPedia; *Wired* How To Wiki);
- **Supplementary wiki**: a supplement to a piece of original journalism, an "add-on": "A tab to a story that says: Create a wiki for related stories" (Francisco, 2006) (CNET's India Tech Wiki; parts of the *Wired* How To Wiki);
- **Open wiki**: an open space, whose subject matter is decided by the user, and where material may be produced that would not otherwise have been commissioned (Wikipedia and Wikinews);
- **Logistical wiki**: a wiki limited to in-house contributors that enables multiple authorship and may also facilitate transparency and/or an ongoing nature (Dewey Answers; N&Opedia).

This taxonomy can be mapped out as follows:

Wiki journalism: a taxonomy of types

	User-defined topic?	User-created draft?	Impossible without wiki?	Infinite?	Professionally edited?
Second-draft	NO	NO	NO	NO	YES
Crowdsourcing	NO	NO	YES	YES	YES
Supplementary	NO	YES	YES	YES	NO
Open	YES	YES	YES	YES	NO
Logistical	YES	YES	YES	YES	YES

This taxonomy is not definitive, but indicative: it is possible, for example, to have a Second-draft wiki that was ongoing (infinite), or an Open wiki that was frozen at a certain point (as Wikinews is), but the suggestion is that this would be atypical.

So far the most highly publicized experiments with the form (the "Wikitorial"; *Wired*'s wiki article; the *Esquire* Wikipedia article) have been of the Second-draft variety, relinquishing the least amount of control over content, and incorporating wiki technology into pre-existing work processes. The subject of the article is still chosen by editors, the first draft is written by a journalist, and only then does the wiki community take control, taking a role as a second journalist/editor in the process.

In these cases the article has also been "frozen" at some point for publication, often only days after first being published online, something that could be seen as "unnatural" for a wiki. Furthermore, freezing wikis reduces the opportunity to allow vandalism to be cleaned up over time (Cannon-Brookes, 2006), under-exploits the ability to look at various "edits" of an article/topic/event as it develops over a long period of time, and reduces the opportunity to build an online community.

In contrast, outside of traditional news operations, Wikinews and Wikipedia have adopted a more open model, relinquishing almost all control, with huge success for Wikipedia but less so for Wikinews, perhaps because of the inclusion of "short-shelf-life" and frozen material.

Timescale appears to be a key variable in the success of wiki journalism. Between these two types on the wiki journalism continuum, the most successful models have involved subject matter with a long shelf life and ensured that the site builds—and taps into—a community that is wiki-literate and willing to contribute. This management of communities is likely to prove crucial to the shape that wiki journalism takes. As Boczkowski (2004) points out,

> at least two transformations appear to distinguish the production of new-media news from the typical case of print and broadcast media: The news seems to be shaped by greater and more varied groups of actors, and this places a premium on the practices that coordinate productive activities across these groups. (p. 183)

Not only is creating a community difficult, but once created it may not act in ways the wiki owner wants it to (Shirky, 2002). Still, investment made in building this community can produce significant results, and there are increasing examples of "crowdsourcing" methods, of which wikis are just one, being used to build journalism projects that would otherwise not have taken place (Howe, 2006).

This inevitably raises issues of access. Although Bruns (2005) proposes that citizen journalism marks a fundamental change in the processes of information gathering, he notes that "There is no automatism at work here which will inevitably lead to the emergence of multiperspectival news" (p. 27). At the same time, he also argues that "in itself this does not undermine the project of open news any more than the fact that not everyone is a software programmer undermines the project of open source: even those who do not engage with the deliberations taking place within open news can still benefit from their outcomes as they emerge" (2005, p. 74). Relevant here is Pavlik's (2001) observation that "The classical media are subject to the same knowledge-gap effect [and] if anything, new media present a possible reversal of the knowledge gap by eliminating the barriers to entry into the journalism marketplace" (p. 144).

As the taxonomy proposed above illustrates, "wiki journalism" is so multifaceted as to be rather difficult to effectively capture in a straightforward overview. There is a pressing need for research into individual forms of wiki journalism, in my view, especially those forms that have only been briefly mentioned above, such as internal wikis and citizen-based forms of wiki journalism taking place outside of traditional news organizations. Moreover, longitudinal studies would help us to look at the development of wiki communities over time at sites such as the *San Diego Tribune*'s AmpliPedia (as the CNET wiki illustrates, wiki communities often need long periods of time to build quality content). Other studies might investigate what compels users to contribute to wikis, and how under-represented groups might be encouraged to participate.

CONCLUSIONS

A number of ongoing projects indicate that we may be seeing a new stage in the evolution of wiki journalism. In Rushkoff's (2003) terms, we are witnessing three stages of development in the growth of citizen media—deconstruction of content, demystification of technology, and do-it-yourself or participatory authorship—that need to be grasped simultaneously in conceptual terms so as to discern how they interconnect. I wish to suggest that some publications, in particular the *San Diego Tribune*'s AmpliPedia and *Wired*'s How-To Wiki, are emerging from the first stage of deconstruction of content. In my view, if wiki journalism is to become part of the online journalist's toolbox, the next challenge is the further demystification of wiki technology, with time and money invested in facilitating participation.

Wikis are "blogs 2.0": like blogs, they provide an arena for readers to critique and correct, to self-publish, and to form communities. But while they share many characteristics with blogs and older technologies such as discussion forums, the significance of wikis lies in the way they move away from the linear call-response communication models that those technologies reflected. If blogs are a distributed discussion (Bowman & Willis, 2003), then wikis offer a single place for that discussion to reach (ongoing) consensus.

The range of voices editing each other tends to result in a fact-based piece of work that represents the "Neutral Point Of View" (NPOV) formalized by

Wikipedia, and which, potentially, avoids some of the biases inherent in individual, commercial journalism. Lih (2004) notes, for example, how "the Wikipedia community's tendency to avoid the use of the word 'terrorist' is similar to the policy adopted by the Reuters news agency" (p. 11), while Allan argues that the NPOV provides a new approach to the "longstanding, if in my view highly problematic, principle of impartial journalism...to the extent that it is made possible by collaborative contributions from across the community of users" (2006, p. 138; see also Thorsen, 2008), while also noting that "No undue influence is exercised by corporate proprietors, nor are market forces brought to bear, when determining what counts as a newsworthy event deserving of coverage" (Allan, 2006, p. 140). In other words, impartial journalism may, at least in theory, be more achievable when facilitated by wiki technology. Whether this potential is realized depends on the investment and understanding that is brought to any wiki project.

Weaknesses identified, such as vandalism and inaccuracy, can be addressed if staff are assigned to monitor and facilitate the wiki in order to prevent legal problems, attract A-List contributors (and monitors), and build genuine online communities. This will involve a new skills-set for those involved, as well as a fresh look at copyright, legal, and ethical issues. Hardest of all, it will involve relinquishing control over what has traditionally been a news organization's biggest asset—content—in order to rebuild another that has recently been neglected: the community. Finding better ways to serve that community will be key to journalism's future, both editorially and economically.

Note: an extended version of this chapter is available as a wiki that will remain live and editable on an ongoing basis. To contribute, visit wikijournalism.pbwiki.com and log on with the password "wikiwiki."

ACKNOWLEDGMENTS

The author would like to thank Dennis Foy, Chris Jennewein, Ken Liu, Mindy McAdams, and Robert Niles for their contributions to the wiki of this paper and via email correspondence.

REFERENCES

Allan, S. (2006) *Online news*. Maidenhead and New York: Open University Press.
Boczkowski, P. (2004) *Digitizing the news: innovation in online newspapers*. Cambridge, MA: MIT Press.

Bowman, S., & Willis, C. (2003) *We media, the media*. Reston, VA: Center at the American Press Institute.

Bruns, A. (2005) *Gatewatching*. New York: Peter Lang.

Bruns, A. (2006) "Wikinews: the next generation of alternative online news?" *Scan Journal*, *3*(1), n.p.

Cannon-Brookes, M. (2006) "When wikis don't work—mass journalism." *Rebelutionary*, 6 September.

Dominguez, Eva (2006) "Wiki journalism. La Vanguardia.es." 14 September.

Dorroh, Jennifer (2005) "Wiki: don't lose that number." *American Journalism Review*, August/September.

Ebbs, Susan (2006) "N&Opedia: the newsroom wiki of The News & Observer." Special Libraries Association 2006 Annual Conference, 12 June.

Francisco, B. (2006) "Why media will embrace wikis", *MarketWatch*, December 28.

Gillmor, Dan (2004) *We the media: grassroots journalism by the people, for the people*. Sebastopol, CA: O'Reilly Media.

Howe, Jeff (2006) "The rise of crowdsourcing." *Wired*, 14 June.

Howe, Jeff (2007) "Did assignment zero fail? A look back, and lessons learned." *Wired*, 16 July.

Hughes, Jennifer (2007) "The wiki defense: what Floyd Landis taught the press about drug testing." *Columbia Journalism Review*, May/June.

Hume, Ellen (2005) "Resource journalism: a model for new media." *Ellenhume.com*.

Hunter, Jim (2006) "Dewey answers: a newsroom wiki." Special Libraries Association 2006 Annual Conference, 12 June.

Jacobs, A.J., et al. (2005) "Wikiworld." *Esquire*, 1 December.

Kolodzy, Janet (2006) *Convergence journalism: writing and reporting across the news media*. Lanham, MD: Rowman & Littlefield.

Lasica, J.D. (2003) "What is participatory journalism?" *Online Journalism Review*, 7 August.

Levine, Robert (2006) "New web sites seeking profit in wiki model." *The New York Times*, 4 September.

Lih, Andrew (2004) "The foundations of participatory journalism and the Wikipedia project." Conference paper for the Association for Education in Journalism and Mass Communications, Communication Technology and Policy Division, Toronto, Canada, 7 August.

Mayfield, Ross (2005) "Wikitorials." *Corante*, 13 June.

Meiners, Mike (2006) "Research wiki at *St. Louis Post-Dispatch*." Special Libraries Association 2006 Annual Conference, 12 June.

Pavlik, John V. (2001) *Journalism and new media*. New York: Columbia University Press.

Rayport, Jeffrey (2007) "Advertising's death is greatly exaggerated." *MarketWatch*, 8 June.

Reynolds, Nick (2008) "BBC blogging guidelines nostalgia 2." *Nick Reynolds at Work*.

Richmond, Shane (2007) "Wild wild west." *Telegraph Blogs*, 17 January.

Rosen, Jay (2006) "Why we're doing this." NewAssignment.Net.

Rushkoff, Douglas (2003) "Open source democracy: how online communication is changing offline politics." *Demos*.

Shirky, Clay (2002) *Broadcast institutions, community values.* September.

Singel, Ryan (2006) "The wiki that edited me." *Wired,* 7 September.

Terdiman, Daniel (2005) "Esquire wikis article on Wikipedia." CNET News.com, 29 September.

Thelwall, Mike, & Stuart, David (2007) "RUOK? Blogging communication technologies during crises." *Journal of Computer-Mediated Communication, 2*(1), 523–548.

Thorsen, E. (2008) "Journalistic objectivity redefined? Wikinews and the neutral point of view." *New Media and Society, 10*(6), 935–954.

Weiss, A. (2005) "The Unassociated Press", *New York Times,* February 10.

Wikipedia (2007) "Wikipedia. Wiki. Wikipedia." *Wikipedia.*

Winston, Brian (1998) *Media technology and society.* London and New York: Routledge.

Yamamoto, Mike (2005) "Katrina and the rise of wiki journalism." CNet News Blog, 1 September.

CHAPTER TWENTY ONE

The Future OF Citizen Journalism

MARK DEUZE

In order to predict a possible future for citizen journalism, it would be useful to consider its meaning from three distinct perspectives. First, using the perspective of industry, citizen journalism can be seen as a way to generate news and marketing opportunities at little or no cost, using the free labor of citizen-volunteers. Second, we can consider the perspective of the audience, where people's generally very personal and opinionated contributions to citizen news can be interpreted as expressions of an extremely individualized and to some extent rather solipsistic engagement with society. Beyond such skeptical views, a third perspective would be a more optimistic note on participatory media culture, civic emancipation, and an emerging new humanism in media professions, where we can focus on the efforts of professional news organizations to genuinely collaborate with (and thus invest in) their constituencies. This "third way" is the framework of convergence culture—a concept I deploy in this chapter in terms of potential strategies for a future citizen journalism where professional reporters and engaged citizens indeed co-create a public sphere within their communities of reference.

JOURNALISM AND CITIZENSHIP

During the 20th century, professional journalism emerged as one of the foundations of democratic societies around the world, and its practitioners came to see their work and their product as the cornerstone of the modern nation-state. "Journalism is another name for democracy or, better, you cannot have journalism without democracy. The practices of journalism are not self-justifying; rather, they are justified in terms of the social consequences they engender, namely the constitution of a democratic social order" (Carey, 1996). In this context democracy is seen as a form of "publicness," where journalists would use the awesome power and responsibilities they got during the heyday of mass media to empower, engage, and in fact "reconstitute the public in the journalists' imagination" (Rosen, 1999, p. 69).

The key to this brief history of journalism is to understand its professionalization process as including a growing disconnect (and alienation) between the journalist and his or her audience. With the gradual demise of the mass media system and its corresponding mass audiences since the 1980s, it is possible to see the contemporary emergence of citizen journalism as tied into earlier trends in, for example, the United States, toward a civic, communitarian, or public journalism—different approaches to the news yet all advocating deeper connections and closer relationships between the journalist and citizens (Black, 1997). Today, citizen journalism can be practically defined as, in Jay Rosen's (2008) words, "when the people formerly known as the audience employ the press tools they have in their possession to inform one another, that's citizen journalism." This definition pushes the long process of increasing collaboration between users and producers of news another step further, in fact taking the earlier presumed necessary role of professional journalists as society's intermediaries out of the equation. This supposed dissolution of remaining distinctions or boundaries between what is a "journalist" and what is a "citizen" (and what behavior counts as such) can be tied to broader social trends. Hartley (2008, pp. 48–49), in particular, suggests the emergence of a global society in which everyone is a journalist or can be, and where everyone has a right (and, increasingly, access to the plug'n'play technological equipment and know-how) not just to express but also to circulate information and opinions. Thus, when we consider citizen journalism, a first step toward an assessment of what it is, and what it may become, is the acknowledgement that the journalist and the citizen are one and the same person, sharing an identity.

The identity of the contemporary citizen has as its principal component what Schudson (1998) calls a "monitorial" capacity: scanning all kinds of news and information sources—newspapers, magazines, television shows, blogs, online and offline social networks, and so on—for the topics that matter to her or him personally. People are not necessarily disengaged from societal and political processes, they just commit their time and energy to it on their own terms. This individualized enactment of citizenship can be linked to the act of the consumer, as Scammell (2000) argues. "The act of consumption is becoming increasingly suffused with citizenship characteristics and considerations. Citizenship is not dead, or dying, but found in new places.... The site of citizens' political involvement is moving from the production side of the economy to the consumption side" (p. 351). Monitoring is indeed the act of the citizen-consumer, participating in society (whether that "society" equals virtual, topical, or geographical community, one's role within a democratic nation-state, or within a translocal network) conditionally, unpredictably, and voluntarist (Deuze, 2006, pp. 67–68).

Reporting on studies in 43 countries, Inglehart (1997) observed a global shift of people in their roles as citizens away from nation-based politics and institutional elites, toward a distinctly skeptical, globally interconnected, yet deeply personal type of self-determined civic engagement. As the rift between the individual and the nation-state widened, Norris (1998) observed the emergence of a new type of deeply critical global citizen who is excited about the ideals of democracy but is losing confidence in its national practice. "We are undoubtedly living in an anti-hierarchical age," concludes Beck (2000, p. 150). It is in this context that we can read the emergence of the citizen journalist, as well as the ongoing deterioration of the traditional community, the increasing cynicism toward social institutions (such as journalism), and the declining audiences of mainstream news. The interdependent, perhaps synonymous relationship between citizenship and journalism is thus not so much the celebration of a reconstituted public in the imagination of journalists, but a partly deliberate and partly contextual shift away from and against professional journalism altogether. It is within this framework that I discuss the three futures of citizen journalism from the perspectives of industry, audience, and convergence culture.

CITIZEN JOURNALISM AND INDUSTRY

> Newspapers have long been a centerpiece of local community life, but paper publishers are recognizing the need to foster community in new ways through their Web sites.... For newspaper sites in need of creating more volume, enabling user-generated content 'is the cheapest way to foster bigger growth,' said Ken Doctor... User-created content can double inventory volume at a production cost of one to three percent the cost of staff-produced newspaper content, Doctor added. (Kaye, 2007).

The above quotation, taken from a story on the American digital marketing news site *Clickz*, provides an important clue to the reason for news companies to engage the consumer as a co-creating colleague: it is cheaper. A couple of points stand out. The first is the perceived need for fast and continuous growth for a news website, which cannot be guaranteed or fueled alone by existing staff. Hiring new staff is generally seen as either too expensive or problematic in terms of the uncertainty involved with lack of tested business models for news online. Making existing staff do more tends to be a popular option, which in turn is understandably resented by reporters and editors involved (Deuze, 2007b). A second note can be made regarding the reference to "news" as "inventory volume," stipulating the commoditization of news. This, for example, means that the unique elements of the news—the reporting, fact-checking, editing, and other acts of journalism that went into producing the story or segment—are not seen as creating added value anymore. With news as a commodity, what generates additional market opportunities are the services and user experiences that can be generated around the news. It is at this point in the industry equation where citizen journalism comes into focus.

A similar trend can be observed in the advertising industry, where the move online of branding opportunities, strategies, and ad spending has come at the expense of creative spending—and served as a boost for marketing and public relations (Ries & Ries, 2002). Worldwide spending on marketing services, such as sponsorships and PR, is growing at a consistently faster rate than for traditional advertising in recent years.[1] At a time when job cuts across the media industries are at an all-time high, hiring in marketing and PR is increasing at a steady pace, according to 2007–2008 census reports in, for example, the United States. The key to this subtle but pervasive shift is a trend away from creative, top-down, professionally produced storytelling formats to an economy of interactive services and user experiences, where value gets (or is expected to be) extracted from building and sustaining relationships with clients, customers, and companies. A May 2008 report from the *Direct Marketing Association* (DMA) investigated the Web 2.0 phenomenon—including blogs, virtual worlds, social networks, user-generated content, RSS feeds, and wikis—as a platform in which all marketing converges. The lead researcher of the report was quoted as saying that "Web 2.0…enables marketers to create a real-time dialogue with each individual customer. It invites both marketers and their customers to work together to create the content that would increase brand awareness, improve brand perception, and generate both sales and leads" (Direct Marketing Association, 2008).

The future of citizen journalism from an industry perspective is about creating brand communities around the news. In some ways, this explains why most successful citizen news projects are distinctly "hyperlocal," as Jan Schaffer (2007) notes in a report on citizen media in the United States. In other ways, citizen (or "social," "participatory") media projects have been particularly successful in the realm of other domains where communities of interest already exist, such as professional sports. Excellent examples would be fantasy football for the National Football League in the United States, and Barclays Premier League soccer in the United Kingdom, where fans form their own teams and play their own league games next to, but distinctly part of (the brand environment of) the existing professional competition. In this context, it is important to note that citizen journalism on a local level, as a way to connect the product—news and information—with a specific community, is nothing new. What is perhaps "new" about it is that it happens in the context of a bloodletting of creativity, or—in other words—of outsourcing salaried labor in newswork to unpaid volunteers, and interpellating the aforementioned citizen-consumer as a citizen-colleague without necessarily investing in training, monitoring, moderating, or protecting arrangements.

CITIZEN JOURNALISM AND AUDIENCES

Consider the following conclusion from a series of research projects by the US Pew Research Center for the People & the Press in 2005:

> Sitting down with the news on a set schedule has become a thing of the past for many time-pressured Americans.... More people are turning away from traditional news outlets.... At the same time, public discontent with the news media has increased dramatically. Americans find the mainstream media much less credible than they did in the mid-1980s. They are even more critical of the way the press collects and reports the news. More ominously, the public also questions the news media's core values and morality. (Pew Research Center, 2005, p. 42)

Reports in most well-established democracies around the world signal similar trends. The global PR firm Edelman conducts annual surveys on trust and credibility among college-educated, middle-class, and media-savvy adults in 18 countries. What the firm finds is a gradual erosion of trust in governments, traditional institutions, and elites (especially in Brazil, Canada, Germany, the Netherlands, Spain, Sweden, and the United States) in favor of "a person like me" as someone considered to be the most credible source of information (Edelman, 2008). Likewise, the primary groups that people turn to for sharing or discussing information that they care about are friends and family, with professional networks and co-workers a distant second.

In the way people respond to social institutions in general and the news industry in particular, as well as in the way we assign prominence and privilege to whom we trust and where we turn for "the truth," we catch a glimpse of what is behind citizen journalism from an audience perspective. It is not about people interacting and collaborating with each other through news organizations (or brands), nor about citizens interacting or co-creating with journalists. It is about citizens engaging in peer-to-peer (P2P) relationships with each other independent of—and perhaps most often in direct opposition to—the mainstream news industry (Benkler, 2006). Here we must consider that people's engagement with the social structure around them has become, as mentioned earlier, monitorial and in essence highly individualized while at the same time generally anti-hierarchical. The critical consequence of such a particular and voluntarist type of civic participation is that it coincides with a macro-level move away from institution-based representation to a type of temporary and unpredictable social cohesion that is in fact grounded in an impotence of people in their identities as citizens, consumers, and workers "to shape their own social environment and [to] develop the capacity for action necessary for such interventions to succeed" (Habermas, 2001, p. 60).

Sure, we can wax poetic about the promise and practice of discussion forums, wikis, and (group) weblogs online, but none of these forms of distributed conversation have real, permanent, or stable political power. To some extent this is precisely because the Web 2.0 environment is premised on a combination of technologies that can be switched off without consequence and a cultural context that privileges solipsistic engagement. In this context Zygmunt Bauman poignantly remarks that "network is not community and communication not integration—both safely equipped as they are with 'disconnection on demand' devices" (quoted in Deuze 2007a, p. 674).

CITIZEN JOURNALISM AND CONVERGENCE CULTURE[2]

Beyond such critical perspectives, a third view of the future of citizen journalism can be a more optimistic note on participatory media culture, civic emancipation, and an emerging new humanism in media professions. Convergence culture, as a concept, articulates a fundamental shift in the way global media industries operate and how people as audiences interact with them (Jenkins, 2006). From a top-down perspective, convergence signals the emergence of cross-media and trans-media storytelling formats, produced by loosely integrated and hierarchical networks of corporations, companies, clients, and cultural producers. Convergence from the bottom up happens as media users are concurrently immersed in multiple media technologies, channels, and genres, and more often than not act as co-creators of media content and experiences when doing so. When applied directly to the theory and practice of journalism in a new media environment, the emergence and rise of citizen journalism can be seen as one of the ways convergence culture gets meaning in newswork.

The often bewildering variety of citizen journalism cases around the world—as documented extensively in this book—suggests that approaches to some kind of participatory (citizen and journalist) newswork, with which commercial and non-profit media organizations are currently experimenting, are complex and anything but uniform. As Outing (2005) suggests, "Citizen journalism isn't one simple concept that can be applied universally by all news organizations. It's much more complex, with many potential variations...from dipping a toe into the waters of participatory journalism to embracing citizen reporting with your organization's full involvement." It is important to study these different approaches in some detail, both as an object of study in their own right, in the context of social software and so-called Web 2.0 phenomena, and as pathways toward future configurations for culturally convergent models of journalism.

News organizations do not necessarily engage the citizen on a more or less equal footing, because the professionals involved are universally convinced that the breakdown between users and producers of news provides society with better information. Often a clear commercial motive is at work: the pursuit of additional sources of revenue, the potential to sell targeted advertising across online and offline media, and the winning back of otherwise non-reading newspaper audiences (Deuze, Bruns, and Neuberger, 2007). At the same time, this convergence of industrial and participatory journalism cultures does not occur in a uniform, painless process. Nor does it occur in a vacuum. Coping with the emergence of hybrid producer-user forms of newswork is easier for some than for others and tends to clash with entrenched notions of professionalism, objectivity, and carefully cultivated arrogance regarding the competences (or talent) of what Jay Rosen (2006) has called "the people formerly known as the audience."

Ultimately, convergence culture in journalism relies on cultural changes and significant investments on both sides of the equation: participants must bring or build an understanding of how to operate in a co-creative news production environment just as much as journalists must develop a sense of how to reinvent themselves as co-creators of culture. Indeed, journalists as the traditional regulators and moderators of public discourse should focus particularly on solving the conflict between open access and the quality of communication (Neuberger, 2006). Further, it also seems incumbent on both sides to ensure that this convergence process is not limited to isolated sectors and groups only, as this—far from bridging the rift between citizens and journalists—would serve mainly to create new divisions between those who participate in convergent citizen journalism environments and those who do not. As work on digital divide issues additionally suggests, access to the internet and all it has to offer is neither random nor dynamic, and indeed tends to reinforce existing institutional arrangements and social inequalities (Dutton, Gillett, McKnight, and Peltu, 2004). These kinds of reproduced systems of exclusion and reconfigurations of access must be critically acknowledged by scholars studying citizen journalism before making claims about the participatory or democratic nature of a site.

In a 2006 global industry overview based on consumer surveys and expert interviews, accounting and consultancy firm PricewaterhouseCoopers (PWC) signaled the rise of "Life Style Media" as "the combination of a personalized media experience with a social context for participation," which will create a media marketplace that is "a platform that connects media providers and media seekers through an organizational and technical infrastructure" (PricewaterhouseCoopers, 2006, pp. 6–8). In its analysis, PWC implicitly referred to the blurring of the boundaries between media producers and consumers (which has organizational consequences), supercharged by the rapid appropriation of new media by people to produce, edit, share, and distribute content themselves, on their own terms (which has a distinct technological dimension). The industry's framing of this newly empowered consumer is not without problems. Turow, for example, considers the construction of 21st-century media users by marketers, advertisers, and consultants as chaotic, self-concerned, and willingly contributing to a pervasive personal information economy as serving only an emerging strategic logic of mainstream marketing and media organizations "to present their activities not as privacy invasion but as two-way customer relationships, not as commercial intrusion but as pinpoint selling help for frenetic consumers in a troubling world" (2005, p. 120). Indeed, the audience has never been a given but must be seen as a socially constituted and institutionally produced category. Whereas in an age of mass-mediated culture such an audience was constructed as an amorphous mob that had to be told "All The News That's Fit To Print" (the 1897 slogan of *The New York Times*), in a convergence culture this same mob—consisting of largely similar people—has now turned into an unruly, self-expressive, narcissistic, yet also deeply interconnected creative class (Deuze, 2006).

There is no doubt that a future news system will be based, at least in part, on an interactive and connective mode of production where media makers and users will co-exist, collaborate, and thus effectively compete to play a part in the mutual construction of reality. On a hopeful concluding note, some consider such a shift toward a more engaged, emancipatory and participatory relationship between media professionals and their publics an example of a new humanism in the domains of public relations, journalism, and advertising, constituting "an antidote to narrow corporate-centric ways of representing interests in modern society" (Balnaves, Mayrhofer, and Shoesmith, 2004, p. 192). This may be true, but if so, one must understand this humanism not only as antidote but also as an inevitable side-effect of current corporate practices as well as a result of industry and scholarly constructions of present-day publics.

DISCUSSION

Considering a future for citizen journalism along the lines of industry, audience, and convergence culture shows a rather inevitable yet problematic plethora of possibilities. There is no reason to assume that people empowered through their newfound publishing freedoms will, at some point, stop blogging, posting, chatting, podcasting, or vlogging. It also seems quite clear that journalism has to permanently engage with this mass of individuals in ways that somehow make sense to the entrenched professional identities and occupational ideology of its newsworkers. Yet this engagement must also make sense to its marketers and advertisers—to the news industry as a business. Similarly, the commoditization of news also does not show signs of relenting. So for commercial, cultural, and technological reasons, it is in the self-interest of (most) journalism to become much more a part of the community it claims to serve. If only for that reason, one cannot study or practice citizen journalism without considering how the discourse of industry, the jargon of academia, and the behavior of audiences are all writing the same narrative—a story that, as it is told today, increasingly seems to be all about outsourcing salaried newswork to the realm of an increasingly skeptical and self-interested citizenry. This trend could go either way: toward finally establishing the ideals of journalism and democracy to enable citizens to be self-governing, or to supercharge the social fragmentation of society into countless individualized public spheres.

NOTES

1. International trends available from a GroupM study from December 2007; some specific trends in the United Kingdom and Sweden, where online ad spending is significantly larger than in the United States, for example as reported in *The Guardian* of January 3, 2008.
2. Some of the material that follows in this section is taken from earlier published work: Deuze, M.; Bruns, A.; and Neuberger, C. (2007), "Preparing for an age of participatory news," *Journalism Practice, 1*(4), pp. 322–338.

REFERENCES

Balnaves, Mark, Mayrhofer, Debra, & Shoesmith, Brian (2004) "Media professions and the new humanism." *Continuum: Journal of Media & Cultural Studies, 18*(2), 191–203.

Beck, Ulrich (2000) *The brave new world of work*. Cambridge: Polity Press.

Benkler, Yochai (2006) *The wealth of networks*. New Haven, CT: Yale University Press.

Black, Jay (Ed.) (1997) *Mixed news: the public/civic/communitarian journalism debate*. Mahwah, NJ: Lawrence Erlbaum.

Carey, J. (1996) "Where journalism education went wrong." 1996 Seigenthaler Conference, Middle Tennessee State University.

Deuze, Mark (2006) "Participation, remediation, bricolage: considering principal components of a digital culture." *The Information Society, 22*(2), 63–75.

Deuze, Mark (2007a) "Journalism in liquid modern times: an interview with Zygmunt Bauman." *Journalism Studies*, *8*(4), 671–679.

Deuze, Mark (2007b) *Media work*. Cambridge: Polity Press.

Deuze, Mark, Bruns, Axel, & Neuberger, Christoph (2007) "Preparing for an age of participatory news." *Journalism Practice*, *1*(4), 322–338.

Direct Marketing Association (2008) "DMA releases 'New media emergence in DM & brand'; to host May 7 virtual seminar." *Direct Marketing Association*.

Dutton, William H., Gillett, S.E., McKnight, L.W., & Peltu, M. (2004) "Bridging broadband internet divides: reconfiguring access to enhance communicative power." *Journal of Information Technology*, *19*(1), 28–38.

Edelman (2008) *Edelman trust barometer 2008*. London: Edelman.

Habermas, Jurgen (2001) *The postnational constellation*. Boston: MIT Press.

Hartley, John (2008) "Journalism as a human right: the cultural approach to journalism." In Martin Loeffelholz & David Weaver (Eds.), *Global journalism research* (pp. 39–51). Malden, MA: Blackwell.

Inglehart, Ronald (1997) *Modernization and postmodernization*. Princeton, NJ: Princeton University Press.

Jenkins, Henry (2006) *Convergence culture: where old and new media collide*. New York: New York University Press.

Kaye, K. (2007) "To build inventory and ad revenue, newspaper sites let users socialize." *ClickZ*.

Neuberger, Christoph (2006) "Nutzerbeteiligung im Online-Journalismus: Perspektiven und Probleme der Partizipation im Internet." In Harald Rau (Ed.), *Zur Zukunft des Journalismus* (pp. 61–94). Frankfurt: Peter Lang.

Norris, Pippa (Ed.) (1998) *Critical citizens: global support for democratic governance*. Oxford: Oxford University Press.

Outing, S. (2005) "The 11 layers of citizen journalism." *Poynter Online*.

Pew Research Center (2005) *Trends 2005*. Washington, DC: Pew Research Center.

PricewaterhouseCoopers (2006) *The rise of lifestyle media*. London: PricewaterhouseCoopers.

Ries, Al, & Ries, Laura (2002) *The fall of advertising & the rise of PR*. New York: Collins.

Rosen, J. (1999) *What are journalists for?* New Haven, CT: Yale University Press.

Rosen, J. (2006) "The people formerly known as the audience." *PressThink*, 27 June.

Rosen, J. (2008) "A most useful definition of citizen journalism." *PressThink*, 14 July.

Scammell, M. (2000) "The internet and civic engagement: the age of the citizen-consumer." *Political Communication*, *17*(4), 351–355.

Schaffer, J. (2007) *Citizen media: fad or the future of news? The rise and prospects of hyperlocal journalism*. College Park, MD: J-Lab.

Schudson, M. (1998) *The good citizen: a history of American civic life*. New York: The Free Press.

Turow, Joseph (2005) "Audience construction and culture production: marketing surveillance in the digital age." *The Annals of the American Academy of Political and Social Sciences*, *597*, 103–121.

List of Contributors

Stuart Allan is Professor of Journalism in the Media School, Bournemouth University, UK. He is the author of *News Culture* (1999; 2nd ed. 2004), *Media, Risk and Science* (2002), *Online News: Journalism and the Internet* (2006); and co-author, with Donald Matheson, of *Digital War Reporting* (2009). His previous edited collections include *Journalism After September 11* (2002; with Barbie Zelizer), *Reporting War: Journalism in Wartime* (2004; with Zelizer) and *Journalism: Critical Issues* (2005).

Ian Ashman is Senior Lecturer at the Lancashire Business School, University of Central Lancashire, UK. He has recently authored and co-authored a number of articles on subjects including journalism ethics (with Jane Singer), business ethics, leadership, emotion work, and research methods. Many of those articles draw upon and reflect his particular interest in the application of existentialist philosophy to management theory and practice.

Paul Bradshaw is Senior Lecturer in online journalism, magazines, and new media at Birmingham City University, UK. A former magazine editor and website manager, he continues to work as a freelance journalist and media consultant. He has contributed to a number of books, including the second edition of *Investigative Journalism* and the forthcoming book *Web Journalism*. Since 2004 he has published the Online Journalism Blog, one of the world's most popular journalism blogs.

Axel Bruns is Senior Lecturer in the Creative Industries Faculty at Queensland University of Technology in Brisbane, Australia. He is the author of *Blogs, Wikipedia, Second Life, and Beyond: From Production to Produsage* (Peter Lang, 2008) and *Gatewatching: Collaborative Online News Production* (2005) and co-editor of *Uses of Blogs* (2006). He blogs at snurb.info.

Bart Cammaerts is Lecturer in the Department of Media and Communications at the London School of Economics and Political Science (LSE), UK. His most recent publications include *Internet-Mediated Participation Beyond the Nation State* (Manchester University Press/Transaction Books, 2008) and *Understanding Alternative Media* (Open University Press, 2008; with Olga Bailey and Nico Carpentier). He chairs the Communication and Democracy Section of ECREA and is vice-chair of the Communication Technology Policy section of IAMCR.

Nico Carpentier is Assistant Professor in the Communication Studies Department of the Vrije Universiteit Brussel (VUB—Free University of Brussels), Belgium. He is co-director of the VUB research center CEMESO and vice-president of the European Communication Research and Education Association (ECREA—formerly ECCR).

Cynthia Carter is Senior Lecturer in the Cardiff School of Journalism, Media and Cultural Studies, Cardiff University, UK. She is co-author of *Violence and the Media* (2003; with C.K. Weaver). Recent edited books include *Critical Readings: Media and Gender* (2004; with L. Steiner), and *Critical Readings: Violence and the Media* (2006; with C.K. Weaver). She is founding co-editor of the journal *Feminist Media Studies* and is an editorial board member of various journals.

Jia Dai is a doctoral candidate in the School of Journalism, University of Texas at Austin. A former journalist for Chinese Central Television and the Xinhua News Agency, her published research includes articles in *Journalism & Mass Communication Quarterly* and *Journalism Practice*. Her research interests include new media and social transformation, citizen journalism, media sociology, and global communication.

Ludo De Brabander studied Communications Sciences at the University of Ghent, Belgium. He is currently working as a Lecturer in the Department of Social Work Education at the University College Arteveldehogeschool. He also works as a member of staff at Vrede, a peace organization. He is an editor for several magazines and e-zines on international policy, war, and peace.

Mark Deuze holds a joint appointment at Indiana University's Department of Telecommunications in Bloomington and, as Professor of Journalism and New Media, at Leiden University, The Netherlands. Book and journal publications include *Media Work* (Polity Press, 2007), and he has published in several open-access journals such as the *International Journal of Communication*. His research interests are creative labor, media work, and social theory. Weblog: deuze.blogspot.com.

Thomas E. Fiedler is Dean of Boston University's College of Communication, which he joined in 2008 after a 36-year career as a journalist. During those years, he earned many of journalism's highest honors for his work as an investigative reporter, political columnist, White House correspondent, war correspondent, editorial-page editor, and, ultimately, as the executive editor of *The Miami Herald*. His investigative report into an extremist cult's political tactics was part of a *Herald* series that won a 1991 Pulitzer Prize. During his 2001–2007 tenure as executive editor, the newspaper was awarded two additional Pulitzer Prizes.

Olga Guedes Bailey is Senior Lecturer at Nottingham Trent University, UK. She is the chair of the section "Migration, Diaspora and Media" of the European Communication Research and Education Association—ECREA. Her latest publications include a co-authored book, *Understanding Alternative Media* (Open University Press, 2007) and an edited collection, *Transnational Lives and the Media: Re-imagining Diasporas* (Palgrave, 2007). She is currently working on her book *Media and Ethnicity: Representation and Resistance*.

Amanda Lee Hughes is a doctoral student in Computer Science at the University of Colorado at Boulder and also holds an ME in Computer Science. She is a research assistant in Palen's ConnectivIT lab and has published papers in crisis informatics. Her research focuses on designing and building technologies that gather and interpret online information in times of crises.

Gholam Khiabany teaches in the Department of Applied Social Sciences, London Metropolitan University, UK. His research interests center on media and social change, and the relationship between communication, development, and democracy, with particular reference to Iran.

Sophia B. Liu is a doctoral student in the Technology, Media and Society interdisciplinary program in the Alliance for Technology, Learning and Society (ATLAS) Institute at the University of Colorado at Boulder. She is also a research assistant in Palen's ConnectivIT lab and has published papers in the emerging area of crisis informatics. Her research focuses on designing social media technologies to support crisis-related heritage production.

An Nguyen is Lecturer in Journalism Studies in the Department of Film, Media and Journalism at the University of Stirling, UK. He is the author of *The Penetration of Online News: Past, Present and Future* (VDM Publishing, 2008) and numerous research articles and reports on online journalism, online news audiences, journalism professionalism, and science journalism. Before joining academia, he was a science and health journalist in Vietnam.

Joyce Y. M. Nip is Assistant Professor at the Department of Journalism, School of Communication, Hong Kong Baptist University. In 2004–2005, she was a Fulbright Visiting Scholar affiliated with the University of Maryland, College Park. Before joining academia, she was a journalist, and has worked in television, newspapers, and magazines in both English and Chinese. Her research interest is the civic use of the media and journalism issues.

Leysia Palen is Assistant Professor of Computer Science and faculty affiliate of the Institute of Cognitive Science and the Alliance for Technology, Learning and Society (ATLAS) Institute at the University of Colorado at Boulder. She directs the ConnectivIT Lab, which researches human computer interaction (HCI) and computer-supported cooperative work (CSCW). Her work focuses on the social implications of technology use, including safety-critical systems, personal technology such as mobile telephony and texting, and crisis informatics.

Stephen D. Reese is Jesse H. Jones Professor of Journalism and Associate Dean for Academic Affairs in the College of Communication at the University of Texas. He is co-author of *Mediating the Message: Theories of Influence on Mass Media Content*, editor of *Framing Public Life: Perspectives on Media and Our Understanding of the Social World*, and area editor for "Media Production & Content" in the *International Encyclopedia of Communication*.

Lee Salter is Senior Lecturer in Journalism and Media Studies at the University of the West of England, Bristol, UK. His research and teaching interests focus on public communication, media and politics, and online journalism. He is also a participant in Indymedia UK, union branch press officer, and occasional journalist.

Barry Saunders is an online producer and researcher who has worked for Indymedia, Vibewire, and the World Wide Fund for Nature. He is the Research Coordinator for Democratic Renewal at the Centre for Policy Development, and writes about the intersection of journalism, independent media, and governmental transparency. He blogs at investigativeblog.net.

Jane B. Singer is the Johnston Press Chair in Digital Journalism at the University of Central Lancashire, UK. Her research explores digital journalism, including changing roles, perceptions, and practices. A former print and online journalist, Jane serves on the editorial boards of several academic journals and is president of Kappa Tau Alpha, the national US journalism honor society. She is on leave from the University of Iowa School of Journalism and Mass Communication.

Prasun Sonwalkar teaches at the University of the West of England, Bristol, UK. A former journalist, he worked on *The Times of India*, *Business Standard*, and the *Press Trust of India* and was Head of News of the Zee News channel.

His research has been published in edited collections and journals such as *Media, Culture & Society, Gazette, Contemporary South Asia,* and *Critique: A Review of Indian Journalism.*

Annabelle Sreberny is Professor of Global Media and Communications and Director of the Centre for Media and Film Studies, SOAS, University of London, UK. She is also President of the international Association for Media and Communications Research. She has been researching issues on Iranian media and gender for over 30 years and is co-authoring a book with Gholam Khiabany on Iranian blogging, *Blogestan,* for IB Tauris.

Jeannette Sutton is a sociologist who specializes in collective behavior in hazards and disasters. She works as a Research Coordinator at the Natural Hazards Center at the University of Colorado at Boulder. She conducts research on warnings and risk communication, disaster preparedness and response, and the uses of information and communication technology in disaster.

Einar Thorsen is Senior Lecturer in Multimedia Journalism at the University of Teesside, and a PhD candidate in Journalism Studies at Bournemouth University, UK. His thesis examines citizen voices on the BBC News website during the 2005 UK general election and is funded by the AHRC. Recent articles focus on Wikinews and the Neutral Point of View, the history of BBC News Online, and the development of public service policies in an online environment.

Sarah Vieweg is a doctoral student in the Technology, Media and Society interdisciplinary program in the Alliance for Technology, Learning and Society (ATLAS) Institute at the University of Colorado at Boulder, and also holds an MA in Linguistics. She works as a research assistant in Palen's ConnectivIT lab and has published in human computer interaction research communities. She studies online help through an ethnomethodological lens, with a focus on large-scale emergency situations.

Farida Vis is an ESRC Research Fellow at the Centre for Research on Socio-Cultural Change (CRESC), a research collaboration between Manchester University and the Open University. Her work is concerned with the reporting of global crisis, threat, and security, with a particular interest in visual mediatizations. She is currently involved in a research project with the National Centre for e-Social Science to further develop methods for analyzing media texts.

Melissa Wall is Associate Professor of Journalism at California State University, Northridge. A former journalist, she has also reported for Seattle's homeless newspaper, advised a Los Angeles student-radio project affiliated with Pacifica, taught journalism in Ethiopia, and studied township publications in Zimbabwe. Her research, focusing on international news as well as new media, has been published in journals such as *Media, Culture & Society, Journalism, New Media & Society, Gazette*, and *Journalism Studies*.

Jason Wilson is a Research Associate in the Creative Industries Faculty at Queensland University of Technology in Brisbane, Australia. He has written and published internationally on citizen journalism, video games, and mobile media. Recently he has been closely involved in two major ARC-funded citizen journalism initiatives, Youdecide2007 and Qlddecides, which covered two Australian elections.

Chang Woo Young is a Professor in the Department of International Administration at the Catholic University of Daegu, Korea. He holds a PhD in Political Science from Konkuk University. Recent publications include articles in *Korea Observer*, the *Journal of Contemporary Eastern Asia*, and *Korea Journal*.

Heba Zayyan is a Palestinian working woman and a mother. She holds an MBA from the Islamic University in Gaza and a BA in English Literature from the University of Jordan. She has been working in civil society organizations in Gaza for about seven years and is now working for an international organization that supports gender equality and women's empowerment.

Ethan Zuckerman is Research Fellow at the Berkman Center for Internet and Society at Harvard Law School. He is the co-founder of the international citizen media community Global Voices and previously founded Geekcorps, a voluntary organization that supported technology projects in sub-Saharan Africa.

Index

Simon Cottle, *General Editor*

From climate change to the war on terror, financial meltdowns to forced migrations, pandemics to world poverty, and humanitarian disasters to the denial of human rights, these and other crises represent the dark side of our globalized planet. They are endemic to the contemporary global world and so too are they highly dependent on the world's media.

Each of the specially commissioned books in the *Global Crises and the Media* series examines the media's role, representation, and responsibility in covering major global crises. They show how the media can enter into their constitution, enacting them on the public stage and thereby helping to shape their future trajectory around the world. Each book provides a sophisticated and empirically engaged understanding of the topic in order to invigorate the wider academic study and public debate about the most pressing and historically unprecedented global crises of our time.

For further information about the series and submitting manuscripts, please contact:

> Dr. Simon Cottle
> Cardiff School of Journalism
> Cardiff University, Room 1.28
> The Bute Building, King Edward VII Ave.
> Cardiff CF10 3NB
> United Kingdom
> *CottleS@cardiff.ac.uk*

To order other books in this series, please contact our Customer Service Department at:

> (800) 770-LANG (within the U.S.)
> (212) 647-7706 (outside the U.S.)
> (212) 647-7707 FAX

Or browse online by series at:

> www.peterlang.com